ST. JOSEPH'S ACADEMY NEAR EMMITSBURG MD.

MEMOIR,

LETTERS AND JOURNAL,

OF

ELIZABETH SETON,

CONVERT TO THE CATHOLIC FAITH, AND

SISTER OF CHARITY.

EDITED BY

RIGHT REV. ROBERT SETON, D.D.,
PROTHONOTARY APOSTOLIC.

Who shall find a valiant woman? far, and from the uttermost coasts is the price of her.—*Prov.* xxxi. 10.

VOLUME II.

NEW YORK:
P. O'SHEA, PUBLISHER, 27 BARCLAY STREET.
1869.

CONTENTS.

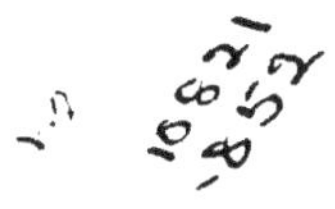

APPENDIX.

MEMOIR AND LETTERS

OF

ELIZABETH SETON.

1808.—Letters.—Removal to Baltimore.—Journal.—Letters.

TO MRS. SCOTT.

January 16th, 1808.

My Darling Julia,—I have met with a very serious loss in the death of Mr. James Barry, who I believe I told you sought me out with his dear wife, and presented themselves, entire strangers, solely for the esteem he had had for my husband, which at once opened my whole heart to them. And from that hour they have shown me and my darlings the most uniform, unwearied affection I have ever known. Miss Barry is in a decline, and her mother will take her a voyage as soon as the cruel embargo is raised. Then, adieu to every inducement to go to town, independent of St. Peter's. Your Anna's progress in music is uncommon for her age, and every new lesson she excels in, pictures to me the delight they who are gone would have had in hearing her. She is very neat at her needle and pen, and translates French with facility and pleasure. She is fond of occupation, but, like her poor mother, is attached to reading and writing only. Her health and beauty would delight you; and that reserved, quiet manner, the result of natural temper, saves her from a thousand difficulties I encountered at her age. Yet there never was a more joyous creature when she meets her favorite—Aunt Cecilia.

HARRIET TO ELIZABETH.

WILDERNESS, *Jan. 27th*, 1808.

MY DEAREST, BEST OF SISTERS,—To say your little note gave me comfort, would be to tell you what you must already know too well. I received it at a moment in which I wanted something to rouse my drooping spirits. I felt very unwell,—had been abed from twelve until past six in the evening. It was late before the boy came, and I was left to my own reflections longer than I have ever been this year. I thought of you, of my B——,[1] of my own future destination; whether *He* would ever deny me the comforts of that dear faith I love so much. At one instant I was all hope, in the next all despair. I reflected, likewise, on my present unhappy situation. If I had that faith to support me under my trials, I could bear them with patience; nay, even with cheerfulness. It would be

[1] She was engaged to be married, it will be remembered, since 1804. Her family, rare beauty, and many accomplishments had made her an object of much attraction in society; but deprived of the guidance of a parent, she had been so imprudent as to bestow her affections somewhat inconsiderately. B—— was at the date of this letter in the West Indies.

all for Him, and for Him I could suffer all. I expect to suffer much, very much before the combat is over. I look to that union, my sister, with a sorrowful heart as it respects a possible change in my principles. Do you think it will, it can ever be so? Perhaps you know him better than I do.

Dearest brother has just come in. I have not seen him since Tuesday morning. The little dears are almost frantic with joy, and he quite as much so to see them. He would have forgotten the note, had I not said: "What! no letters." Say to Cecily I was all astonishment at not seeing her. But it is always so whenever she goes to see you; the fates have ordered it. I have no doubt but it will rain or snow until Saturday.

The children have been very good, and quite as attentive to their studies as if she were here. They are calling me to go to vespers,—'tis past eight. I shall pray for you all with fervency, do so you for me: one good act deserves another.

10 *o'clock.*

I have passed a sweet, silent hour at prayer; my heart feels light after it. Oh! were I transformed to be near you. Tell Anna she shall have a long note soon. Yours, with truest affection.

FROM MR. CHEVERUS.[1]

BOSTON, *February* 3*d*, 1808.

DEAR AND RESPECTED MADAM,—Your esteemed favor of January the 12th did not come to hand till last night,

[1] It is sent "to the care of the Rev. L. Sibour, rector of St. Peter's, New York."

and the stamp of the post-office in New York is of January 26th. Had I received it sooner, I would have answered it immediately.

Our worthy friend, Mr. Tisserant, was well on the 8th of October, date of his last letter, which we received on Christmas-eve. We had before received several other letters, dated in July, August, and September. In all of them he expresses his wish and resolution to return to us in the course of the spring; but although I doubt not his sincerity, I entertain but faint hopes of seeing him here, unless the United States remain at peace, and the war continue in Europe, so as to make his situation in England rather unpleasant, and prevent his going to pay a visit, as he intended, in case of a general peace, to his sisters in Germany. In every one of his letters he speaks of you, of his sincere and affectionate respect for you, etc., etc. Had I known you had been so long without hearing from him, I would certainly have communicated sooner the above intelligence, and should I hear something more decisive about his return, I will write immediately. I have also the pleasure to[1] inform you, that, on the 20th of January, I received a letter from our dear Mr. Filicchi, dated Leghorn, October the 3d. Since the day it came to hand, I have been writing to you, or at least resolving to do so, and would certainly have done it in the course of this week. Your goodness will forgive the delay, and, to obtain my pardon, I copy the words of your amiable and worthy friend:

"Mrs. Seton, under date of the first of July, mentions her having received some fresh account of me through you . . . . . At such a distance, and in the uncertainty

[1] The Abbé Cheverus's letters are all in English.

of the safety of one's letters, I have been and am very backward, indeed, in addressing any of my best friends. My last letter to my virtuous friend, Mrs. Seton, at New York, was dated in June, and I reproach, almost to no purpose, my own inertness."

I shall write to Mr. Filicchi as soon as there is any opportunity, but when this will be I know not.

Dr. Matignon unites with me in respects to you, and compliments and love to your dear children. His health is tolerable, although he is often troubled with the rheumatism. I was unwell for some time last autumn, but am now in very good health. May the Almighty preserve yours till you see all your children *grounded in the faith and immovable in the hope of the Gospel.* To see them and you, to rejoice together in our common faith would be a heartfelt pleasure for me, but I dare not flatter myself of enjoying it very soon. I must forewarn you, however, that, whenever you see me, one of the heroes of your evening stories will shrink into a little ordinary man.

As you do not give me any direction, I shall direct the present letter to the care of the Rev. Mr. Sibour. I rejoice that you find a tender friend and adviser in your pastor. Give him my best respects, and those of Dr. Matignon. Your letters will be always welcome messengers, and can never be troublesome. It will be always a real satisfaction for me to correspond with you, and to be reckoned in the number of your friends.

Your affectionate and respectful humble servant,

JOHN CHEVERUS.

My compliments to Mr. Morris, if you see him. My respectful compliments to your interesting sister. Say something about her in your next.

In the month of March Mrs. Seton lost the society of her best Catholic friend in New York, the excellent Mrs. Barry. It would be sufficient to mention the high idea of her Christian virtue which Bishop Carroll entertained, and his great friendship for herself and family, to show the true worth of this lady. The tender affection that Mrs. Seton felt for her and her daughter may have been strengthened, in the circumstance of this one's illness, and the almost desperate resolve of going on a voyage in quest of health, by the recollections of her own feelings, that time she also had set out with one she heroically loved to seek a milder climate.

ELIZABETH TO CECILIA.

March, 1808.

At eight o'clock this morning at the altar[1] with dear Ann and her mother. At ten on board their vessel.[2] Received the last adieus. You, dear, were affectionately remembered in them. My heart aches, yet there is a heavenly comfort in trusting to Him at such an hour above all others.

How I would love to rest my weary head on your dear shoulder, but how much more to kneel with you on Sunday. Dear, dear Lord, comfort us. Is there any

[1] For Holy communion.

[2] The "cruel embargo" mentioned in a former letter was not repealed until the 27th February, 1809 (to take effect from the 4th of March next following); but Mrs. Barry probably sailed in a man-of-war, or in some vessel in ballast.

thing so dear to us as hope? Heavenly hope! Cherish it, my darling, it will carry us through triumphant. Do you remember the last chapter[1] of the *Spiritual Combat?* If not let me send it to you.

Not a word from sweet Harriet, perhaps she is at Mary Hoffman's.

TO THE SAME.

Friday.

Please send little Page's things as soon as you can. I often imagine you nursing the poor sick girl. It is trouble sent by sister, but it will be rewarded by our Jesus—our all. Oh! my darling, is it possible He loves us and accepts even our most imperfect actions! Do you wish to have the *devotions* again? Mrs. Barry has given me hers, and you shall have it as long as you please. My heart and soul yearns to see you, dearest. Ever yours.

TO MRS. SCOTT.

April 23d, 1808.

. . . . . Reverend Mr. Dubourg, the President of St. Mary's College, in Baltimore, to whom I communicated my anxiety, has offered to give me the formal grant of a lot of ground situated close to the college, which is out of the town, and in a very healthy situation; and to procure me immediately the charge of half-a-dozen girls, and as many more as I can manage. Added to this he will take my boys in the college, and the entire charge of

[1] "On the Deceits of the Devil at the hour of our Death," the 66th and last chapter of this golden book of devotion which St. Francis of Sales thought equal to the *Imitation of Christ.*

them for a very small consideration, in order that Mr. Filicchi's money may assist me in another way. . . . . . Anna is my companion, friend, and diligent assistant.

FROM REV. DR. DUBOURG.

St. Mary's College of Baltimore, *May 2d*, 1808.

Dear Madam,—I have this moment written at length to our worthy Boston friends, to submit to their consideration the scheme which now engrosses all my thoughts. Should they approve of it, I would be for your coming hither in two or three months, and taking the lease of a newly-built house which, in every point of view, would perfectly suit all our ideas, at least during the first year, which would give you sufficient time to reflect and consult on the propriety of building, and on the most eligible spot and plan.

Our two dear little girls[1] impatiently wait for you; but now, assuredly more than ever.

The rent would be about $250 per annum.

Your most respectful, devoted, and hurried friend,

Wm. Dubourg.

Please give my tenderest respects to the Rev. Messrs. Sibourd and Byrne, and to the Alomys (?) family.

FROM REV. MR. CHEVERUS.

Boston, *May 12th*, 1808.

Dear Madam,—The Rev. Dr. Dubourg, in a letter to the Rev. Mr. Matignon, of the 2d instant, says he has

[1] His nieces.

had the pleasure of seeing you and conversing with you on the project of an establishment in Baltimore. Dr. Matignon and I agree on all points with him and the Rev. Mr. Sibourd. Such an establishment would be a public benefit to religion, and, we hope, a real advantage to yourself and amiable family. We infinitely prefer it to your project of a retreat in Montreal.

Mr. Dubourg writes that Mr. Filicchi has authorized you to draw on his correspondent in New York for any sum necessary to begin a useful establishment, and this same worthy friend wrote to me on the same subject these very words: *Money shall not be wanting*. . . . . .

I have not received any letters from him (Mr. Anthony Filicchi) since the one I mentioned in my last to you, but I have heard by a gentleman who left Leghorn seventy days ago, that he and his family were well. The last letters from our dear Mr. Tisserant were dated the 25th of December and the 1st of January. He was well, full of projects for his return, but uncertain when he could put them in execution.

Dr. Matignon desires his respects, and I unite with him in begging to be remembered to your dear children and sister. We present our respects to the Rev. Mr. Sibourd and other clergymen of the church.[1] Remember us in your prayers, and believe me, with the most sincere respect and esteem, dear madam, your most obedient, humble servant,

JOHN CHEVERUS.

This letter from her enlightened friend, and the earnest solicitations of Dr. Dubourg, determined Mrs.

[1] In New York.

Seton to make the change from New York, where her existence was miserable, and no way of improving it, to hospitable Baltimore, which was then as now the central point of Catholicity in the United States. She was assured of the sympathy there of all Catholic hearts, and of the material assistance of the Rev. President of St. Mary's, in an undertaking such as she was prompted to try. Her good friend at Philadelphia, Mrs. Scott, had asked her as soon as she heard of the proposed removal, to pass through that city on her way to Baltimore, and rest herself and children in her house, besides making, in the same amiable and delicate manner as before, generous offers of pecuniary aid.

She left New York with her three daughters in one of the Baltimore packets on the 9th of June.

TO CECILIA SETON.

Thursday, 9th June, 1808.

My own Cecily would scarcely believe that we are only now passing the light-house thirty miles from New York. All the fatigue and weariness of mind and body are passed—the firmament of heaven so bright; the cheering sea-breeze and merry sailors would drive care away indeed, had I the company of the *five* dearest beings who bade adieu in the little room. Every one is so kind! A very mild-looking, modest young man came down before we had been half an hour on board, and said: "Madam, my name is James Cork,[1] call on me at all times; I

[1] He was the mate.

will help you in every thing." And so it is. Oh! sweet mercy! how kindly you are mixed in every cup. How soothing to look up and think of it all. Again and again this poor heart is offered in every way He will make use of it. How small a tribute for the daily debt! My Cecily dear, dear friend of my soul!

Friday, Saturday, and Sunday are passed, my dear one, with many a prayer, many a sigh. We are rocking and rolling without getting on. Ann is suffering; she is very low spirited, and refuses to go on deck. The ladies on board, Mrs. Smith and her daughter, so good to us! I said vespers during a storm; very fervently you may be sure. This morning we are again in sight of land and near Cape Henry. . . . . .

Tuesday.—Here we are flying up the Chesapeake: a fairer wind and lighter hearts never went through it, I believe. The sun is setting gloriously: are you looking at it? My soul flies up with the Miserere;[1] it is wrapt in yours, and for our own Harriet it sends the sigh. To-morrow do I go among strangers? No! Has fear or an anxious thought passed my mind? No! Can I be disappointed? No! There can be no disappointment where the soul's only desire and expectation is to meet His adored will and fulfill it.

Wednesday Evening.—Once more good night, sweet love, aboard the *Grand Sachem,* not yet in Baltimore Bay. Hope is on the wing, expecting to-morrow morning. What

[1] She had long been in the pious custom of saying the 50th Psalm at sundown.

are you doing? Happy child whom God employs! How contrasted to the giddy round of beings who play away their happiness both present and eternal.

Thursday Morning.—Corpus Christi. My dear, all I can tell you is, a carriage conveyed us to the seminary. The organ's solemn peal, then the burst of the choir. This is the moment of consecration of Mr. Dubourg's chapel. We entered without a word; prostrate in an instant. Human nature could scarcely bear it. Your imagination can never conceive the splendor—the glory of the scene. After mass I was in the arms of Mr. Dubourg's sister; surrounded by so many caresses and blessings. My wonder is how I got through it all. The feelings were lost with delight.

Friday Evening.—Received our all. Oh! how fervently! So much all combined turns my brain. Masses from daylight to eight. My dwelling, the most complete, almost adjoining the chapel. Vespers and benediction every evening. Every heart caressing us; the look of love and peace on every countenance. Hush! oh my soul. Cecily, Cecily, that soul cries out for *you.* It can not do without you. It must claim you in life and in death. There is a little mount behind the chapel called Calvary,—olive-trees (?) and a cross. At the foot of it are four graves. "There is your rest," said Mr. Dubourg, as we passed it this morning. It must be yours too, my lovely, dear sister.

On her arrival at Baltimore, Mrs. Seton and her daughters were received by the hospitable Mr. Dubourg and his sister's family with that open-hearted courtesy that distinguishes educated French people. Every thing that refinement could suggest was placed at her disposal, and she found among her new friends not only religious sympathy, but also many of those little comforts of life that the French know so ingeniously to create, in the midst even of people whose manners and ways of living are different from their own.

The following was written by Father Babade, and spoken by Mr. Dubourg's niece on the Thursday evening of Mrs. Seton's arrival in Baltimore:—

COMPLIMENT D'AGLAE DUBOURG AUX DEMOISELLES SETON À LEUR ARRIVEE À BALTIMORE, ET CONTRACT D'AMITIE ENFANTIN.

O vous si longtemps attendues
Recevoz nos embrassemens;
Nos deux familles confondues
Ne font plus qu'une en sentimens.

Votre Mère sera ma Mère.
Aglaé sera votre sœur;
Nous n'aurons plus qu'un même père
Nous n'aurons plus qu'un même cœur.

Bientôt dans un même langage
Nous aurons un nouveau lien;
Celui du cœur a l'avantage
Qu'on l'entend toujours assez bien.

De vos plaisirs et de vos peines
Je vous demande une moitié;
Vous aurez aussi part aux miennes;
Tout est commun dans l'amitié.

Ou plutôt ces mots tout de glace,
Le mien, le tien ne doivent plus.
S'entendre ici, ni trouver place
Dans cet asile des vertus.

Suivant la remarque d'un sage
Ces mots si froids de *mien*, de *tien*,
Furent bannis au premier âge
Du vocabulaire chrétien.

Le mot *nôtre* a bien plus de grâce
Il ne fit jamais de jaloux.
Mien et *tien* il faut qu'il remplace;
Tout sera *nôtre* parmis nous.

Je ne dirai plus; Mes poupées,
Mes joujoux, mes fleurs, mon jardin,—
Tout est à vous, sœurs bien aimées,
Tout sera nôtre dès demain.

Communauté délicieuse!
Charme jadis de l'âge d'or!
Reviens d'une famille heureuse
Faire le plus riche trésor.

ELIZABETH TO MRS. DUPLEX, IN IRELAND.

BALTIMORE, 20*th June*, 1808.

You will be much surprised, dearest, to hear that we are no longer in New York. We removed to Baltimore the middle of June, and I find the difference of situation so great that I can scarcely believe it is the same existence. All these dear attentions of human life which I was entirely weaned from, are now my daily portion from the family of Mr. Dubourg whose sister and mother are unwearied in their care of us. We are treated as a part of their family, and in every respect my condition is that of a new being. The fence of our boundary is the only division from a beautiful chapel which is open from daylight till nine at night. My prospect of an establishment I leave to God Almighty. The two nieces of Mr. Dubourg are all I have; but after the summer vacation, when the inhabitants return, the prospect will be better. . . . .

We are away from all to whom we are allied by natural affection, aliens to our nearest connections and seeking bread among strangers—in one sense of the word, but not strangers in kindness or love. Madame Fournier, the sister of our Superior, assists me in all the little cares for my children. There is also a branch of the Barry family here, who are as kind to us as was our dear Mrs. Barry in New York. Mrs. Barry and her husband omit nothing that generosity or kindness can dictate, and I do not fear that they will be wearied in their attentions, because I know the principle on which they act. You would be pleased to see our good old Bishop Carroll when he is in the midst of us—of all his children as he calls us.

Anna is the admiration of every one, more for her discretion and propriety of behavior than even for her beauty. Rebecca is not so handsome, but is so full of expression you would not wish her to be lovelier. My sweet Cecilia is still in New York. Her being with us, you may be sure, is the first wish of our hearts; but James Seton was so positive on the necessity of her staying with him till his family is settled, that she could not properly insist; but I shall have a great deal more care and occupation until she come. She writes me that B—— is expected next month; poor Harriet is truly unhappy.

TO MRS. SCOTT.

BALTIMORE, *4th of July*, 1808.

After our arrival here I went immediately to Washington for my boys, and having my family to settle, house to arrange, etc., and such heat to support as was almost insupportable, it has really been very difficult to write even a line. You would scarcely believe the change I experience in my manner of life since I am in my new home. After so long a period of trouble and confusion, to lead a life of regularity and comparative repose, accustomed to find recreation and amusement only in books, and considering every visitor a thief upon my few precious moments, and almost an intruder; my poor heart was wrapt up in its own solicitudes. But such is the contrast of my present situation, I scarcely dare think of it. We were received by each of the reverend gentlemen of the seminary as their adopted charge. Mr. Dubourg's sister is a most amiable, affectionate character. She arranges my affairs for me with an ease and gayety of manner, as if the favor were all on my side. I have the advantage of procuring every thing I use from the seminary, which, as they engage by the gross, makes a difference of at least a third less expense on every article. My boys are finally received in the college without the least expense, by the voluntary offering of these kind beings, who are the professors. Mr. Robert Barry, the consul for Portugal, with his amiable wife, are unceasing in their kindness. The children are in a dream of delight at being once more united and so much cared for, but it is all a novelty, and consequently bears its best appearance; it is liable to change. However, I shall not be disappointed.

CECILIA TO ELIZABETH.

NEW YORK, *June 28th*, 1808, 9 *o'clock*.

. . . . . . It is late, my beloved sister, for an invalid to be writing; but, strange infatuation! when I once commence writing to you, I know not how to stop, and have so much to say, I know not where to begin. Will my love for you be ever the same? Will its fervor never abate? Heaven forbid it should be other than it is. Our ties are too closely united with our love for Him. Is it not so? Give me a description of the chapel and the many altars, in place of our solitary *one*—but that one, how sweet! There have we mingled our tears, and there together we have poured forth our souls to Jesus. Can we ever forget those hours? Never, never, never. I participate in your joy at seeing your dear boys. How poor mother's heart must have felt at the first sight! They are grown, I suppose, very much; tell them to think sometimes of Aunt Cecily. I believe the Rev. Mr. Hurley has left you before this—may I expect a letter? Perhaps he is afraid to leave me here. Some parts of the family have great hopes of bringing the "stray sheep" back to the fold, now the principal obstacle (as they imagine) is removed. Are you fearful of me, my sister? Or does it make you laugh? Pray for me that my faith may be strengthened. I am not wavering, but it does not do to be too confident. Be my guide and counselor. Dear remembrance to Mr. Dubourg. Ask him to remember me in the Blessed Sacrifice, I greatly need his prayers. Kiss and bless my darlings for me. Tell Anna to write me a line. I know not how to leave you, yet I must. Dearest, best of sisters, when shall we meet again? *He* only knows. Your own in life and death.

CECILIA.

TO THE SAME.[1]

BARCLAY STREET, *July 6th*, 1808.

DEAR BELOVED SIS,—Will you believe it? I am once more in town, seated in Mr. Sibourd's room. I can not tell you how thankful I am of being once more able to renew the delightful employment of writing to you. Mr. S. has just shown me your letters. My heart jumped at the idea of being with you, but the sacrifice must be complete. Every day do I make the silent offering. It can not be; my friend advises me to stay, as circumstances are at present. Do you fear I shall not be able to go through *all?* But *He* will give strength equal to the burden. Is it not so, my darling? Can He leave a soul that clings to Him as mine does? Never! Our dear Harriet is in trouble. She is now at Charlotte's,[2] where they wish her to make a promise of never joining our church, which she positively refuses. My soul feels light, and flies up to Him when I think how happy I am to bear something for Him who bore so much for me. My sister, dear, dear sister, remember I am *yours*. I can not help cherishing the idea that something may yet arrive to unite us. Kiss my pets. Best remembrance to Mr. Dubourg. Your own.

The Abbé Sibourd, in his letter[3] to Dr. Dubourg inclosing the above, says of *l'angélique Cécile* (for so he calls her): "Let us leave to time and Providence the task of deciding which among the many plans of bringing the two so tenderly to one another affectioned friends

[1] Under cover of one from Father Sibourd to Dr. Dubourg.
[2] Mrs. Ogden. [3] In French.

together, should be adopted. If it please Heaven that they should not be separated, nothing, you know, on earth can hinder that they live united."

TO THE SAME.

Friday, July 7th, 1808.

I received your letter, my sister, just as I was leading the darlings[1] to prayers. My heart was too full. I dared not open it until I renewed my promises to heave no sigh, or feel any anxious thoughts, about being with you. What a description of your happiness! Well may you wish me with you. The tears flowed fast. I did not stop them, for they were not tears of regret for sister, or impatience to be with her; but of a soul wholly resigned to her God,—desiring only His will, and even feeling happy at being permitted to make so great a sacrifice. When I wrote you, there was every reason for me to suppose I should soon join you. I thought when —— had once been explicit with her grandmother, that my situation would forthwith be decided. But it seems not. All that has passed is unknown to ——. As it respects myself, their cold, mysterious manner to me, certainly denotes something. I anxiously wait the result.

Saturday, 8th.

Oh! my sister, what a world of sin!—angry words and cross looks are all I meet with. But how sweet it is to feel that we suffer with and for Jesus.—My soul truly rejoices. The cup is at first bitter; but in it there is an

[1] Her little nieces.

unknown delight for those that love. Dear, dearest sister, if I were with you I should not have these tears,—these many offerings to make. I fear my scales would then be very light.

Thursday, 21*st*.

Is it possible, my precious sister, so long a time has passed since I wrote one line; I trust you have not been uneasy. Nothing but sickness could have prevented me. I have been staying a week at Westchester to regain my strength, and am once more well and back at the Wilderness. But once at communion since your departure. I think of your happiness and heave the sigh upwards. Every means has been tried to get me with you, but none will succeed, and I think my situation is now determined for the summer. I look to God to carry me through it. I saw your friend, Mr. Cooper, on Sunday, he is very silent and retired. Mr. Sibourd is so good and so kind to me—consoles me every way. My fear has left me, and I can now open my heart to him without trembling, which is my greatest earthly happiness.

Friday, 22*d*.

It would be impossible to tell you all I have suffered this day. Mrs. H——n has been here, the *abominations* of my religion was all her conversation. Is it not hard to have to hear what we hold dear and sacred abused? She says I will bring her to the grave, and that I *must* leave the children. She refuses entering the house while I am in it. In such a situation, my sister, what am I to do? I have used every argument with brother to permit me to leave it. He will not hear of it, and I must submit. I at least try to make him happy by appearing cheerful, but in appearance, indeed, for there are hours when I can not conceal my feelings. Daily and hourly pray for your Cecilia. Were there not an all-wise Creator to direct, and a Jesus to recompense for our pains, I know not what I should think of my situation. Oh, my sister! if I could only get out of New York, I would go anywhere, and be the most menial servant.

Thursday, 28*th*.

I must add a few more lines, my soul's sister, if it is only to say how truly I love you. No one can ever know our love that has not known its source. Our day of deliverance will come, that we may rejoice together. Our dear Harriet spent yesterday with me. Farewell, my beloved sister, keep my little room in readiness. "He will deliver." Kiss all my pets for me. Love and pray for your own—she is truly your own—THERESA.[1] Write me how dear Mr. Dubourg is, if he is yet well.

Wednesday, August 3*d*.

Precious, dear sister, I could not let Mr. Cooper depart without a line from your Cecily. The grain of sand is heavy, but I make out to get it up hill. It would be easy enough with sister's assistance. My soul is with you, but still I am contented and resigned, notwithstanding Baltimore is the uppermost wish of my heart. Your letter, when it comes, will be a precious one. I have been so long expecting it, yet, in reality, it is not so long since the last. Mr. Sibourd leaves for the Springs on Saturday.

[1] Confirmation name. She frequently signs with it.

I received *my all*[1] this morning. Was it not sweet? almost too much for a mortal to bear. Yet what would we do without it? My heart is so full, the tears start at every line. My sister, my friend! when shall I see you, when shall we go together to the dear altar? Will it ever be? That thought must not enter. To an Almighty Providence I trust all. I am in His hands, and I am under good direction. Remember me to your Rev. friends. Farewell, beloved, your own,

THERESA.

POSTSCRIPT FROM MR. SIBOURD.

Aug. 4th.

I have permission to join in the sisterly correspondence, and I shall not let this letter go to the post-office without a few lines of my handwriting. Though it was intended for Mr. Cooper, who left town last night, I thought it more proper to dispatch it by mail. I am to embark the day after to-morrow on the steamboat, and do not expect to be back before the middle of September. My earnest wish was for withdrawing from the rectorship of New York, but heavenly injunctions seem to be against man's determination. I must submit to my case, hard as it is. I trust in God's assistance, who alone can make it light. I can not express how much I feel for my child in Christ, and admire her Christian fortitude. How invincible are those who have God's support on their side? She would be too happy with you, but her happiness will be the greater when the stress of weather drives her to you. God only knows when this will be the case. Be pleased

[1] Holy communion.

to remember me to the Rev. gentlemen in the seminary and college, chiefly to the president. Your boys and girls are constantly present in my prayers, in yours think of your respectful servant, L. SIBOURD.

TO CECILIA.

Friday, 12th August, 1808.

Sister writes with an overflowing heart. It is St. Clare's day. What did *she* not suffer in opposing the world? How tender and faithful was the love of her Agnes who followed her. Shall *we* one day be so happy, my dear one? He only knows who holds us in His hand; but this we know, that "sorrow is not immortal," nor can we suffer long whether severed or united. The Angelus bell rings morning, noon, and night: at half-past five in the morning precisely, a quarter before two in the day, and a quarter before eight at night. Meet your own soul's sister in the angelic salutation. I say it with particular attention, and always on the knees, because there is an especial indulgence attached to it, which indulgence and every other I can gain I offer to God, after the example of Rev. Mr. Dubourg, for the departed.

My dearest child, you must not think sister neglects you. I have so little time and so much writing to do. When I write a letter, some of my prayers must always be given up; many a visit to the blessed sacrament is resigned for this purpose. Tell my dear Mrs. —— she must take your letters as written to herself. Do you never see dearest Harriet? Oh! sorrow, sorrow; and Eliza, too, is banished! We are monsters indeed. But I would not change one of my half-hours with the good folks here for their whole life put together. Oh! Cissy dear, if they had one substitute for all riches and pleasures.

If you will prepare a hundred letters, they can all be brought to me by Mr. Redmond from Georgetown College, who will call for them before the 15th of next month. I give you all a long time for writing.

TO THE SAME.

BALTIMORE, *5th September*, 1808.

SWEET CIS,—I am almost afraid you are ill, it is so long since your last. I inclose you, now, a little letter for Harriet. Oh! do tell me every thing about her. All the people there are very silent; but to live forgotten and unloved is a part of Christian perfection. And what is all the world to you and me? *We* are in the secret of His tabernacle, and there alone is safety, true liberty, and content. If I were to write you a thousand sheets, I could never tell the love of the heart that doats on you, and never loved you as at the moment I read the sweet words "my mother," added to the many precious titles which unite us. Yes! in life and death we will be united to our Jesus; and I shall be your mother, sister, friend, and you my darling of darlings. And so Harriet was really permitted to see you! Thank Him for all that. I concluded that, from her delicate position, she would have had to forego a pleasure so dear to her. But not one word of our dear Eliza! Oh! how I long to see you all. What delight, dearest child, I yet anticipate in our reunion! Every thing you wish to know of me is said in few words. In the chapel at six until eight, school at nine, dine at one, school again at three, chapel at half-past six, examination of conscience and rosary. Sometimes before that hour a visit to some one in our limits, or a walk; and so goes day after day. But I should rather say, where are you my love? I fear your sufferings are proportioned to my ease. Oh! Cecily dearest, why can not I exchange with you? In an instant I would take your stormy station, were it His will, to give you even a taste of my spiritual enjoyments. But how soon may they pass, at least in their form, though in principle we know they are unalterable. Poor Cecily! so you were but once at church the whole time of Father Redmond's visit to New York. Oh! oh! he was sorely disappointed at not seeing you, but he remembers you in the great sacrifice. The prayer at the end of your Georgetown prayer-book will explain the *Agnus Dei*[1] he left you. Ann and Aglaé always wear one around the neck with great devotion.

A young gentleman of St. Mary's College promised me faithfully to call on Mr. Byrne for your commands before the last of this month.

[1] The *Agnus Dei* (literally "Lamb of God") is a small piece of pure wax, bearing the impress of a lamb supporting the standard of the cross, which, encased in precious metal, or in some rich stuff, is worn devoutly about the neck, or suspended in a glass frame from the wall.

The remote origin of this celebrated devotion may be sought in the morsels of the Paschal candle blessed the preceding year, which were distributed to the faithful on Sunday *in Albis*. In this form the *Agnus Dei* is traced back to the fourth century; but as it now exists, medallion-shaped, and imprinted with the lamb, it dates from the sixth century, the earliest instance on record being one sent by Pope Gregory the Great to Theodolinda, Queen of the Lombards.—Martigny, *Dict. des Antiquités Chrétiennes, Art. Agnus Dei.*

At the present day the confection of these waxen images is a privilege of the Cistercians, and their benediction reserved to the Sovereign Pontiff.

HARRIET TO ELIZABETH.

GREEN-HILL, *Aug.* 12*th*, 1808.

MY SISTER,—Exquisite, indeed, would be my happiness, if permitted to rest my head on that dear shoulder, to utter unreserved every thought and express every sentiment of a heart that feels for you an attachment no language can define. I yet hope the day may come when I can fly to your arms and find a shelter from every sorrow. Of B——'s coming I know not what to say. September is soon here; but I fear it will not bring him. So it is, my dear Sis, I am always disappointed. Perhaps it may be another year or two before the meeting—God only knows. When I think of the many trials yet to come, I shudder, but resign my fate with perfect confidence in His Divine Providence, and offer Him all my anxieties and sorrows. Let what will come, I have no doubt it will be for our mutual advantage. To you, my sister, I owe more than I can express, for instilling principles that will make the rugged path of life smooth and easy; from you I have received a treasure that can not fail to make me happy even in adversity.

Tuesday, 13*th*.

A few lines from B——, which I have just finished reading, have, as I had been hourly expecting, destroyed every hope of his arrival. How I should like to take a peep into the book of fate to know what leaf would be next turned over! Some propitious breeze may, perchance, blow it aside and disclose a few happy days to come. "Poor Harriet!" you will exclaim, "sister pities you;" and well she may. Dear Cecily sat an hour with me this morning: our thoughts involuntarily turned to our dear absent friend. You may be sure I had, as usual, a number of questions to ask. I am to pass Wednesday with her. What a precious creature she is! To be separated from her would be more than I could support. When I behold her in such a trying situation, so young, yet so perfect, I am astonished. My heart, indeed, bleeds for her; and I should be miserable did I not know she possesses that *peace which passeth all understanding*. We very often picture you in the little chapel, and admitted in spirit we almost forget we are separated.

Pray, without ceasing, my Sis, the scene may change. When you write, always inclose to Cecily for peace's sake. Embrace my precious darlings with tenderness for me, and never let them forget me in their prayers. By you I am certain of being remembered. Farewell, my dear sister. Your's eternally,

H. SETON.

ELIZABETH TO CECILIA.

BALTIMORE, *6th October*, 1808.

MY DEAREST, MOST PRECIOUS CHILD,—Sister's joy is but an anticipation of yours when you will hear that the best, most excellent assistants to dear Mr. Sibourd who could be obtained, are on their way to our poor, desolate congregation at New York. I can not speak my joy, as it will so much glorify the Divine Name. Your precious letter with the lovely profile are come safe to hand. All the girls, my Aglaé and Celanine[1] among the rest, are wild to see their

[1] Rev. Dr. Dubourg's nieces.

Aunt Cecilia. Aglaé is the fairest, most perfect child you can imagine; diligent and faithful in every duty, always remembering our dear Lord's eye is upon her. What would we ask in this world if Cecily and Harriet of the Wilderness were with us? In my dear, sacred communions, which are almost every day, often my soul cries out so much for you all, that it seems impossible to express the desire in any words. A deluge of tears is the only relief. Yes! every morning in the week at communion, except some particular circumstance prevents; living in the very wounds of our dearest Lord. What more shall I say? The children sing *Adoramus* all day long; after morning school our Litany of Jesus, when afternoon class is over, our Rosary. What more should I ask in this world but Cecily and Harriet? But it is expected I shall be the mother of many daughters. A letter received from Philadelphia, where the Rev. Dr. Dubourg is now on a visit, tells me he has found two of the sweetest young women who were going to Spain to seek a refuge from the world, though they are both Americans, *Cecilia* and *Mary*, and now wait until my house is open for them. Next spring we hope. He applies to me the psalm in our vespers: "The barren woman shall be the joyful mother of children," and says: "I promise you and wish you many crosses, which it will be my delight to bear with you, my daughter; but they will brighten our crown, and glorify His name whose glory is our only desire."

I have a lovely picture of Saint Mary Magdalen de' Pazzi, who is kneeling in her religious habit before a crucifix standing upon a little altar, on which is written her motto, *Ne point mourir mais souffrir*, but I dare not send it you for fear of trouble. But you shall have your own little crucifixion[1] framed. Oh, Cecily, my soul's treasure, let us beg our Lord to hasten the time of our reunion . . . . . Having other letters to write, I can only recommend you to show, as you have ever done, whose child you are, by your patience and resignation.

It will be seen by the above that the Rev. Dr. Dubourg was prudently leading Mrs. Seton on, with the help of God, to a more useful, and to herself more perfect life, in the foundation of a religious community. In her own letters will best of all, not, indeed, in detail, but still sufficiently, be traced out the commencement and success of a work which has been so fruitful of good to the church in the United States. In a letter to her friend Julia Scott, written in October, she playfully hints at a possible change of life, where she says: "I determined that nothing should prevent my asking you before night the question, whether you thought any longer of your poor little *nun?*" In the same month her sister, Mrs. Post, writes a terribly long letter from New York, all to express her surprise, "that she can contemplate any change that must necessitate separation from her children." As to separating herself from her children, so long as they stood in need of maternal care, Mrs. Seton had no such intention, nor would she in any case have been allowed to do so by her ecclesiastical superior, because the church teaches her children to perform first

[1] This is an exquisite *aqua forti* engraving of Rembrandt's Crucifixion, by the celebrated K. E. C. Hess. It was brought from Holland by my grandfather Seton.

the natural obligations of their position, and *then* to proceed to works of perfection. But Protestants are profoundly ignorant on questions of Catholic practice as well as belief.

A few months later a young non-Catholic relative, Mary Wilkes, with more common sense and less bigotry than most outsiders, writing from New York to learn somewhat of the new foundation, says: "The Sisters of Charity! I am anxious to hear the particulars of this institution. Various are the accounts of it here, and I am convinced they are all founded on ignorance."

HARRIET TO ELIZABETH.

November, 1808.

Whenever I can catch the little moment to give you pleasure, I count it a year of happiness to myself. Four months, and not one single line from B——. 'Tis strange. They bluntly tell me at —— he never will return. Is it not cruel to torture my mind by such observations? My heart feels a thousand pangs that are indescribable. I wish more ardently than ever to be with you, if it were only for ten minutes, to explain to you several little circumstances, and ask your advice as it respects *conduct*. I would not dare do it by letter, fearful of accidents. This winter I am determined to enter no society whatever. My mind is not in a state to enjoy it. I trust soon to spend a little time with my precious Cecily.

FROM THE SAME.

WILDERNESS, *Nov. 29th*, 1808.

I promised, my dear sister, in my last letter, that I would write again when at the Wilderness, at last I am here, close by my Cecily. It is here alone that my poor heart feels some little cessation of pain and sorrow. What anguish, the most acute could not be hushed in her dear society? Her presence actually works like a charm upon my mind. Oh, my dearest Sis, how sweetly we could pass the winter together, thinking, speaking of, and writing to you! The world would be forgotten with all its vanity, and we would lose ourselves in thoughts of heaven. Let me share a portion of your thoughts the 29th of December.

For many years back I have been accustomed to receive from you some rules of conduct for the new year—some little affectionate letter of advice and comfort blended. I now stand more in need of this than ever, and shall sigh for the day that brings me, if only one line, to say I was remembered at the foot of the cross.

ANTHONY FILICCHI TO MRS. SETON.

LEGHORN, *Nov. 30th*, 1808.

Your two letters, dated Baltimore, July and 20th Aug., 1808, are before me. I am extremely pleased in seeing you out of New York, among true Christians, surrounded by all your children, and under the holy direction of such worthy persons as those you mention. To promote the establishment so much approved of by my Cheverus and Matignon, you will please to draw on our friends, J. Murray & Sons, of New York, one thousand dollars, charging the same to the account in the world to come of my brother Philip and of Anthony.

My wife and children are in perfect health. Be sure that none of the Filicchis has forgotten or will ever forget Mrs. Seton. Pray only for us, and particularly for good Philip's health, which appears to be much impaired since my return from America. He is actually at Pisa, where, as in a milder climate, he proposes to pass the winter season. He has received your letter and will answer it. Abbé Plunket is very well; but Doctor Tutilli is no more since April last. We must all go one after the other. Blessed those who, by their faith and good works on earth, are entitled to look at that last hour as to the beginning of a new life.

I was last summer in expectation, from week to week, of addressing you a long letter by the newly elected Bishop of New York, Monsignor Concanen, a learned Irish Dominican friar from Rome, of a truly venerable sweet aspect and manners; but the American vessel on which he expected to take his passage was prevented from putting to sea, and he was obliged to return to Rome until God's will would furnish him with some other opportunity in the next spring for his going to take charge of his flock. He will bring along with him the necessary bulls, etc., for the consecration of our Cheverus as Bishop of Boston, of Reverend Egan as Bishop of Philadelphia, of Reverend Flaget as Bishop of Bardstown, and of Bishop Carroll as Archbishop of Baltimore.[1] When you write to our ad-

[1] Pope Pius VIIth erected these four bishoprics on the 8th of April, 1808, by a bull given from Saint Mary Major's, and at the same time and place Baltimore was made an archbishopric with the new creations for suffragan sees. Bishop Concanen

mired Cheverus, pray remember me to him. Though lazy in writing (particularly at such a distance, and at a time of so much provoking uncertainty for the safety of one's letters), my American friends, you and he above all, are and will ever be deepest stamped on my mind and heart.

Believe me, most sincerely, and daily more your friend,

ANTHONY FILICCHI.

Writing again to Mrs. Seton, about the same date, he says: "The inclosed letter to Bishop Carroll is from Bishop Concanen. Be so good as to deliver it into his own hands with my most respectful regards."

ELIZABETH TO MRS. SCOTT.

18th December, 1808.

MY OWN DEAR JULIA,—How long a time you must have been uneasy for your poor friend! The sight of the dear amiable J. C. brought the whole recollection with full force, and convinced me that the hours and days pass with me much faster than I calculate. From half-past five in the morning until nine at night every moment is full; no space even to be troubled. There is very little time for writing; even at this moment the pen is falling from my hand, so completely is nature wearied. Many very advantageous offers of assistants have presented themselves; but in the present state of my pupils we are so happy, and live so much as a mother surrounded by

was detained by adverse circumstances at Naples, whither he had gone in hopes of obtaining a passage to the United States, and died there in 1810 her children, that I can not resolve to admit a stranger, yet it must be eventually.

I am obliged so strictly to avoid giving offense, that as I could not leave home at any time without the greatest inconvenience, I do not pretend to leave it at all; and this is one of the charms of my situation, which truly and indeed is most congenial to all my ideas of happiness. Oh, how sweet to be every moment employed in the service and in the sight of the dearest and most generous of Masters, who repays with the tenderness of compassionate love, even the good-will of His child, however imperfect its execution. My dear Julia, when I think of you, my first friend, who are so unchangeable through so many changes, I would wish to do something—any thing—that might be the least expression of my attachment to you and yours; but such is the Divine order that the good must be received on my part, not bestowed; and I must be content with that dispensation which lightens favors by conveying them through a hand so dear and beloved.

I am now so well, so free from weakness of the breast, that I can hardly believe it; but winter has always been my cheerful season; and here I am sheltered from cold and changes of weather, wet walks, etc. May a thousand blessings, and the first and best of blessings, be yours the ensuing years, even to eternal ages.

1809.—LETTERS.—ARRIVAL AT BALTIMORE OF CECILIA AND HARRIET SETON.—MRS. SETON TAKES VOWS.—REMOVAL TO EMMITSBURG AND FOUNDATION OF ST. JOSEPH'S COMMUNITY.—CONVERSION OF HARRIET SETON.—HER DEATH IN THE LORD.—LETTERS.

CECILIA TO ELIZABETH.

N. Y., *Jan. 8th,* 1809.

MY BELOVED SISTER, FRIEND, AND MOTHER,—I can never tell you half my feelings on seeing once more your dear handwriting. Mr. Redmond gave me your letter at half-past ten this morning. My heart was too full; I dared not read it till I got to a silent corner at the Wilderness. Then, offering my heart to Jesus, I opened it; there was no restraining the tears. I did not wait for your letter to be firm and resolute. Did you then think your Cecily could trifle with another's happiness? Never, dearest friend. I again repeat that my heart belongs only to my Lord: 'tis His alone, and I trust will *ever be.* I feel my situation daily more painful; God only can know all.

There is so much discontent shown at all I do, that I have been asking permission once more to join you. *They* tell me that it is the will of God that I remain where I am. I will fight it out as long as I can support it. *He* only knows how long that will be. One thing I know, that I shall have strength according to the weight of my cross. Yet it seems to me He will not let it remain long so. I am hourly in fear of splitting on the many quicksands and rocks which surround me. Ah! dearest sister, can you not write me oftener? No one can know half the pleasure I feel on reading your letters. But do not indulge me if you must give up any visits to the dear chapel. My conjectures were then right about Christmas-eve. I imagined how *you* would spend it. I little thought when you left me, we were to be so long separated. No, my sister, I expected long before Christmas to have been one of you. I saw Zide[1] on Sunday. She says you must not think she neglects you. But she can not write without being obliged to show her letters, and in that case it would be pleasure neither to you nor to her. My fingers are almost frozen, I can scarcely hold the pen. My heart is too full to write in the parlor. Friday night I staid in town with Mrs. Wall. I stood godmother to Mrs. Fowler's child; she is a convert. Was at church before eight; at communion at sunrise. You have that happiness every morning. Farewell, your own forever.

CECILIA THERESA.

ELIZABETH TO MRS. SADLER.

Jan. 20th, 1809.

. . . . . The truth is I am a coward in thought, and try to drive away the past as much as possible, in whatever occasions regret. To receive the daily bread and to do the sacred will—that is the fixed point. But I find in proportion as my heart is more drawn towards the summit, it looks back with added tenderness to every one I

[1] Elizabeth Farquhar, of whom in a former note, she was twenty-one, and well disposed to Catholicity.

have ever loved; much more to those who have long possessed its entire and truest attachment.[1]

In February Elizabeth received a short letter from Mrs. Barry, announcing the death of her daughter Ann, at Madeira, on the 21st of August preceding. It was sad news, for she was sincerely attached to this gentle-hearted girl, whose personal merits lent a charm to the kindness of her parents towards the convert. Mrs. Barry writes: "My angel frequently spoke of you and your sweet children. You and they will not forget her. Her last words to me were pray, pray." Anna Seton was particularly affected by the loss of one who had been an intimate companion and example of all the virtues that should adorn a Christian virgin.

ELIZABETH TO MRS. DUPLEX.

February, 1809.

My Dear Friend,—I must beg of you to give me some account of your health, as I have heard that you have been much indisposed. How much my heart prays for you, and how tenderly it is attached to you, you can never know until we reach the source of light who will make all things evident. Oh! dear sister, to us who look

[1] This passage and many others breathing the same spirit, which occur in Elizabeth's letters and papers after her conversion, are another proof of the assertion that the Catholic religion, far from drying up in the heart, which tending to perfection offers itself entirely to God, the love of natural affection, expands it, elevates it, and gives it with supernatural intensity relation to an Infinite Object—to God who is charity.

beyond the pains and separations of our present existence, how sweet is the hope of an eternal reunion in the presence of our Lord! I know that all your hopes are fixed on that happy time, which makes me love you with a love which is inconceivable to those who do not find their center in the sacred hearts of Jesus and Mary. But He knows with what tenderness I present you to Him in my happy communion and the daily masses I assist at. I hope you never forget me in yours.

There is no news of our dear Mrs. Barry. No doubt our angelic Ann now remembers us who have been so fondly attached to her. Dear, dear friend, my tears flow at the thought of her happiness, and the heavenly hope that we shall share it with her. Oh! let us not stop a moment, but sigh incessantly for that happy hour when we will be together, absorbed in the ocean of His love who is now our life, our hope, our consolation.

Dear friend, do not be displeased that I am so much at liberty in writing to you: loving you in God, I can not speak any other language. That we may be happy in the ages of eternity is the fervent new year wish of your affectionate friend.

Your handsome present was far too handsome for me, dear friend. I have long ago offered it to God in the service of the altar in your name, which was the greatest pleasure I could have.

In the month of February Mrs. Seton's attention was more seriously than ever turned towards the formation of a religious community to which she was invited to belong. Her co-operation was of a very modest kind.

It had already long before entered into the heads of the zealous and far-seeing French clergymen in Baltimore and Boston, to prepare a society in this country in which women, while attending in a special manner to their own sanctification, might bestow a care upon the young in schools, asylums, and such like institutions. This is apparent from the letters of Cheverus, Matignon, and Dubourg, in all of which they deprecate Mrs. Seton's idea of removing to Montreal, although Mr. Filicchi favored it, and they would not have thwarted his wish without some particular reason. There can be no doubt that these three distinguished priests, and Mr. Tisserant also, early contemplated the establishment for females of a religious house, with a constitution as well adapted to the necessities of the country as circumstances would allow. An occasion only was wanting to carry out their plan; and this the pious ecclesiastics knew would not remain unrevealed if their design entered into the views of God. It was no harm to wait, since any hasty action might ruin all.

Mrs. Seton was first to establish herself in Baltimore, to breathe an atmosphere wholly Catholic; to exercise herself in the duties of mistress of a school, while following, at the same time, what might almost be styled a semi-conventual mode of life, and attending with fixed attention under enlightened direction to advancement in Christian perfection. During this period of preparation, Mr. Dubourg and others were to look about for persons who could join Mrs. Seton, and for the material means with which to execute their cherished project. They were successful in both points: to them, to members of the *Clergé Emigré*, belongs pre-eminently the honor of having founded Saint Joseph's House, and, consequently, of introducing the Sisters of Charity into the United States.

ELIZABETH TO MRS. SCOTT.

BALTIMORE, *March 2d*, 1809.

MY JULIA,—As you have so long shared all my pains, how much pleasure it will give you to know that Providence has disposed for me a plan after my own heart. A benevolent gentleman[1] of this place has formed a scheme of establishing a manufactory for the use of the poor, and includes in his intention the education of children, rich and poor. He is about purchasing a place at Emmitsburg, some distance from Baltimore, and has offered me the department of taking care of the children who may be presented, or rather of being the mother of the family. This pleases me for many reasons; besides I shall live in the mountains and see no more of the world than if I were out of it. A very amiable young lady,[2] who has been my assistant these two months past, will accompany me; and with Miss Nicholson, whom I before mentioned to you, and Mr. Dubourg's niece compose an amiable society.

[1] Mr. Cooper, a convert, of whom in a former letter.
[2] Miss Cecilia O'Conway.

CECILIA TO ELIZABETH.

WILDERNESS, *March 5th*, 1809.

MOST DEAR FRIEND,— . . . . . Mr. Kohlman[1] seems more and more averse than ever to my leaving New York. He has gone so far as to tell me I can not go unless in opposition to his advice and the will of God. That in Baltimore I can do no good. He is to write you a few lines about it. We move in town next month. One consolation, my sister, I am in the hands of God, and He will direct all for my salvation. If I am not to be with you, I can only say: "Thy will be done." If otherwise, with what joy and gratitude would I fly to the arms of my more than mother. But, hush! I could fill pages on that subject. Mr. Kohlman has so well regulated my hours for the course of the day that every thing comes much easier, and I have more time for study, which is a great object for me at present. I am no longer permitted to rise at four—six is the hour. It makes a vast difference. But obedience renders all sweet and easy. My May expedition is entirely given up.[2] In the first place, S——[3] says he will not go with me, and Mr. Redmond tells me it is foolish to think of it; moreover it would be a great *self-indulgence*. Never mind, it will all come in good time. Every day I think how sweetly you must pass the season of Lent. I have made out very well so far. I must not wish to pass it with you, for then it would no longer be a

[1] A Jesuit priest stationed in New York.

[2] She alludes to a proposed *visit* to Baltimore. Cecily and her friends disposed one way, but softly God another.

[3] One of her brothers.

time of penance. Dear friend, farewell. I hope your reverend friends all remember me at the Divine sacrifice. Your own forever,

CECILIA THERESA.

FROM THE SAME.

March 20th, 1809.

I know, beloved sister, you must be somewhat astonished at not hearing from me last week, in answer to your two letters which I received the same day. Could you, then, doubt of your Cecily's being willing to join you in any way, or any part of the world? I did not wish to write you until I had seen Mr. Kohlman. He had not then heard from the bishop. He said if it was the will of God I should go, but he thought it would be better put off until the fall, until E——'s return from school, as she would then be of an age to take charge of the little ones. Ah, my beloved dear friend, my soul truly sighs for the hour of peace and retirement. You know the dear beings that draw my heart most to New York. Harriet is the chief. When I mentioned to her my idea of going, she could not restrain the tears. She said I ought not to leave her now, as there was so great a prospect of her being married in the summer. B—— has settled at Jamaica,[1] and is to take her there for the first six or seven years. I am confident I should suffer much in parting with them; but, at the same time, both they and you must be assured how much happier I would be at Emmitsburg. If the anticipation is so sweet, what will the reality be? Yet do not think, my beloved, I expect a life of

[1] West Indies.

ease and pleasure. No, I seek the glory of God, and expect a life of penance and humiliation. I shall be very anxious to hear from you. Do, dearest, write soon. If I can, you shall hear from me in a few days. I thought my cough was over, but it has only been kept off. It has now returned worse than ever. So, my beloved, do not be astonished if you do not hear from me, for when I cough much my head is so giddy and eyes so blind as not to let me read or write.

Pray, pray for your own dear

CECILY.

ELIZABETH TO CECILIA.

March 26th, 1809.

MY DEAR CECILIA,—The first news I had of your suffering and illness was from a letter of ———, which, at the same time, gives the hope that you will soon be with us. I can not but expect you with joy such as you alone can believe who know how much my happiness is connected with yours. Do not bring any other clothes but *a black gown*. Keep your heart in peace and as composed as possible in parting with so many most dear to you. Look up and remember what poor sister has gone through. And our dear Harriet and Eliza! But He who is our only support will sustain them. My darling, I shall count every hour till you are in the arms of your own dear sister in Christ.

CECILIA TO ELIZABETH.

WILDERNESS, *March 27th*, 1809.

Since my last letter, my beloved sister, my prayers and communions have been offered to our adored Jesus to know His will, and to place me in that state which will tend most to His glory. After having disclosed with sincerity to my director every circumstance and every feeling of my heart I rest quiet, earnestly begging the assistance of our Lord, who, I am sure, could never leave in error one who so sincerely desires to do His will. You must know little, my sister, of your Cecily's heart if you doubt for a moment her love for a religious life. I told Mr. Cooper how much I desired to be with you. He thought I was called to that state. Yet, my sister, when I think of the dear children, of the change it will be for them when I leave, I know not what to think of it. On the other side, by remaining in the world I am exposed to innumerable dangers. My love for a religious life may be weakened. All this I told Mr. Cooper, but he bid me trust in God and fear nothing. Do, do pray for your own. Oh! my sister, your Cecily fears so to be deceived. Will not Mr. Babad sometimes offer the blessed sacrifice for me?

The health of Cecilia Seton began to show alarming symptoms early in the spring of this year, and it was determined, after many entreaties on her part, to permit her to join Elizabeth, without whose society it would seem as if she could not live, for her position among Protestant relatives in New York had sharpened the anguish of separation from the only one who could, to natural affection, add the charms of religious sympathy. She arrived in Baltimore towards the end of April in a very feeble condition, accompanied by her sister Harriet, and a brother who returned to New York after seeing them safe; but her sister remained with her.

It is easy to imagine the welcome of Christian love the long-wished for Cecily received from Elizabeth. The evening of her arrival the kind-hearted Father Babad[1] sent her a paper with the following pretty little verses:—

Colombe entre dans l'arche
Renferme toi dans son sein;
Un nouveau patriarche
T'y conduira de sa main.

Que le peuple volatil
Entonne ses chants joyeux:
La colombine Cécile,
Ciel! est rendue à nos voeux.

Après un long voyage,
Qu'il est doux d'entrer au port!
Quand battu de l'orage,
On a vu de près la mort.

[1] The Rev. Peter Babad was a Sulpitian, and as learned, zealous, good as the rest of his venerable *confrères*. He came originally from the village of Pont-de-Veyle, in what is now the department of the *Ain*. On a paper of his in my possession, of the 6th of May, 1809, he has jotted down, in French, the following memorandum of himself: "Born on the 10th of June, baptized on the 11th, in the year 1763, feast of the Sacred Heart of Jesus. Cast into prison for the faith of Jesus on the 20th of June, also the feast of the Sacred Heart." This holy priest was commonly called by the simple endearing title of *Père*. His many gentle qualities made him a universal favorite in Baltimore. He had, moreover, the truly apostolic gift of accommodating his words to the intelligence of his hearers. Some of his first communion instructions, written for one of Mrs. Seton's two youngest daughters, are admirable for their simplicity, joined to sufficiently ample development. He had, also, an excellent voice, and a facility for turning ideas into verse; truly one of those, "Such as by their skill sought out musical tunes and published canticles in writing."—*Ecclesiast.* xliv. 5.

Que le peuple volatil
Entonne ses chants joyeux:
La colombine Cécile,
Ciel! est rendue à nos vœux.

Mrs. Seton having been joined by several pious ladies intent on their own spiritual advancement, and desirous of serving the poor, it was thought proper that they should assume a semi-religious habit. This was a plain black gown, and cap of the same color, with plaited border, and pendant from a cincture, a chaplet of beads.[1] Mrs. Seton was further admitted to the three customary simple vows[2] of religion, which, as she says in a letter to a friend, she took in the hands of Bishop Carroll, on her knees before a crucifix, to be binding for one year's time only, but to be renewed at stated periods, if she should so wish to engage herself, and were approved by her ecclesiastical superior.

From this time those who had united with her, looked upon themselves as her spiritual children, and began to address her by the beautiful title of Mother.

[1] Elizabeth's beads were given her by Mr. Dubourg's sister. They are large, black, and solid—meant for use not ornament—with a brass medal of the B. V. attached between the decades and the initial string, which has a silver ring and crucifix at the extremity. Around the ring is engraved: *cor unum—anima una.* On the back of the cross: *Charitas christi urget nos: Pauperes evangelizantur*, and on the face, under the figure of our Lord: *Tibi Soli.*

[2] Vows in the Catholic Church are either *simple* or *solemn*. The latter kind are officially accepted by her, the former not. Both equally oblige in conscience, but differ widely in their dignity and effect.

TO JULIA SCOTT.

BALTIMORE, *9th May*, 1809.

The superior[1] of the Seminary here, who is graced with all the venerable qualities of seventy-five, which is his age, a mind still strong and alive to the interests of our little family as if we were all his own, and one of the most elegant men in his manners you ever met with, is going to take charge of our community, and reside at Emmitsburg. This is a great consolation in every sense, since he will say mass for us every day, regulate our religious exercises, etc. . . . . The views of Mr. Cooper have always been to afford instruction and consolation to the poor in every way it can be applied to them. To speak the joy of my soul at the prospect of being able to assist the poor, visit the sick, comfort the afflicted, clothe little innocents, and teach them to love God! There I must stop.

In the month of June Elizabeth, her two sisters-in-law, her daughter Anna, and one of the pious ladies who had joined her,[2] left Baltimore for Emmitsburg, a small village of Frederick County, in the northernmost part of Maryland, between the upper streams of the Monocacy and the Catoctin ridge of the South Mountains. It was

[1] The Very Rev. Francis Nagot. He was born at Tours, in 1734, and came in 1791 with three other Sulpitians to Baltimore, where he founded Saint Mary's Seminary, and became its first superior. Something intervened, probably his health, to hinder him from going, as he had intended, to direct the infant community at Emmitsburg. He died in 1816, full of years and good works.

[2] This little party went on first, principally to make a few necessary arrangements against the coming of the rest, but in part to give Cecilia, whose health was fast growing worse, the benefit of purer air.

there the generous aid of the Rev. Mr. Cooper, seconding Mr. Dubourg's plan, had located the new establishment, of which Elizabeth has spoken in her letters. The route of the little party was by way of Westminster, going diagonally across the State almost to the Pennsylvania line, and passing through a region, in some parts beautiful, in others monotonously ugly; yet the eye could generally turn as a relief from the unpicturesqueness of immediate surroundings to a range of blue hills on the left, rising in the distance into mountains. The journey was made amidst the cheerfully borne discomforts of heat, dust, bad roads, streams unbridged, joltings, crowding, fatigue, and fear of freshets, partly on foot and partly in one of those huge, canvas-covered, creaking wains in use among the country people of Maryland. The expenses of the expedition amounted to fifty dollars.

On arriving at Emmitsburg the women found the building on the property, purchased by Mr. Cooper, unfit for immediate occupation, and were fain to accept the shelter of a log-house, about two miles from the village, which Mr. Dubois, the missionary priest of the district, had built on the side of the mountain, a little below Saint Mary's church, and which he gave over to their occupancy, while he moved into new buildings further down, intended for a college.

The while this band of devoted women, pioneers of, in some sense, a new religious order in the United States, were peacefully living on the mountain side in a lowly house, in humble attire, busied in prayer and homely occupations, occurred the much-hoped conversion of Harriet Seton. As the feast of Saint Mary Magdalen drew near, all her friends redoubled their prayers in her behalf. Two days before it the incomparable Father Babad addressed her the following letter :—

J. M. J.[1]

BALTIMORE, *20th July*, 1809.

MOST DEAR CHILD,—After to-morrow, the day of St. Mary Magdalen, do join your Father in the solemn offering of the Great Sacrifice of the altar for your eternal concerns. Let us give thanks to Jesus for the favors he conferred on the loving Magdalen and through her intercession, let us beg for you the same grace and mercy. Faith will necessarily augment the merit of your love. Love, then, with all your heart Him who has eternally, from all eternity, loved you so generously, so purely, so disinterestedly, who has suffered so much for you, who has so patiently waited for you. Be ready to return Him love for love, and sacrifice for sacrifice. In your name, and as your representative, your interpreter at the altar, I will offer Him the sacrifice of your understanding, disposed to believe whatever He has taught us, the sacrifice of your tender heart choosing Him for the only object of your love, the sacrifice of your will ready to obey all His commandments, the sacrifice of your body prepared for mortification and penance. Amen.

[1] *Jesus, Mary, Joseph.* This good priest invariably headed his letters with a crosslet and the initials of the Holy Family.

Early in the day of the blessed feast of the Magdalen, Elizabeth, after pouring forth her own fervent prayers, and uniting her intention with that of the good Fathers Dubois and Babad in the holy sacrifice, made the following:—

Memorandum.—Saturday morning, July 22d.—Two masses said for poor Harriet: one in Baltimore, the other on St. Mary's Mountain.—Angels of heaven offer thy prayers.

So many petitions, such powerful intercession, so much grace of the all-merciful God, were not without fruit: Harriet was a Catholic in the evening. Among her papers is the following note relating to this event and subsequent religious acts:—

I formed my first resolution of becoming a Catholic on the 22d of July, Saint Mary Magdalen's day, in the little chapel on Saint Mary's Mountain. On that day the pastor of two happy souls I was ardently attached to, offered up the Divine sacrifice of the mass for my conversion.

September 24th.—Day of the Blessed Virgin of Mercy.—Received my first communion. On the same day made a renewal of my baptismal vows, and was entered in the sodality of the Sacred Heart. Hour of adoration, seven o'clock in the morning.

On *Tuesday the 25th* made my second communion, and was entered in the sodality of the Rosary of the Blessed Virgin Mary.

Verses of Father Babad to Harriet after giving her first commnnion and aggregating her to the sodality of the Sacred Heart.

J. M. J.

ST. JOSEPH'S VALLEY, 24TH OF SEPTEMBER, 1809,

DAY OF THE B. V. DE MERCEDE.

Jadis, chère Harriet, aujourd'hui Magdeleine,
Souviens-toi qu'à tel jour, qu'aujourd'hui, tu reçus
Ton Dieu Sauveur, ton Roi, ton Epoux, ton Jésus,
Que ton âme de Lui demeura toute pleine:
Qu'après L'avoir logé dans ton cœur tout amour,
Je te logeai toi-même en ce cœur tout tendresse,
Où tu trouveras tour à tour,
Et ton appui dans ta faiblesse,
Et dans l'angoisse et la détresse:
Ta consolation jusqu'à cet heureux jour
Où le bonheur commence, où finit la tristesse.
Plonge-toi dans ces divins Cœurs
De la compatissante Mère,
Et de son Fils, Jésus le débonnaire,
Source de tous les biens, abîme de douceurs.

Soon after Harriet's conversion the little party, which had meanwhile been joined by those who had remained in Baltimore, left the temporary dwelling on the mountain and removed to the valley.

The house first occupied by the community of Saint Joseph's, was a small two-storied building with a high porch in front and an open passage running behind. It stood about a quarter of a mile to the right of the public road, between the mountain and the village, surrounded by a few trees, and on a gentle rise some hundreds of yards from the valley stream. Here the pious women assembled with an appropriate ceremony of taking possession, which was conducted by the Rev. Mr. Dubois, and consisted in blessing the place according to the form in the ritual,[1] and sprinkling it with holy water. They then went in procession to a little wooded knoll, still used by their successors as a place of assemblage for recreation and out-of-door prayer, and recited the Litany of the Saints. The community was, also, with special invocation, placed under the patronage of the glorious patriarch St. Joseph.

On the 10th of August following, the first mass was said in the house, and all who could[2] received holy communion in honor of the blessed martyr Lawrence.

The community was now fully and fixedly established.

The Rev. Father Dubois[3] was indefatigable in his exertions to assist the new-comers, and when not obliged

[1] *Benedictio Loci*, in rituali Romano.

[2] Harriet and Rebecca had not yet made their first communion.

[3] John Dubois was born in Paris, August 24th, 1764. He left France on account of the revolution, and in 1791 arrived in the United States. "Bishop Carroll welcomed the faithful exile, and authorized him to exercise the functions of his holy ministry, first at Norfolk, and afterwards at Richmond. Recommended by General La Fayette to the Randolphs, Lees, and Beverleys, to James Monroe and Patrick Henry, he received the kindest and most respectful attentions from these distinguished statesmen and their numerous friends, and for want of a Catholic chapel said mass in the *Capitol*, and there administered the sacraments to the few scattered Catholics who could avail themselves of his ministry."—*Discourse on Bishop Dubois* by the Very Rev. Dean McCaffrey, D. D. In 1794 he was appointed pastor at Frederick, Md., and in 1826, after long and faithful services, was made Bishop of New York, in which city he died December 20th, 1843. He was of those who "have gained glory in their generations, and were praised in their days: . . . . men of mercy whose godly deeds have not failed."—*Ecclesiast.* xliv. 7, 10.

to say mass at the village or the mountain church, he used to go to the modest little chapel fitted up in one of the rooms at Saint Joseph and say it there. This excellent clergyman was later superior of the Sisters, and continued for many years to give them his untiring attention. On Sundays and holydays of obligation the community heard mass at one of the two parish churches attended by Father Dubois, until, as the number of inmates increased, a priest was appointed to go regularly to their chapel.

The women entered at once upon their occupations, which were to teach poor children, visit the sick, sew, knit, and make clothes.

A boarding-school for girls, whose parents could afford to pay for their education, had been contemplated; and not long after the occupation of Saint Joseph's the first pupils were received. All idea of a *manufactory* that Mr. Cooper may have entertained, and which Elizabeth mentions in a letter, appears to have been soon given up.

REV. MR. SIBOURD TO ELIZABETH.

September, 1809.

My Dear Daughter,—Though I seldom write, yet I always think of you; your little ones, and dear Cecilia, whom I offer to God every day at the altar—the place, you know, you all like best to be remembered at. I give you joy for your solemn renunciation of the world, of this deceitful world, wherein nothing is to be found but grief and vexation of spirit, to espouse Jesus Christ, who will be your joy and never-failing happiness.

But for my bad eyes and impaired health by cold climates, I should have taken up my residence near the holy mountain, there to be once more the confidential father of my dearly beloved child in Christ, M. A. Seton. . . . . . On the 25th ultimo you had my blessing, and the holy sacrifice of mass was offered in your intention. May the Almighty prosper your future exertions for the institution of St. Joseph. Amen, amen, amen.

L. SIBOURD.

ELIZABETH TO MRS. SCOTT.

EMMITSBURG, 20*th Sept.*, 1809.

O MY JULIA,—What a letter have I received from you! How could you write to your friend she seemed to have forgotten you? Yet you know not that the nearer a soul is truly to God, the more its sensibilities are increased to every being of His creation; much more to those whom it is bound to love by the tenderest and most endearing ties. You will hear a thousand reports about our community, which I beg you not to mind. The truth is we have the best ingredients of happiness—order, peace, and solitude. There are only sixteen now in the family; a steward supplies all out-door wants. Nothing can be more pleasant than our situation as to woods, meadows, and a gentle stream that winds behind our house. With regard to Anna,[1] all will be right at last with the excellent examples

[1] Elizabeth's daughters lived with her at Saint Joseph's. Her two sons were admitted into the college, newly opened by Mr. Dubois, at the base of the mountain. They used to walk over once a week to see their mother and sisters.

she has in both her aunts. Cecilia's complaint of the chest remains. B—— has written poor Harriet a proposal that he should remain eight or ten years longer in Jamaica to obtain a fortune. She is so shocked at a proposal which evidently shows his indifference to her, that it seems to disgust her with every thing of the kind. However, I hope he will know how to appreciate her merit and constancy, and things may be accommodated in a shorter time. She has resolved to wait the event patiently, and make the best use of her time in the interval. Ann and Cecilia are the gainers, as she is determined to hide her disappointment in our mountains, and keep out of the circles of fashion this winter, which would be impossible if she returned to New York . . . . . I think you will come to see me next summer, and take a peep at our black gowns and demure looks, which hide, however, a set of as lively, merry hearts as ever met together. If you knew half the real good your friend possesses, while the world thinks she is deprived of every thing worth having, you would moralize an hour at least, and allow that she has really and truly the best of it. If I am not strong in health, it is because my constitution is broken. Air, exercise, good food, and content ought to strengthen me; but so long a combat as I have gone through will leave its vestiges, yet there is no settled complaint of any kind. What are you doing darling, dear Gloriana? You are well, you have many comforts, but you have not all. When you are taken to the sick-bed, what will you say? You will acknowledge then you have enough—too much of this world, because it has bound you. You will feel a want, then, which nothing can supply. The long, long life in perspective will seem a strange land with strange inhabitants. Think about it a little. Do you know, dearest, that after all my neglect of you, and the little reason you have to think I love you with the boundless tenderness I do, God is my witness I would this moment gladly give my life to obtain for you the comforts to be obtained in that hour; the peace of a soul going to its kindest, dearest, most tender Friend. You understand. When I think of you, sometimes I could go and tear you away from all, and wrap you in the bosom that loves and has loved you long. What would I not do to give you only a little taste! Dear, dear friend, you laugh; but while you laugh consider what an extravagant idea it is that piety creates gloominess and disgust. Who think so are unacquainted with the anticipations of a soul whose views are chiefly pointed to another existence; it is inconceivable what liberty it enjoys. The cares and troubles of life surround it, to be sure, as others; but how different their effect! Human passions and weaknesses, to be sure, are never extinct, but they can not triumph in a heart possessed by Peace. She is lovely, Julia. Make acquaintance with her. She will not be angry you have neglected her so long. Tell me in your next how you like her. Forever your own friend,

E. A. Seton.

In the month of October the Right Rev. Bishop Carroll visited Emmitsburg, and administered confirmation on the 20th. Among those who received the sacrament were Harriet and Anna Seton.

TO CECILIA FROM ONE OF HER BROTHERS.

NEW YORK, *October 29th*, 1809.

Harriet gives your bad health as her principal reason for remaining at Emmitsburg all winter, and wherever I go I am asked whether she is really a Roman Catholic. My answer is: "That is the report."

A singular circumstance happened yesterday. I had been shooting with John near Newark, and had made a stop to lunch, when the Diligence stage came along with three female and two male passengers. As soon as the conveyance drew up, they commenced a conversation about the Setons at Emmitsburg. You may imagine my curiosity. I turned my head towards the stage, but was not near enough to hear much. One of the ladies asked if Cecilia was not her name? The reply was: "Yes, Cecilia Seton; there are three sisters there." At that moment I was on the point of saying: "And pray, madam, what do you know of the three sisters. If you know any thing, speak! for they are near and dear to my heart," when the stage drove off apace. One of the ladies was remarkably pretty, and had a little child in her arms; and one of the gentlemen left a stick which I have now in my possession, and look at every day as if it had something to reveal, but not a word can I get out of it. I think the best way to get the full story of the three sisters, will be to advertise the stick . . . . .

The news of Harriet's conversion brought down upon her quite a little storm of letters full of horror and indignation at such a treasonable act. Mr. and Mrs. Ogden, her sister and brother-in-law, in whose family she had lived in New York, considered themselves the most aggrieved. The two following letters contain the usual appeals to the feelings and temporal interests which are thought by some to be such powerful arguments with any who differ from them in matters of religion. They also curiously show how consistent Protestants are in the inconsistency with which they visit persecution on persons logical enough to think for themselves from the premises of their religion. It is simply ridiculous to have a Protestant reproach a convert to the Catholic Church with *instability of faith*;[1] but the other letter is unusually brutal and oafish, even in the customary anti-Catholic line of argument. Mr. Bruté summed it up mildly when he wrote on the back: *Poor controversy.*

MR. OGDEN TO HARRIET SETON.[2]

NEW YORK, *November 27th*, 1809.

Your letter of the 12th instant, my dear Harriet, to your aunt, announcing the reality of our fears respecting your first concerns in this life, has this day been received. From all that had already passed in our family on the subject as it respected Cecilia, from the peculiar manner in which you left us, and above all from the solemn assurances you gave us both before and after your departure,

[1] If Bossuet could come to life again and bring his *History of the Variations of the Protestants* down to 1869, "The world itself would not be able to contain the books that should be written."—*John* xxi. 25.

[2] What is italicized is underlined in the original.

we confidently hoped that a temporary absence, in the discharge of the duties of a sister, would preserve your mind and judgment uncorrupted by the artifices and temptations to which you would be necessarily exposed. In addition to these, I must confess I had great confidence in your discretion and good sense, that you would not hastily have abandoned the faith in which you had so far progressed towards immortality, and through which you had enjoyed all the consolation and comfort this transitory life can require. But permit me, before I go further, to pass a candid opinion upon the letter alluded to, and if I shall doubt the *sincerity* spoken of in it, I shall not so much impute it to your guileless heart, as to another *head* which, I think, dictated it: to that fatal influence which has not only brought on us extreme distress, but has drawn you aside from the straight path towards heaven, and from the society of your family and friends. Permit me, then, to say that, judging from all that has passed, in my opinion, your mind was poisoned before you left us; that opportunity alone was wanting for the poison to show itself: and most unfortunately for us and for yourself, that opportunity occurred by the illness and consequent voyage of Cecilia. Far be it from me not to allow that the affection of a sister was in some degree a motive; but I must think it was not the only, and but a secondary one; and if so, tell me in the name of heaven, why not have mentioned your doubts and opinions before you left us? Why turn so suddenly, without mature inquiry, from the sacred pale of our and your church, to seek refuge and salvation within that of another, whose tenets, whose rites, and whose doctrines were to be declared and explained (or had been so) by one of its devotees, uncontradicted by the unanswerable arguments of the members of your former church? Had you avowed your determination to embrace the Catholic faith, or even your disposition to do so, before your departure, with one accord we would have taken measures to remove your doubts, to quiet your scruples, and to put *that Monitor* at rest who has been so imperious during your absence from us. But you did not think proper to do so; and, therefore, I think you have not acted with your usual candor—the loss of which I can only attribute to your change of principle. And now let me say a few words in relation to your new *faith*, for I can not call it a religion. In doing this I shall not attempt any more learning than that of the most common layman; and, of course, not pretend to discuss the merits or errors of either side of the question. . . . . . . [Primitive purity of the church. Corruption. Popish errors. Dark ages. Superstition. Second dawn of pure and undefiled religion. Luther and Calvin. The Church of England. Glory, glory, glory. "Fire and rolling smoke." . . .] . . . . At this moment we see the Pope a cipher on earth, a mere nothing in temporal and spiritual power. The prophecies within the last few years have also been examined with peculiar learning and care, and their explanation and daily fulfillment abundantly demonstrate the near and final overthrow of the chair of this *vicegerent of Heaven*, and unfold to the world the falsity of his faith and their delusion. Believe me, dear girl, for many ages it has been a persuasion calculated only for the government of the most ignorant part of Europe. It has so far degenerated from its original purity as too often to be a mask for the perpetration of the most dreadful crimes; and really, at this time of day, to see a Protestant forsaking the church for worship in a Roman chapel, is a phenomenon not to be accounted for, unless through the means of undue influence. . . . . . Harriet, let me ask you, how is it possible that you can pin your faith upon the sleeve of another, relinquish the sacred observance of our former worship, the society of your friends, and bid defiance, without due reflection, to the opinion of the world? You say your eternal welfare is at stake. I grant it; but is the opinion of a woman (or of two or three priests paid for their profession) to prevail over the most learned and numerous body of divines in the world? men, the most enlightened ministers of God's Word here below, who are all equally concerned with yourself, and interested for their individual welfare hereafter, and who have pronounced the Catholic faith (as now used and emanating from the Pope) not orthodox, and bordering on profanation and idolatry. . . . . You must then perceive the immense difference between worshiping an Invisible and Infinite Trinity in spirit and in holiness, and the senseless addresses to wooden images or imaginary saints. The former is in union with our rational and established religion, the latter with superstition, ignorance, misguided zeal, and degenerate Catholicism. Yet, important as this subject is to you, as you acknowledge it is, how have you acted? Why, I will plainly tell you. Immured in the solitude of your retirement, you have lent a willing ear to the persuasions of Mrs. Seton, the only person in her situation in the United States, a constant witness of the external performance of her devotions, your heart has yielded to the delusion; your mind thus seduced has embraced and avowed *her* faith, not because internally convinced of its purity, but from the strong impression of her manner, and the want of opportunity of worshiping after your former custom, from the absence of other society; and, in short, from your want of discretion. This, then, on my solemn belief, has been the cause of our present distress, and of your lamentable and hopeless condition. Thank God! there is yet a remedy in your own hands—suspend, or rather recall the rash resolution you have made . . . . . It would be useless for me to describe the pain and anguish of mind which now distract the family on your account, more particularly your aunt, who really mourns as for the loss of a child, and with whom we have had but one conversation on the subject, and that was short, for it was intruding on grief. But I do not wish to address your feelings, but rather your reason. Suffice it to say we are *really distressed* . . . . In addition to what I have already said on the merits of the unhappy subject of my letter, let me draw your attention for a moment to some other considerations which, perhaps, are entitled to some weight, even on the ground of *policy*. Reflect then on your situation, supposing the hand of death has laid Mrs. Seton and Cecilia in the grave. Unfriended and deserted by relations, you will find yourself immured in the gloomy recesses of your mountains, dependent on the scanty provision of the sisterhood, and perhaps under the control of another less indulgent superior. Really, I should pity you. But to this, methinks, I hear you say, in the jargon of a convent, *my religion will support me under every trial.* Believe me, then, these are unnecessary trials, never intended or imposed by our Heavenly Father; but, on the contrary, militating against His express commands. Besides, let me remark that the establishments at Baltimore and Saint Joseph's are novel things in the United States, and would not have been permitted by the populace in any other place than in the democratic, Frenchified State of Maryland. The religion they profess is uncongenial to the habits, manners, and nature of Americans, and I predict ere long, from many causes, the demolition of every building in that State in any wise resembling a convent or Catholic hospital. Yet do me the justice to believe that nothing contained on the last page is in any manner intended as *in terrorem.* I only wished to bring to your view probable events in which you are materially concerned. . . . .

MRS. OGDEN TO HARRIET.

GREENWICH, *Saturday night, Dec. 9th,* 1809.

Oh, my dear Harriet, how have you disappointed those hearts that were so tenderly attached to you! what painful affliction you have caused your first and truest friends! How could you in a few short months throw aside, without the smallest hesitation, all those to whom you were endeared, to whom you were united in the tenderest sentiments of love, and to whom you were bound by gratitude[1] and duty? How could you desert us to pursue a path so exactly opposite to our wishes? How could you embrace a religion which holds forth that its sacred ceremonies will lead you safe to heaven, while your family, though Christians of a somewhat different faith, shall be driven to an abyss I shrink from mentioning; and embrace it, too, without hesitation, without that consideration and reflection so sacredly necessary on an occasion of such infinite import-

[1] Harriet had lived with her sister since their father's death.

ance? What an unaccountable infatuation! You in whom we placed the fullest confidence, both as it respected the stability of your faith, your judgment and discretion; you who gave the most solemn assurance of your speedy return with unchanged sentiments, to tell us without any previous intimation of that state of doubt which must have preceded it, that you have changed your religion, and have forsaken us forever! I am almost inclined to disbelieve it. Harriet, my dear girl, if the thought of relinquishing the society of all those so dear to you was not sufficient to induce you to act with more sincerity and candor, the ties of gratitude and *implicit duty* should have brought you to the bosom of your adopted mother, imploring her counsel and advice before so unfeeling a desertion. And even now *imperious* duty should bring you like a pleading culprit to beg that counsel which some enthusiastic vision has caused you to forego. Could you see the various and contending emotions depicted on my countenance when your name is mentioned, your heart would feel a sorrow that would make you repent the rash resolution you have taken. I love you as a sister, but I have felt for you as one that was unworthy of the name. Your conduct to the family that gave you protection has been unjust, ungenerous, and insincere, so much so that unless you make a recantation, principles of the strictest justice would forbid them ever proffering you an asylum at your once happy home. Do you look forward to your situation, my darling Harriet? If B——, under existing circumstances, should refuse to unite his fate with yours, where then would you retire to? What would become of us? Would you make inroads upon our happiness, and give up all for the sisterhood? Heaven forbid! I look forward with the brightest hope for the revival of that happy day when we shall be once more united. As for me, I lament much more your ungracious conduct towards us than your change of religion. Alas, there is no end to the separations of our family. You have now given the finishing stroke, for in your letter you have left us with little hope of ever seeing you again. I hope, my dear Harriet, you will look with a favorable eye on my husband's letter, and impute nothing he has there said to any other motives than affection and a wish gently to reprehend your inconsiderate conduct. He loves you much, and unites with us in wishes that it were in our power to repair the breach you have made in our shattered family. Take it in good part, he will be much pleased if you assure him from your own hand you have done so. Your bosom friend Eliza[1] feels your loss most sensibly,—so unexpected! She has not yet reconciled her mind to such an unhappy event. S——[2] is very disconsolate, he blames himself very much for suffering you to stay.

I am bound, in honor, to deliver a message from Mrs. Hoffman, that neither you nor Mrs. Seton will ever write to Emma or any of the girls. I shall expect to hear from you the next post after you receive this.

Your truly affectionate sister,

CHARLOTTE OGDEN.

These and other letters received after her conversion deeply wounded Harriet's feelings, without in any way moving her from the position she had taken. The hand

[1] Farquhar. This young girl who had excited such hopes of conversion, never became a Catholic.

[2] A brother.

of God, gently all things disposing, had drawn her *out of her country and from her kindred,* "To seek a tranquil death in distant shades." Nature taking a wrong turn, she died most unexpectedly in the bloom of youth and beauty, on the 23d of December, 1809. Her last moments, described by Elizabeth in a letter to a friend, were highly edifying. As death approached, she begged to be frequently sprinkled and blessed with holy water, and recommended her soul with earnestness to the prayers of Father Babad, to whom in great measure she attributed her conversion.

Harriet Seton was buried under the spreading branches of an oak-tree, in a little wood, a few hundred yards from the house, that had been chosen for a graveyard. She would have joined the community, following her sister Cecilia's example, as a religious, had she lived a few months longer; but our Lord did not permit this consummation of her generous sacrifice.

The blessed inmates of St. Joseph's have, nevertheless, always considered her one of their own, and her body reposes in the community burial-ground—the Valley premices of them that "are gone before with the sign of faith, and rest in the sleep of peace."

A few weeks after Harriet's death, Elizabeth wrote thus to the young man to whom she had had the misfortune of being engaged.

My Dear B.,—Before this time you have, no doubt, heard many different accounts of the departure of our beloved Harriet. I know letters were written you immediately, and thought it best to wait until your mind would be composed before I wrote you any thing on the subject.

By your letters to her after her leaving New York, you appeared to be acquainted, in part, with the circumstances of dear Cecily's illness, and the manner in which they were again re-united to me at Baltimore. From thence we came to the Mountain, where both Harriet and Cecilia soon obtained a great share of health. We were accustomed to walk every afternoon in the woods which led to the height of the mount on which we lived half-way up, and a little higher than our log cottage stands our chapel, which Harriet never entered till some time after we came here, but always walked in the forest with Anna when Cecily and I went there. Neither of us ever asked why she did not come in, well knowing that in her situation it would be imprudent in her to take any share in our religious exercises, but when of her own accord she did come in and take great delight in joining us in them, we surely never advised her to stay out, or showed any other opposition than asking her if she had considered how it would be thought of at home. She then, with many tears, related to me how completely unhappy she was in that home (the which I fully knew before I left New York); said she would rather die than return to it; represented how little hope she had of being united to you from the different accounts and reports she had of you from persons who intimately knew your situation and habits; showed a letter you had written which mentioned the story of a young man who left his mistress, youthful and lovely, and was so long separated that he found her old and ugly, asking if she had not lost her bloom, etc., which letter she burnt in great agitation, and declared she would make her determination forever and not separate from Cecily and me, and by uniting herself to us she was sure of peace and tranquillity, at least, which was all she asked in this world.

After that, Aunt Farquhar wrote her that you wished her to join you in the West Indies, or that you were coming for her, to which she replied in a manner expressive of her unchangeable affection and attachment to you, and that she was ready to prove it at any hour; and, I believe, wrote you to the same effect, as I remember she was two or three days writing you and sent a very large package. . . . . .

ELIZABETH TO JULIA SCOTT.

27th December, 1809.

My own Dear Julia,—I have had many heavy hours since I wrote you last from the extreme illness of Cecilia, and now from the death of my sweet and darling Harriet, who was the life and joy of my heart for many months past. Her illness has been long; that is since she first complained of the sick-headache she has been long subject to. But sometimes better and other times worse, I had not the least alarm till her complaint took another turn.

So it goes with your friends: tribulation is my element; if it only carries me home at last, never mind the present. Year after year passes—the last must come. Foolish and extravagant as your own friend now appears to you, when the scene is about to close, things will wear so different an aspect you would be very glad to have been among the number of those who look beyond it. Our mountains are very black, but the meadows still green, and my dear ones[1] skipping upon them with the sheep, except poor Anna, who deeply feels the loss of her companion, friend, and adviser. They always walked, read, and worked together. Yet I am much reconciled to our loss, as her situation with B—— was so distressing. . . . She was truly an angelic girl, and her death is one of the hard blows destined for your friend. Yet *as He pleases and when He pleases;* but, to be sure, when my turn comes I shall be very glad. . . . . . They tell me a hundred most ridiculous stories are going about relative to our manner of living here, but I hope you will not listen to them a moment if they should reach you; and believe me, again, when I assure you that I have true peace and comfort in every way. As to sickness and death itself, if they come to us again, we know that they are the common attendants of human life, and it would be madness to be unhappy because we are treated like the rest of human beings.

1810.—Letters.—Bounty of Rev. Mr. Cooper.—Death of Cecilia Seton.—Visit of Bishop Cheverus.—Letters.

ELIZABETH TO MRS. SADLER.

Emmitsburg, *9th January,* 1810.

My Dearest Eliza,—A letter from sister Post last week tells me you are safe arrived and very well. A few

[1] Her two little girls, Kitty and Rebecca.

days before I began a letter to you, not knowing where it would find you; and now I do entreat you to take the first stormy day when visitors are quiet, or the first hour of night you can bestow, to satisfy a heart that loves you more than you are conscious of. It is more than nine months since I have heard any thing direct from you. . . . The darlings you have so long cherished are as when I last wrote, full of health and innocence, except poor Anna, who is more than affected by the death of Harriet. . . . . The different reports you may perhaps hear of our situation, will make it doubtful what it really is; but if you recollect the system of the Sisters of Charity before and since the Revolution in France, you will know the rule of our community. You may imagine my content in such a situation: it is almost inconceivable to myself that I possess it. Now, our chief occupation is spinning, knitting, etc., to obtain clothing for ourselves and the children in our charge, who are educated with the care the principle inspires on which our good Sisters act. They are truly good Sisters: you would be delighted with their simplicity. Every occasion to visit the sick is embraced; but the villages around us are not very large. Our mountain seems the limit of the world to us; but beyond it, dear Eliza, you know we have many most dear interests. . . . . Rev. Mr. Tisserant is not yet returned, but still expected; the death of a sister in Germany has delayed him. We have reason to hope Mr. Tisserant will be our chaplain when he returns.

TO MR. WEISE.[1]

Sunday night, 7th January, 1810.

MY FRIEND,—Your kind letter was, as always a letter from you must be, very, very welcome. My not writing to you was, to be sure, from a very bad cause, being cross, sick, and lazy: but these things will happen, and you must forgive. Your troubles, I find, like my own, are multiplied; and so will our comforts be when this dark night of life is over. I do not grow very strong in the body, yet the soul is so well at liberty that every thing except eternity seems but a dream.

Be good, Mr. George, and tell your dear little wife I think of her and pray for her continually; and she must pray that I be good, that my prayers may be accepted. As for you, I hope your cross may increase till it purifies you like pure gold; and woe to you if, knowing so well how rich a treasure you have, you do not let it work its effect in you: as you are not sure you would be safe without this very one, which, I grant, is hard enough to bear, but might be yet harder if compared with all that is due to our adored Master. Tell our dearest *Père* that we have all adopted his motto at St. Joseph's: "Well enough to work, bad enough to suffer;" and are proud to share the cup with him. You will be anxious for Annina. Her situation is not dangerous for the present, I hope, but the complaint is very obstinate and the fever constant. Good Susan is recovering; little Mary continues ill. Tell our

[1] A gentleman living near the seminary in Baltimore, who had been very kind to Mrs. Seton; and the attentions of his excellent wife to Cecilia when she arrived ill, from New York, were most affectionate.

dearest *Père* the thought that we are always in his prayers is my greatest consolation next to the Adored. We are all praying for him continually. Best love to your dear Minon.[1] Have confidence. Never let the comparison of time and eternity slip an instant from your mind. I find this cures all sorrow. L. J. C.[2] *Béni, adoré.*

Your friend,

M. E. A. SETON.

After Anna's recovery she was invited by one of her mother's friends to come and stay some time with her in Baltimore, where her health would improve amidst the comforts that the rigorous season made so welcome to a delicate girl, and the poverty of the little community at St. Joseph's could by no means afford.

From Baltimore she writes:—

To the Dearest of Mothers: Union in Eternity with Him.

MY MOST PRECIOUS MOTHER,—No letter! well, my Jesus, Thy will be done. O my mother, my dear mother, what shall I say? all uncertainty. I know not what to think; but, O my mother, pray, do pray for that dear soul.[3] I can not tell you how much I loved her: she is as it were the subject of all my prayers and sighs. Oh, how much I love you! You are my dearest, and soul's dearest mother. I have a question to propose to my mother, and you alone shall decide. The girls are going

[1] Mrs. Weise.

[2] These initials are often used by Elizabeth, who took the pious custom from Father Babad. They stand for *Laudetur Jesus Christus:* Praised be Jesus Christ.

[3] Harriet.

to have an exhibition, and they wish me very much to be in it; but I do not wish to have any part in it. They begged me very much, and still I refused. Well, they begged me again. At last I said : Well, whatever mother says. Do not you think I had better not act? but whatever you say. Most precious, dear mother! it has been a long time since I have received a little word from my mother. If you can, do write me a little word and tell me your opinion.

Your ever-loving and affectionate child,

ANNA-MARIA.

J. M. J.—My Jesus, bless my mother.

In the month of February the house at St. Joseph was suffering for almost the necessaries of life, but several good friends came forward with assistance, and chiefly the Rev. Mr. Cooper, who sent from Philadelphia a large stock of provisions and material for clothing. His charity is particularly mentioned, with gratitude, by Mrs. Seton, in a letter to Julia Scott. After enumerating some of the articles forwarded by Mr. Cooper, she says: "He will never let us want what he can give. We never see him or even thank him for his pure benevolence. Many strange beings there are in this world, dearest." This generous benefactor of St. Joseph's disliked to have his charitable acts alluded to, and would receive no acknowledgment of them: he left all to God.

ELIZABETH TO MRS. SADLER.

8th March, 1810.

MY DEAR, DEAR ELIZA,—Both your first and second letter reached their destination, which I know were to my very heart. They have said all that could be most grateful to it. It seems to me I can see you and look within yours as it was while you were writing; every article of furniture, plants, etc., around you, and the spot where each thing stood, I can bring to the mind's eye as distinctly as if they were in view but an hour ago; even the features and expression of the beloved Pauline are exactly present. Have you this treasure of memory? Some persons can never recollect features: all the past is confusion. If you have this privilege, you must often look towards the dear uncle's dwelling with sensations—*I feel for you.* Sweet Lord, what a being is ours? obliged to reduce our aim to a simple view of the little part we fill, and in quiet acceptance insure tranquillity, or engage in the torrent of recollection which carries—oh, my Eliza, where would mine carry me if it was not resisted? therefore, a transient glance behind, with me, is quickly followed by a strong look upward which the mid-day sun himself can not repel. . . . . . I can not say more now without missing this week's post. My earnest love to Craig. If ever you see dear Mary, try to do away the bad impressions I find she has of Anna. Oh, if God would ever grant that I should once again have an opportunity of cultivating her and Helen's sisterly love, how thankful I would be! You know, writing them the kind of letters I should be obliged to write, would be nonsense; nor have I the time. But time and patience will do something, perhaps. All I can say is my heart now hangs round them all more than ever.

Soon I expect, my dear, dear, a thousand times dear Cecilia will take her flight. Oh, Eliza, how many strings draw up as well as down! Yet my heart faints when I think of this separation; no one can ever conceive what she is to me, but—but—*fiat*.

Dear Mary B—— and her lovely family—do say a word of them. That partiality will go with me to the grave, as will my true and faithful affection for you.

TO MRS. SCOTT.

26th March, 1810.

MY OWN DEAR JULIA,—Your account of yourself and of what is dear to you, is more interesting to the very soul of your friend than you can imagine.

So you have been told we are all suffering, sick, etc. It has been so in part, but not as much so as report would have it. Harriet's death, while it wounded me sorely in one way, was easily reconciled in others. If I had an hour's conversation with you on her situation with the Farquhar family on one hand and B—— on the other, you would see that with her sweet, heavenly dispositions, she is just where it is best she should be, and all this starting of nature from death and separation is often more selfish than rational. Cecilia will very soon follow her—I think in a few months, more probably weeks. What can I say? They are both far dearer to me than myself—we part, nature groans, for me it is an anguish that threatens dissolution, not in convulsive sobs, but the soul is aghast, petrified; after a short while it returns to its usual state, and all goes on as if nothing had happened. This same effect has followed the death of all so dear. Why, Faith lifts the soul, Hope supports it, Experience says it must, and Love says—let it be. . . . . Dear Anna is beginning to feel her mother's fate, and mixes the attention of a friend with the duty of a child. How happy she is to learn experience at the school of a mother, there are so many ways of sweetening the lesson, and it makes her cautious and solid in her hopes! You have given her completely the means of independence, and I assure you she acts with great propriety, and considers her little sisters as in her charge. The boys are very happy and truly good. I have enough, dearest, for this world, be assured. What I would now most earnestly ask would be to see you quietly and alone for a few hours, perhaps before next winter. Say yes, though they tell me it is a tedious journey from Philadelphia. Mr. Cooper says you are very well, building a new and handsome house. What would I consider my life if I could obtain you true happiness! You know what happiness; not that of the present passing hour, of course, but that which is infinite. Do not imagine your own friend is looking on the gloomy side for that soul so precious. Not so, but wishes, ardently wishes, that you could taste the peaceful disengagement which some are enjoying without being indifferent to their active duties. But, patience, dearest. Only be not insensible to the thousand motives we have to love the best of Beings, and it will grow right at last; that is, if you will love. For my part I find so much contentment in this love, that I am obliged to think with consideration to find out how any one can raise his eyes to the light of heaven and be insensible to it. . . . . I never recollect hearing you express any other sentiment than simple veneration, but I know your heart is all alive, and may be acquainted with a language in which it has never spoken to its friend. Love me dearly, as I do you.

In the month of April Cecilia's complaint took a sudden and final turn. She was suffering from consumption, and it was deemed advisable to take her to Baltimore. Her sister-in-law accompanied her, and they arrived at the house of Mr. Weise on the 19th of April, where the invalid received many religious attentions which were impossible at Emmitsburg, whose single priest was so harassed with duties that it is a wonder of that missionary spirit, for which the French are distinguished, that any man could have performed them alone. The good *Père*, by whom Cecilia had been greeted on her arrival from New York the preceding year, now became her assiduous spiritual attendant. He had never, indeed, been heedless of her precious soul even when she was at St. Joseph's, as the following little letter received by her a day or two before she left it will prove. The original is in French.

April 14*th*, 1810.

FOR THE LITTLE DOVE OF JESUS CHRIST.

Have read to you in the morning the 62d[1] psalm, and arrest your thoughts upon the *Gloria Patri*, as on the central point of our Trinity, not only, but of every thing that tends

[1] A psalm of David when he was in the desert of Edom: "O God, my God, to Thee do I watch early.

to God. With what transports do the saints and angels who see Him as He is, and face to face, repeat the heavenly song of praise forever: Holy, holy, holy, and to the Father, Son, and Holy Ghost be glory! How His holiness, His justice, His greatness fills them with wonder! How His goodness melts them! How His beauty does enrapture! With what ecstatic admiration cry they out: Holy, holy, holy, Lord God of hosts! and how, filled with most intense desire, they declare glory to the Father, to the Son, and to the Holy Ghost—*Sicut erat in principio:* as it was in the beginning, is now, and ever shall be.

Oh! He will, indeed, for all ages be what He has been, what He is: holiness itself, justice itself, goodness itself, mercy itself. Consider, then, with what exceeding great delight the blessed Spirits joy to lose themselves in the ocean of His infinite perfections! Oh! dove of Jesus Christ. Oh! I hope that you will join them soon. Strive, then, to begin even here below those sweet acts of purest love which will be in heaven your eternal occupation: for in heaven we continue what has been on earth begun. The more closely a soul has been in this existence united to Jesus Christ, the more intimately will it abide in Him hereafter, to praise Him as He is worthy to be praised. Ah, you are truly happy, because Jesus is purifying you of every thing that is not His. I trust that before long your union with Him will be perfect; and then, Oh, how you will adore! Amen. *Gloria Patri, et Filio, et Spiritui Sancto.*

Cecilia died in peace at Baltimore, on the 29th of April, and her body was brought back to St. Joseph's to be placed beside her sister's in the cemetery.

ELIZABETH TO MRS. SADLER.

EMMITSBURG, *6th May*, 1810.

MY OWN DEAR ELIZA,—I have just returned from Baltimore where I had carried the darling Cecilia, with a distant hope that she might be benefited by the ride, change of air, and consultation of physicians; but *He* said no, and that is enough. A happier, more consoling departure than she took you can not imagine. She was innocence and peace itself. The precious sisters lie in a wood inclosed hard by our dwelling. Every day the hands of affection and love do something to adorn the sacred solitude. . . . . . The mother has made a great sacrifice, and Anna remains in Baltimore for a time with a tried friend and most excellent woman, Mrs. R. Barry, part of the family we loved in New York. She is a European, and will and does keep her always under her own eye. Anna has a very great desire to improve herself in drawing, and will always be busy, so that I can not be uneasy for her; besides, her modesty and reserve are truly angelic.

Anna Seton had been engaged since the spring of 1809, to a young gentleman from one of the French West India Islands, who had been educated at Saint Mary's College. Her mother, in a letter of March, 1810, to a friend in New York, thus writes of Charles du Pavillon:

"Can you think, then, that the sad stories of my dear and precious Anna are true? Indeed, not one sentence more than I now tell you. She contracted a strong affection with a young gentleman in Baltimore, and endeavored to obtain my sanction to their affection. This was not very difficult, as I knew more of him than she did herself, through Mr. Babad, my friend, who is also his, and had always wished Anna might be so fortunate as to gain his affection in the way she has, which seems to be solid and sincere. His fortune is very large and his education of the first kind, with superior talents; his family, only a very tender mother, who resides in Guadaloupe, and I am told is very amiable. So stands the affair: so much and no more. They had one interview in my presence, and I brought her away with me[1] where she is very well contented, waiting for the event with a good grace, as she has sense to know his sincerity is best tried by absence, and that she is yet too young to enter into so serious an engagement. He graduated last month, and still lives with the superior of the college until he joins his mother to make the proper arrangements. I have no reproach to make myself, for it is impossible a child could be more strictly watched or carefully advised than my Annina. He writes always inclosed to me, unsealed. Now, I can do no more than commit all to the Adored." [2]

Poor Anna was but human, indeed; yet the following letters lay open a simple heart, and show the sweet love with which she clung to her mother.

[1] To St. Joseph's.

[2] Elizabeth was very much distressed at Anna's affair, as she says in a letter to a more intimate friend. Her daughter discovered before she died how deeply she had grieved her mother's heart, and all her last letters betray in their sad expressions of love a suspicion of having in some manner disappointed hopes, that she was superior to sentiments which must draw her into the world. It had long been a wish of Elizabeth's soul that she might some time say to her eldest daughter: "I have espoused you to one husband, that I may present you as a chaste virgin to Christ."—2 *Cor.* xi. 2.

FROM ANNA.

✠

BALTIMORE, *Saturday, 5th of May,* 1810.

DEAREST AND BEST OF MOTHERS,—Could you know how much, already, I long to see you, and I know you are as anxious to hear from poor little Annina. I heard by Mrs. Burk, who reached here the day before yesterday, that you arrived safe. I was, though, a little disappointed at not receiving a word, yet I knew you could not write. The 3d,[1] I know you remembered me. I went to the seminary, to our dear father,[2] to receive from his hands our Adored. He dined with us, and Charles also. I send you one of the little flowers blessed and presented to your dear Annina by our father.

To-morrow Charles leaves Baltimore. He has been here these two days successively, and will be here again this evening. Father has spoken to him the other day —about you know what—and seems very well satisfied with his explanation. I have received an explanation of what I wished—very satisfactory.

Do not think, beloved mother, my love blinds me. No; it is, I hope, guided by a submission as much as is in my power to our dearest Lord's will. Mrs. Barry is, as father calls her, a second mother. He says you (best of mothers) are more for my spirit; I, *poor profane I,* want a worldly one, though our dear Mrs. Barry is very domestic. She has been this some time unable to go out of doors by the rheumatism. She desires to be affection-

[1] Anna's birthday. [2] Babad.

ately remembered to you. It rained very hard the day father dined with us. He can never speak of the death of our beloved *Cécile* but with joy. Oh! my mother, here in this wide and spacious city there are scarce any appear to strive to attain that blissful haven for which they were created—perhaps I am among the number.

I have not yet seen the drawing-master, but I hope to begin next week. The bishop has been here twice since you left us; all kindness, as you know. I have not seen Mrs. Burk, yet she stays at M——'s; but I do not like to go there. My excuse is always I don't go out anywhere, which is true enough, except to church. Wednesday there was a review. The children of Mrs. Barry wanted to go and see the soldiers pass. I must confess I had a part in the wish, as we were going to Renaudet's, though not for the same reason. Charles had been here the evening before, and I had a hope of seeing him at Maria's. We staid a little while, and Mrs. Barry asked him to dine with us the 3d, which he did. Dearest mother, write to me as often as you can. I long to hear from you. Remember me at the graves of our dearest angels; when you say beads there pray for me that your daughter may not go unprepared. Oh! my mother, I hope not. I called at Weise's the other morning, as I knew you wished I should, but I did not see anybody, as it was early. I heard our father's half-past six mass. Do not forget to remember me very affectionately to Mr. Dubois, and to the Sisters separately. . . . . Dearest mother, write me all your joys and sorrows: you know, when you pressed me to your breast, you called me your "little friend." You may, I assure you, depend on your Annina. . . . Crosses and sorrows are the way to heaven. I have not yet my share. He who sends them will not give above the strength. I have not yet tasted. Yes, this is Saturday, another week; how the time flies. When I knelt down this morning to say my prayers, though I did not know the hour, yet I thought of you; and at mass with father I was with you. Tell Susan and Véronique to write a few words now and then to me. Give all my best love, and kisses in plenty to the four, dear Kate and Becca, dear William and Richard; you know better than I can pen what I wish to say to them. All, all remember Annina in your prayers. Love and pray for me, my dearest mother. 'Tis He gives and He takes away: *Bénissez le Seigneur.*

Monday, 7th May, 1810.

DEAREST, DEAR MOTHER,—Father had forgotten to give me the first letter till just now. Yesterday I was, to be sure, excessively disappointed at not receiving any by Mrs. Burk, but the mistake is cleared. I wrote to you on Saturday, and sent it yesterday in the morning to Weise's. . . . . . Charles did not go yesterday, as we expected. Something about the sailors and their pay, so he does not start till to-morrow. It was a fine, fair wind yesterday, and as he did not come on Saturday, as I expected, I took it for granted he had sailed in the morning; when, just towards dusk, standing by the street door, as I was thinking of him, he stood before me. You may be sure I was very much astonished, as well as Mrs. Barry—said we thought him soon returned, not in earnest though . . . . Dearest *Père,* his heart was full, and he pronounced over me the prayers and blessing he says over you. I send a copy, for I have another for myself. Mrs. Barry is all kindness. She sends plenty of love and kisses to Kate, Becca, *et la Mère*—oh! I must not forget, to Susan too.

The tops of the houses blackened by the rain, and two or three poplars shining in the sun is the present prospect from the little window of my room, where I now sit; not like the wide expanse of heaven from the great window of St. Joseph's—the beautiful view of the mountain. How happy we might be when the mind is at ease. Dearest, darling mother, this is a wide world, and we are but little people . . . . . The pain in my side has entirely left me, so may your pain in the breast. I shall write you when Charles goes, he seems in high favor with father. I have written two or three words to Veronique. Tell Susan to love me always, and take care of my poor little cabinet in the bustle, and don't let the people plaster it . . . . . Now, dearest mother, I have told you all the nonsense that I had in my head, and made it a little lighter. I beg you to pray, pray, for the prayers of the just shall save the sinner.

Tuesday, 8*th May*, 1810.

Best and Dearest of Mothers,—Mrs. Burk did not go, as I expected, to-day. To-morrow she goes. I must write again.

This morning at four o'clock Charles left Baltimore. He is at last gone; well, so be it. Last night till nine he was here; very kind. You know I felt it, but when he pressed my hand for the last time, I could scarcely contain—yet I did. Yes, mother, I did not shed a tear, but my heart did. Could I help it? Perhaps he will write by the pilot. He goes to St. Bartholomew's, from thence to Guadaloupe.

———

You will, most probably by Mrs. Burk, receive three letters from your Annina. I wish you joy on your rule, perhaps I have need of one, and the retreat. You perceive I have seen your letter to Mr. Weise . . . . . I send in this a little "*Invocation to Hope*," which I think is pretty, and if it is not wrong for nuns to read profane pieces, will my beloved mother peruse it for the sake of the hope that rests in the bosom of her daughter? Our Almighty Father will direct all for the best, and I leave it with resignation to Him. I went this morning to mass at the seminary, to offer it for him, it was Father David's. . . . . . Here I stand, another year, perhaps two. It is a distressing thought. But I must hide that from you. Love me, my mother, more than ever. I try to please you. I do, perhaps; I know I do.

My mother, your loving daughter,

ANNINA.

TO SUSAN.

MY SISTER "SUS,"—I begin, dear Susan, by giving you father's blessing, that's the most valuable part of my letter, and I do sincerely hope it will enable you to fulfill the task of giving tasks—you understand, and to keep silence during the retreat; and, again, to keep your rule as strictly as possible. Therefore, do not read this till recreation. You must take care of all my treasures, send me all my demands, etc., and love me more *absent* than present. Will you? You practice obedience, remember. You perceive I am wilder than ever. I must follow the example of *Mère*, the more trouble I have, the better contented. Tell Sister Bridget or the unknown, that though I have not the supreme honor of being acquainted with her, yet all the *Sisters* are mine—so my best love to my unknown Sister Bridget, and to all the little pigeons you are teaching to say A B C.

Wednesday, 23*d May*, 1810.

BELOVED, DEAR MOTHER,—Again I must write. Already it seems a long time since I heard from you. Joseph came and delivered the letters himself to me last Thursday. How many tears, my beloved mother, I shed over them. Yes, how I longed to be with the dear writers. Already, my dearest mother, am I tired of Baltimore, I wish to be with you again, I can not be happy here . . . . . Here I must hush, I must stifle my grief, there I can indulge it, in part at least. You will excuse all my extravagance, my beloved mother; remember, *you* are the only person to whom I can speak my thoughts, therefore excuse. Monday I received news by the pilot—two letters, I wish I could send them to you. If this went not by post, I would. He does not speak of you; yet I trust, best of mothers, he thinks. He does not forget our dear *Père*. It appears they sprung a leak and landed on the coast of Virginia. His last dated the 15th, but then doubling Cape Henry, though he left this the 8th. I fear they will have a *long* passage. So be it. *Père* was here yesterday; I was out.

We went to that famous spot, on the road as you go up to father's paradise, as he calls it, where *Madeleine, my* mother,[1] etc. ! ! ! you recollect. How foolish I am, yet I can not but remember—at once deprived of all three. *Père* will be here, I expect, some time to-day. He will

[1] Alludes to her mother's meeting Harriet and Cecilia arrived from New York.

send in this effusion of—what? his blessing to sanctify what needs sanctification. Kiss, bless, and love my dear sisters, and William and Richard. When I was with them, I knew not how to love them as I ought, now we are separated . . . . . "When the storm of life is past, oh, receive my soul at last." I often sing that and think—your storms will soon be over, mine are still to commence. I may fall. I am, best of mothers, just at present in a very gloomy strain, so I fear this will be a very dull letter for you. Mrs. Barry, the dear children, and Betsey, send their love to you. Mine you always have, therefore I can not send it. John Scott has been in town these ten days. He tried very much to persuade me to go to Philadelphia for a couple of weeks in the country, but I would not consent, as I knew you did not wish it, and I preferred living in Emmitsburg. He desired me (as he will not now go up to see you, since I will not go with him; he intended, if I had consented, to have gone and asked your permission) to remember him to you, the Catons also, and Miss E. Welch, whom I saw in church. Her brother is married to a young lady of Philadelphia, as rich as himself. Emily and Mrs. Patterson pressed me very much to go and dine with them on Sunday, but I persisted in the refusal. John Scott dined there. I wish to ask you to send for me, I wish to see you and to regain my liberty. You must judge. Never forget to remember me respectfully to Mr. Duboïs.

I must tell you the news, I suppose, if you have not heard it already, that the tyrant Bonaparte is married to a young Austrian princess. She is described in the Gazette as a most beautiful creature, but I fear she will but too soon repent of her imprudence, for he is a second Henry the Eighth. Maria Louisa is her name. What! am I telling the news to the nuns? But it is in recreation, it is all right.

Love, best of mothers, and pray for your *pauvre petite méchante fille.*

ANNINA.

30*th May*, 1810.

DEAR MERE,—It has been very long since I have heard from you. I have written twice by post, but there is no certainty whether you have as yet received the letters. Baltimore is a desert to me. I wish very much to see you. I wish, dearest of mothers, to be with you. I hope by this time Charles is in Guadaloupe. *Père* read his letter and seemed very much pleased—though in appearance more with me than with him. To-morrow is Ascension-day, and I am going to communion. Oh, my mother, pray for me when you receive this, though it will then be passed. I am always in need of your prayers. You know I am no longer the *nun.* I am much worse than I ever was, and you know I was always a wicked piece of furniture . . . . . I believe, dearest mother, there are ifs and buts in every thing. Tell me, my beloved mother, all about St. Joseph's. I love it better now than I did formerly. . . . . . *Père* does not come as often as usual, he has a great deal to do. To-day they are preparing a number of children for first communion to-morrow. I can not help pitying him, sometimes, walking in the heat of the day to the Point.[1]

In about four or five weeks I may expect to hear from Guadaloupe . . . . . You are, my best of mothers,

[1] Saint Patrick's church, on Fell's Point.

quite reconciled, indeed, *happy* now; but would you not be happier to see your dear Annina sitting by you in the delightful task of teaching her little class, instead of sitting here all day, doing nothing, perhaps, but some foolish piece of work or reading a little French . . . . . Dearest, best of mothers, love and pray for your poor Annina. I love you more than you imagine. May He who called the heavy laden and died for sinners have mercy. Your own

ANNINA.

ELIZABETH TO MRS. SADLER.

Monday, 27th May, 1810.

MY OWN DEAR ELIZA, ... If you could breathe our mountain air and taste the repose of the deep woods and streams! Yesterday we all, about twenty Sisters and children, dined in our grotto in the mountain, where we go on Sunday for the divine office. Richard joined his mother's side, but William contented himself with a wave of his hat and a promise of seeing me afterwards; and going home he followed in a part of the wood where he would not be seen, and gave such expressions of love and tenderness as can come only from the soul, but always unobserved, and never forfeiting his character of being a *man*. They are two beings as different as sun and moon; but William most interests poor mother. In the afternoon catechism he was asked if his business in this world was to make money and gain reputation, or to serve God and use all his endeavors to please Him. "My business, sir, is to do both," answered William, with a tone of decision. But I forget, time flies and I have taken up half a sheet with these trifles . . . . . A thousand, thousand loves and benedictions be with you, dear Eliza. My heart feels as bright as the sun now setting.

TO JULIA SCOTT.

30*th May*, 1810.

MY OWN DEAR JULIA,—What is your conclusion? That this world is a changing, passing scene? To be sure, dearest, and happy they who can quit it as my Cecily has done, so peaceful and contented that when the last sad silence came it was more like sleep than death. . . . . . Annina was left in Baltimore with Mrs. Robert Barry, who is kindness personified and a truly amiable woman. It was a very interesting moment for the poor child, as her *much loved* was on the point of departure to his own country, in order to arrange his affairs for—our Lord only knows whether their reunion or separation. I have given the whole business up to that dear Lord who has indulged me so much . . . . . L—— and E—— C—— were often with us. L—— once said: "Come, Anna, stay with us, we will get a much better match for you. You don't know the enchantment of cockades and epaulets," etc. Oh, how my mother's heart felt! We are poor, and let us be so, but free from such ideas of happiness. Poor, poor L——, how she is to be pitied, but we can not change her. . . . . . Now tell me about yourself. I used always to be fearing sickness, accidents, etc., when you were so long silent; but now they say you are so well and strong. Yet well and strong may change quickly, too, like every thing else. Tell me, dearest, how indeed are you, and Charlotte, and brother; but, above all, most dear Maria. There is a most lovely girl (Eleanor Smith, of Fredericktown) in my charge, about sixteen, but so like Maria that she took my heart the moment she lifted her eyes upon me, and many a time I think of Maria while giving her her daily instruction. I have four of them, the same age, as boarders, and many are daily applying.

TO MRS. DUPLEX.

4th June, 1810.

MY OWN DEAR DUPLEX,—Never let it enter your thoughts that time, absence, or all your carelessness in writing, can change, even in degree, a love, a friendship of my soul which for so many years has made yours as a part of my own. I wished you to have written, but can well excuse you, knowing your habitual dislike to letter writing. . . . . . We have a new and handsome house just built on a very large farm, half covered with woods; high mountains all one side of it, and meadows below. Our chapel joins the house, and the parish pastor comes every morning at six to say mass. At eight work begins, and at five is finished. The darling boys are in a branch of the Baltimore College, half way up the mountain, and well taken care of in every way. Without partiality, they are two as sweet fellows in looks, manners, and disposition as poor mother's heart could wish. Richard—always mother's boy—all his desire centers in a farm that he may never quit her. William is the boy of hopes and fears. Reading some lines in an almanac the other day of the whistling of a sea boy in the main-top shrouds: "That's your sort," he cried, "I'm your man;" and always talks of roving the world, but yet has great ideas of being a gentleman in every thing, without knowing that a gentleman without a penny is but a name.[1] However, as his gentleman-notions make him a fine fellow, I trust it will all turn out well, for a more loving and tender heart can not be imagined. The talents of neither of them are distinguished, which does not disappoint me, knowing well they often ruin their owners. Kitty is only less than an angel in looks and every qualification; she rules books, sets copies, hears lessons, and conducts herself with such grace that girls twice her age show her the greatest respect. But what is truly funny is to see Bec, with a little class of six or eight children, holding up her finger in silence, with her pen and ink giving them good points or crosses, and keeping better order than her mother can. Her oldest is her own age, but Bec is a woman to her. And my Annina—my poor Annina—so young, so lovely, so innocent, absorbed in all the romance of youthful passion. She gave her heart, and afterwards what could a doating and unhappy mother do but take the part of a friend and confidant, dissembling my distress, and resolving that if there was no remedy, to help her, at least, by my love and pity. I found her case incurable; nor do I yet know if there will be any cause for repent-

[1] Yet a gentleman of blood and coat-armor as he, albeit penniless, was richer than another who, not one, should have "the wealth of Ormus and of Ind." Sir Alexander Seton, of Foulstruther (who became Earl of Eglinton), is reported to have had two standing prayers in his family, one of which was: "God send us some money, for they are little thought of that want it." But he was a fierce and an odd specimen of the race. Having turned off his chaplain, he used to say public prayers himself; and being a logical Protestant, he interpreted the Bible after his own fashion, and the way he acted upon this very elastic private interpretation principle gained for him the nickname of *Gray-steel*, the suitableness of which is understood from his other standing petition at public prayers in the family, a grimly blasphemous paraphrase of the *lead us not into temptation*: "God keep ill geer out of my hands, for if my hands once get it, my heart will never part with it."—From Kelly's *Scottish Proverbs*, p. 113, in a note to the Preface of The Genealogy of the House and Surname of Setoun.

ance, as her favorite has good talents and a handsome independence—it is said immense wealth; but I never inquired much about it. He is now on his passage to Guadaloupe to endeavor to arrange his affairs and her poor little soul (you may imagine) is tossed by all the hopes and fears. He has appointed six or eight months for his return; but if it will ever be, who can tell? He has been well educated, and is possessed of good principles; but there is great danger, certainly. I always look *directly upwards*. Dearest Harriet and my angel Cecily sleep in the wood close beside me. The children and many of our good Sisters, to whom they were much attached, have planted their graves with wild flowers, and the little inclosure which contains them is the dearest spot to me on earth. I do not miss them half as much as you would think, as according to my *mad notions*[1] it seems as though they are always around me—at all events separation will not be long.

Dearest, dear friend, farewell.

ANNA TO HER MOTHER.

BALTIMORE, 10*th June*, 1810, *Sunday Afternoon*.

DEAREST, DEAR MOTHER,—I think Father Trappist,[2] the

[1] Mrs. Duplex was yet a Protestant.

[2] Some Trappist monks, after unsuccessful attempts to plant their Order in the West, were hospitably received by the holy French priest François Moranvillé (a great friend, *soit dit en passant*, of Mrs. Seton), who served the Mission of Fell's Point at Baltimore. and under whose protection they remained until they removed, in 1814, to New York. When it was finally determined to return to Europe, several Trappist nuns, having been freed from their religious obligations to the Order, united themselves to the Sisters of Charity at Emmitsburg. Considerable light is thrown upon these good women in a number of very interesting letters from Mr. Moranvillé to Mother (then sister) Elizabeth Boyle, which I was kindly permitted to copy by the late Father Madden, of Madison, N. J., in whose possession they were.

person I send this by, is determined he will take enough letters to you. This morning I went to receive our Adored. About a quarter before seven I was in the bishop's chapel—I suppose about the same time my mother and the dear ones were receiving—I was saying the Litany of Jesus; I hoped it was about that time. The bishop said high mass; our dearest father's was either at the Point or seminary, I don't know at which, though he always says high mass at the bishop's on Sunday, and I believe will to-morrow. Remember me on *Corpus Christi*—but I know you will. Oh! my mother, if you could but see this little heart, how it flutters for joy at the idea of being once more with you. There is a Mrs. Caten, father told me of, going to Emmitsburg the 1st of July; he thinks it will be a better opportunity for me to go by than the other one I spoke of. We have had incessant rain these two days past, and have had large fires all over the house. That has detained Father Trappist, I suppose. Oh, I hope soon to be with you, but I submit all to our Lord. I wish it was possible to hear from *pauvre Charles* before I go—but that too in conformity to His adored will. Mr. Barry tells me to inform your mothership that he has received your letter, and will do all he can, and will write you when he has succeeded. The bishop told me, as a secret though, and you will keep it such, that you would probably be down in the fall again, and still more probably that you would not go back. At least, he said, you would be down before October with a few—I hope he means father's—children. Yet, dearest mother, let me come to you. Tell the dear boys I wish to see them very much; you know, even if you were sure of coming down, I must go to see *them*. You know Baltimore is not so attractive to Annina as it used to be. . . . I saw a gentleman yesterday who, when I was made known as Miss Seton, said he knew my father who married Mr. Curzon's daughter; I knew then he did not mean my father, but my grandfather. He said he supposed I could not have been born then, as it was thirty-six or seven years ago, and he supposed I was not so old. A good joke: I could not help laughing. Mrs. Barry desires to be remembered to you, as also Betsey and the Renaudets—I saw Mary on Sunday. As for father, blessings is all he sends. *'Twas all he gave, 'twas all he had to give.* What can I say to you, dearest of mothers, but the old story that I love you most dearly? Give my best love to Véronique, to our Susan, and little May Rose: you know what to tell them. I declare I never thought that those sisters could have clung so tightly to this little stony heart; but I believe the valley heat can melt it down, not to pure gold, but to pure lead.

Love, dear beloved mother, and pray for your own dear, wicked, loving, hoping, ever the same,

ANNA-MARIA.

WORDS OF ANNINA IN A LETTER TO A FRIEND.

19th July, 1810.

How often, at the foot of that altar dedicated to the queen of purity, I have prostrated myself to implore her for purity of soul,—to make me virtuous,—to reform my heart of stone,—to kindle in it the fire of divine love,—to teach it to praise its all-beautiful and merciful God . . . . . Life is frail and of very short duration, but let us fix our hope in Heaven. There, souls which were united here will part no more; there we will be purified; there behold forever the Lord we love. He is as a fire ever burning in the very center of our souls, yet are we cold because we do not stay by it—Oh, our Jesus! when? . . . . .

ELIZABETH TO JULIA SCOTT.

July 20th, 1810.

. . . . . . The situation I am in, as I have told you before, is all I could *even imagine* in the world most congenial to my disposition, sentiments, and views of peace: enjoying the liberty of solitude and country life with every advantage of mental occupation. The thought of living out of our valley would seem impossible if I belonged to myself; but the dear ones have the first claim, which must ever remain inviolate: consequently, if at any period the duties I am engaged in should interfere with those I owe to them, I have solemnly pledged to our good Bishop Carroll, as well as to my own conscience, to give the children their right, and to prefer their advantage in every thing. . . . . When I have seen my Anna in danger of death, I felt a sensation of joy mixed with the mother's pangs; rejoicing in her innocence and anticipating the pressure of human misery. I am for sending my rosebuds to blow in heaven. You, looking over the sharp thorns which will grow on the rising stem, think more of the odor they exhale in your bosom. Ungenerous, selfish little mother, when will you grow wise?

Emily Caton wrote me dear Maria had been ill; and I am afraid they have written to you what they expressed to me—that they considered my situation a hardship and continual fatigue ; but, my own Julia, take the sacred word of your friend that *it is not so.* On the contrary, every person in the house watches even my eye to hinder me making the least exertion, and all my wants are supplied with the kindest attention.

The little fairy is then on fairy-hill![1]—Oh, Glorianna, could I meet you there!—but that pleasure could be purchased only by many pains, for, except the joy of seeing you and yours, I would rather go to the shades of death than to Philadelphia or New York. Tell your darling Maria, Anna is not now in a state of mind to enjoy society. Quiet, silent, and always reflective, if not melancholy, she has no pleasure but in her work or piano.[2] Charles has conveyed two letters to her, already, expressive of the romance of his age; but never could I believe what he says in both of them, that she had not given him the least proof of her affection :—"Anna, you always refused me, and I respected your delicacy; but at the last moment—when I left you, perhaps for a watery grave—could you continue to refuse me one single kiss? one only proof that I was dear to you? The remembrance that you persisted in doing so is a continual cloud of sorrow." This language is trifling;—but to me the music of heaven: —that my darling should have had the virtue and purity of an angel in the first dawn of youthful and ardent affection is a joy to her mother, which her mother only can know.

Emily C. writes me some extravagant story of John[3] (she knows how I love him) about a connection he is in danger of—money, without qualifications, etc. I hope and

[1] In the "new and handsome house," of which in a former letter.

[2] She had returned to St. Joseph's.

[3] Julia's son.

pray it is not so. So write me about him, and all that interests you, love.

So you are growing old! Poor little darling:—truly, to be old and young, too, must be a very troublesome business. Oh, do, do consider, my Julia;—*He* will come —you can not send Him back.

The bulls of the bishops appointed by the Sovereign Pontiff to the sees of Philadelphia, Boston, and Bardstown, and which had been delayed by the untimely death of Bishop Concanen, were received in the fall of the year 1810. The Abbé Cheverus was consecrated at Baltimore on the first of November following, and before returning North he paid a visit to Emmitsburg, where he saw Mrs. Seton for the first time, although he had had so much to do with her conversion, and, by determining her to remove from New York to Baltimore, with the establishment of St. Joseph's.

REV. MR. DUBOIS TO MRS. SETON.

Not having been well, I decline going to attend our venerable bishop to your house, quite assured that you can dispense with my presence.

Respecting communion to-morrow, you are at liberty to do what you please: whether you have church at home or come here. I have no doubt that Bishop Cheverus would most cheerfully agree to stay and to officiate for us on Sunday next, if you could only prevail upon Bishop[1] Egan to give up the prior, but not very essential, claim he

[1] Of Philadelphia.

has to the company of Mr. Cheverus, whom I might send to Conewago next Monday. Exert all your insinuating eloquence upon the old bishop—it will have a good effect, if it has half the influence which it has on your devoted friend and servant,

J. D.

Before Bishop Cheverus left St. Joseph's, Elizabeth asked him to accept a letter of introduction to her friend Mrs. Sadler in New York.

TO MRS. SADLER.

Nov. 21*st*, 1810.

My Own Dear Eliza,—It will please you to see our blessed Cheverus, because he carries your friend and the darlings in his very heart, and we love him with a sentiment not easily described, but which *you* may very well imagine who can conceive what kind of ideas we attach to him,[1] independently of his uncommonly amiable manners and his being the most *cher confrère* of our valued Mr. Tisserant, who has the advantage exteriorly, but not in the *spirit of the mind.* Look at his purple ring[2] and reflect how often *we* kissed it, and if you have the happiness to hear him preach you will participate in the consolation I have greatly wished you to enjoy. Yet everybody has differently colored eyes and different ears on such occasions, and perhaps—perhaps, ours may not agree.

[1] As a bishop in the Church of God.

[2] A sapphire. The mystical signification of this color in an Episcopal ring is said, by Pope Innocent III., to be *Hope.*—*Cancellieri: sopra l'origine e l'uso dell'Anello Pescatorio*, etc., p. 23. How much reason the saintly bishop had to look forward with confidence to the future of the church in his vast diocese, which comprised the whole of New England, is very manifest at this day.

I do not take this excellent occasion to send the book, because I positively expect to see you next summer. It is certain that this so much wished for favor is in the power of Him who grants me so many others, and I ask it of Him with confidence, that you, with our Duplex, will come to the mountain and see your poor friend before she is called, not that I believe the time so short, but, still, *my views are all beyond.*

The excellent Bishop Cheverus made the same good impression upon both Protestants and Catholics in New York that he had already, as a simple priest, in Boston. Mrs. Sadler, writing back to Elizabeth, says that he gave "Confirmation on Sunday to many, and afterwards exhorted them in French and English." He is spoken of by her as having "all that ease and simplicity so much admired in so dignified a character." Without exaggeration may be said of him what Æneas Sylvius of Cardinal[1] Julian Cesarini:—

"He was a noble person and worthy whom we admire, one in whom it was difficult to say whether his doctrine or his eloquence were greater. Pleasing was the appearance of the man, gentle his manners, pure his conduct at every time of life. Zealous for religion, not aught did he desire but for Christ—if for Him, even death was welcome."

[1] The application is perfect even in the dignity, for the bishop was later exalted to the Roman purple.

A FRIEND TO ELIZABETH.

BALTIMORE, *December* 25*th*, 1810.

MY EVER DEAR MOTHER,—Having just returned from St. Mary's, where I heard six masses, at which I did not forget the dear mother and inhabitants of St. Joseph, I will spend part of the day in writing to my "Mountain Mother," as you style her. Bishop Flaget[1] gave us high mass and sermon this morning at four o'clock. The church was so crowded that a great many were outside the doors. I have neglected writing to you before, not knowing of an opportunity. My dear father charged me on the day he sailed, when I went to see him for the last time, to write you his farewell and blessing, to say every thing an affectionate father could say to a dear child, and to recommend himself to your prayers. He left Baltimore the 28th November, and was detained in Hampton Roads until the 8th of December by contrary winds. Every evening since he went away, I say one pair of beads for him, and I want you, as ye say three pair every day, to offer one for that dear father in union with mine; that what my unworthiness can not obtain, may be granted to your united endeavors. Do not refuse me.

Your letter gave me pain. I can perceive by it that your health is declining, and I am afraid you are too indifferent about it. Pardon my freedom, it springs from true friendship. Consider your precious children. Alas, no one could supply your loss. Do, then, be more solicitous about your health, even if it were for their sakes alone.

[1] Of Bardstown, Ky. The Episcopal See has since been transferred to Louisville in the same State.

I purpose paying a little visit to Father Babad. I have looked every day this week for him to call, but I know not how it is, he has never called once. It is strange, as he frequently calls on his way to the poor-house. When I return I will finish my letter.——I have returned without seeing him. The holydays have rendered him invisible, except at the altar, where I see him every day.

27th, St. John's Day.

At last I have seen him, and was almost tempted to scold. He read me a charming panegyric on the beloved disciple of our Adored. I was tempted to wish for you. But, *apropos*, that is a pleasure I soon expect. He has just informed me that it is our dear bishop's intention to send for you on the arrival of Mrs. Barry (who at present is in New York) at Baltimore. Then, oh, then, I shall see my dearest mother. Oh, that I could return with her, and remain with her forever. As to the idea of sending Sisters to Kentucky, I know not where it originated. Your superior dined with us last week at Madame Moreau's academy, being invited there to attend the public examination of the scholars. He came after dinner and sat beside me. The conversation turned on Emmitsburg. I asked him if it was his intention, he answered no, that at present it was impracticable. Perhaps, hereafter, when he becomes acquainted with that country, and finds that such a thing might be effected, he will then endeavor to have a Sisterhood there; but I believe from what he said that day, he will try to establish one here first. If such a thing do take place, it will be for the sick alone—no school. He did not speak of establishing one here as being determined; it is as yet undecided. I did not give him to understand I had heard any thing of sending Sisters to Kentucky. My letter resembles a journal more than a letter; but no matter what form, it will be acceptable to you. *Père* assures me he never enjoyed better health these twenty-five years past than he does at present. He may feel better, but he still looks the same thin, emaciated figure as ever. The report of a Sisterhood being established in Baltimore gains ground. Mr. Fenwyck has arrived here to take charge of St. Peter's church and flock. Mr. O'Brien goes in a few days to New York, but returns here, I believe, in a few months. Our dear archbishop has received accounts which can be relied on, that our head pastor, Pope Pius, was in perfect health about the middle of September last, but still in confinement. This day commences another year, and completes my twenty-third.

January, 1811.

I have just heard that Mrs. Barry is in town at Colonel Howard's. Kiss my sweet Rebecca and Josephine for me. My love to Anna; *Père* often speaks of her. I have been in daily expectation of an opportunity, none has occurred till now. Pray for your poor child,

M. C. G.

Postscript of Father Babad—under the word *Anna.*

"I never lose sight of her. No letter from ——. Such was the case with dear Harriet before her deliverance. Such a disappointment contributed not a little to hasten and accomplish her true and eternal gratification."

1811–1812.—LETTERS.—CONFIRMATION OF THE RULES OF THE SISTERS OF CHARITY.—ILLNESS OF ANNINA SETON.—JOURNAL OF ELIZABETH.—ANNINA MAKES HER VOWS AND DIES A RELIGIOUS MEMBER OF THE COMMUNITY.—LETTERS.—MR. BRUTÉ.—ON THE MOUNTAIN.—IN THE VALLEY.—DEATH OF SISTER MARIA MURPHY.

MRS. SETON TO GEORGE WEISE.

Jan. 15th, 1811.

Véronique[1] has had a dream of a very singular kind about our Harriet, telling her that Cecily was above with the virgins and martyrs, but that she was suffering inexpressibly for sins committed in New York, and will suffer till next October except masses are offered for her continually. True or not, it has awakened the prayers of the whole house for her.

TO MRS. DUPLEX.[2]

Feb. 11th, 1811.

MY DEAR FRIEND,—Your letter of the 8th is just received, and read with the sweet delight which we must forever feel (now) that our Adored has given us hearts to love each other without restraint, calculations, or fears of saying too much or too little. . . . . . Since I wrote you, my peace and quiet are the same, and even increased. The community consists of fifteen Sisters, and thirty

[1] One of the Sisters. [2] She had become a Catholic.

boarders in the school. The very thought of your visiting us gives a delight you can never imagine—the solitude of our mountains, the silence of Cecilia and Harriet's grave, the children playing in the woods, which in spring are full of wild flowers they would gather for you at every step, the regularity of our house, which is very spacious, and in an end wing contains our dear, dear chapel, so neat and quiet, where dwells night and day our Adored. This is no dream of fancy, but only a small part of the reality of our blessing. You must be a witness to believe that from Monday to Saturday all is quiet, no violation of each other's tranquillity, each helping the other with a look of good will which must indeed be seen to be believed. All the world would not have persuaded me if I had not proved it so. You may be incredulous till you come and see. Our mountain pastor[1] is a polished, simple, truly holy man. He says mass for us at sunrise all the year round; if any one has a trouble it is carried to him—they receive consolation, and it is buried in silence. He is the superior of the seminary of the mountain, and doats upon William and Richard. He has had the former in his study, with fire, night and day, because he has at times been threatened with a cough. Annina for six months back is a picture of health, as they all are in color and brightness; but it is a deception of beauty, and requires perpetual care. Anna has her cell in my chamber; and how it would amuse you—so many oddities and fancies. She is always busy; tries much to improve herself, and if her Charles ever claims her, he will find her more than lovely; but that business we must trust to the Adored alone. Dear child! she sees now her want of prudence; and if what is

[1] The Rev. John Dubois.

done could be recalled, would be far from doing the same again; but I know not what to wish for her. She wishes much to write to you, but has, through timidity and aversion to writing letters, partly also from knowing the romantic things which have been said of her among our friends, so long delayed writing any one in New York, that she knows not how to begin. Oh, my Dué, if I could but share with you my comfort, or you your pain with me! My friend, the pen is silent when the heart says too much.

TO MRS. SADLER.

April, 1811.

. . . . . I have told you my present situation is, of all I could imagine in this world, most congenial to my sentiments and disposition. I am at peace; yet this quiet is in the midst of fifty children all day except the early part of the morning and the last of the afternoon. But quiet it is. Order and regularity can not be slipped over here; and I am in the full exercise of that principle which in the world passed either for hypocrisy or a species of it; that manner, you know, of looking upon twenty people in a room with a look of affection and interest, showing an interest in all, and a concern in all their concerns. I am as a mother surrounded by many children of different dispositions—not all equally amiable or congenial, but bound to love, instruct, and provide for the happiness of all; to give the example of cheerfulness, peace, resignation, and consider individuals more as proceeding from the same origin and tending to the same end, than in the different shades of merit and demerit.

TO MRS. SCOTT.

10*th July*, 1811.

MY JULIA,— . . . . . My Anna has endured a similar trial, and with a rational and patient conclusion that it can not but be a good escape to lose a heart which does not know its own inconstancy. The young Du Pavillon, to whom she gave her foolish little heart, found on his return to his family and possessions, some one who seized him on the spot, and saved him the trouble of disposing them for his return to my darling. Well, so much the better. I am very thankful she is left quietly with me, as she seemed to dread the separation, had it been even so small, and had long since felt the imprudence of connecting herself so soon and with so little experience.

And are you not anxious to know if I am alive and unmelted during this hot weather. Indeed, dearest, our New York has refreshing breezes which never reach this land of wood; but also the woodland is inhabited by a heavenly guest I often wished for in New York. So taking all in all, the balance falls this way, and I am better and more active in soul and body than you could believe. I remember Dr. Tutilli, in Leghorn, used to say of Mrs. Filicchi, who always seemed dying, that "she would outlive himself, though he was in perfect health, because her spirit kept her up;" and, true, he is gone, and she is still the same. My spirit, too, whether good or bad supports me; but love for the darlings more than all—the look only of these dear ones who seem to say: "Mother, live for us," acts as a mainspring; but yet it is not the mainspring, for if it were no higher I should be worse than ungrateful. . . . . . .

Oh, dear, dear, a thousand times dear Julia, eternity. Do you ever see it in its long, long, never-ending day or *night?* Peace to you, dearest. I would gladly give my life a thousand times, could I give it so often, to obtain for you the never-ending *day.* Yet, perhaps, in His searching eye you are surer of possessing it than the poor friend who so often begs it for you. . . . . .

Anna bore her mortification with exemplary patience and submission to the will of Him who is "God of all consolation." She gave up, henceforth, every thought of the world, and lived with her mother at St. Joseph's, engaged in the manner of life of the community, and preparing herself to ask, at the proper time, admission into the House as a professed Sister.

ANNA TO HER YOUNG FRIENDS H. AND C. SMITH.

July 3d, 1811.

MY DEAR H—A,—I am very sorry, my love, to have gone so far as to make you cry about our old Hermitage, which exists only in fancy. Never mind, I have some hopes yet that after you have seen a little of the world, and experienced its nothingness, you will come and end your days with Sister Annina of St. Joseph's. I hope you won't be negligent about your prayers. You know death soon takes us, and often unawares, from the greatest pleasures this world can bestow. You will, remember, have a great deal to answer for if you are not a good girl, because our Lord has given you so many opportunities to be good. Don't forget to say the prayers we joined in for a happy death: we ought, you know, to take a little trouble to prepare for that which should be the concern of our whole life. I had the happiness of receiving our Blessed Lord yesterday, the Visitation. Never do I enjoy that happiness, but you are all in my heart. Ah, if my prayers could do you good, what good girls you would be! S. has gone home; B. is going, and as for me, I am going home, too—won't you be sorry to part with me? Mother sends you a great deal of love. Pray for your

ANNINA.

This time last year we were all together. For my part, I remember it only as a dream. Perhaps it is the will of God to separate us in this world that we may take more pains to meet in the next. Oh, my dear ones, when we consider how soon death will cut us off, we ought to forget every thing, to gain the one only thing necessary. I have no news but the old news, how much I love you. When you are tired of the world, I have some hopes you will come and join your *Nun*, though I am so unworthy of the name.

I hope you continue to be as good as formerly, or, rather, better. You must not neglect meditation. Meditate particularly on the miseries of this life, that you may not be too much taken up with its pleasures. Meditate, also, much on death, that you may not be attached to this life; and on the shortness of time, that it may prepare you for eternity. But there is too an endless eternity, where we may feel the most bitter regrets for the loss of that time we now trifle with. How good a use we should make of the few moments God gives us here!

If we neglect them, *we lose an eternity.* I sometimes fear your dear heart thinks too much of this world, of which you have not yet tasted the many miseries. Oh, be not careless. You know, dear love, we can not tell at what moment we may both meet before the awful tribunal; and then, perhaps, you will thank me for reminding you, though I think so little myself. Pray for your Annina.

You wish to be resigned to live in this wicked world as you call it. Ah! Henrietta, you have many opportunities of serving and pleasing our dear Lord in it: make use of them, it is for *them* you will be called to account. Here is the first day of Advent, and we are to keep in mind, chiefly, the judgment. Never cease praying, my sweet friend, that we may meet one another joyfully in that day of terrors. When we think of the eternity which follows, *we may well tremble.* I return you a monthly patron. I hope you have had the happiness of receiving our dearest Lord, and that you did not forget your poor friend. Love and pray for and with your Annina.

Meet me at the foot of the cross next Sunday at eight o'clock.

Our dearest Lord will protect you. May He reunite us all, if it is His holy will, in this world; and if not here, in heaven. Ah, all our endeavors, then, should be to reach that happy abode. The road through life is strewed with thorns—there are many parting tears and many sorrows. We can hardly perceive them fully till youth is past; but we will pray for one another, and walk on resolutely, loving one another, serving our blessed Lord together, that we may love Him for eternity together.

Dearest mother is pretty well, and desires her tenderest love to you all. Beg G. to offer prayers for me. Tell her she shall be paid with mine if I may hope they are acceptable. Don't forget to say your short beads—think how much those poor souls want them. Pray for and love your own affectionate friend in our blessed Lord. Oh, do pray for me, dear girls; say at least a Hail Mary for me once a week; it is not much for a friend. Remember to draw[1] a saint for me—I send you yours.

ELIZABETH TO MRS. SADLER.

22d July, 1811.

. . . . . Anna's countenance and every action inspire the idea of her truly superior mind. She makes more progress in the formation of her character than any one could believe, who did not observe her continual advancement. The intelligence and spirit with which she practices the religion we love, gives her a distinct character from any young female I ever saw, except Ann Barry. But I hope you will be able to judge for yourself, and come and hear the history which has followed her once inexperienced and childish conduct. Oh! how good has the source of all good been to her.

ANNA TO A CHILD AT ST. JOSEPH'S PREPARING TO MAKE HER FIRST COMMUNION.

J. M. J., *November*.

DEAR THERESA,—I write to put you in mind of the great action you are going about. Do, my dear love, try

[1] A Catholic devotion which consists in drawing fortuitously from an urn on the first day of each month, a billet—one of many—marked with the name of some saint and a referable maxim of virtue.

to prepare your heart to receive our Blessed Lord. Oh think, Theresa, how good He is to you in granting you such a favor. Spend every day till Christmas a quarter of an hour in the chapel to offer your dear heart to our Lord, and beg him to prepare it. You can not, you know, do it yourself. Offer yourself to the Blessed Virgin, ask her to make you her child. Beg our dear Lord to be born in your heart as He was in the manger for our salvation. Oh, Theresa! remember you can make your first communion but once; try, then, to make it well. Think, my love, how happy you will be if you receive Him for your salvation. Oh, when death comes how you will wish that you had made it well! but it will be too late then, and how dreadful if you make it ill! Oh! take care. Throw yourself in spirit at the foot of the cross, tell Him you are a weak child—you can do nothing of yourself, but particularly do not forget to say every day one or two verses of the "Come Holy Ghost," and beg our Lord to send the Holy Spirit of His love into your heart to consume it with this blessed love. Beg Him to enlighten your faith, that you may receive Him worthily. Oh, how happy would I think myself if I could again make my first communion! I would think I could never prepare myself enough . . . . Oh, my love, if you knew what I feel for you and the dear girls who are to make their first communion. All I ask of you is to beg Him, and Him alone, to prepare your heart, and to give you a true sense of what you are going about. I should be so happy to think you would be forever *His*. Pray for me, dear love, beg our Lord to make me His, and teach me to love Him.

ANNINA.

Annina had followed for some months the rule of St. Joseph's with extreme regularity; but she was not long able to resist the effects of the many privations to which, in those early years of the establishment of that house, all the Sisters were obliged to submit. At the approach of winter, and the blowing of the mountain winds that sweep down upon the valley, she felt her health with the most alarming rapidity give way. Her mother writes on the 2d of December to a friend: "Anna, my sweet and precious comfort and friend, is undergoing all the symptoms which were so fatal to our Cecilia." She was now confined to a part of the house called the Infirmary, whence, on Christmas-day, she addressed these few lines—the last she ever wrote—to her mother.

Christmas.

My soul's dearest mother, oh! how much I love you. None but our Jesus knows how much. And must I be separated from you? Oh, yes, I must for a time! but I will try my poor best to be good, so that I may be united to you in eternity—and both of us united to our Jesus. Oh, delightful thought! to be forever united to all we love most tenderly, and, above all, to be united to Him who is all our hope. Oh! my mother, my soul's mother, I try to be good, yet still I fall into many faults. Oh, pray for your most loving child, but yet very bad child. Oh, my mother, this is the time of love, and Jesus can refuse us nothing. Oh, my mother, unite with me to beg for "Thy kingdom come." This is written from the infirmary. Your poor, but affectionate and loving child,

ANNINA.

Then with Jesus e'er remaining
In that land of peace and love,
Why? my soul, why now complaining?
We'll hereafter reign above.

ELIZABETH TO FATHER BABAD, IN BALTIMORE.[1]

Between the adoration of midnight and the mass of four o'clock—what moments! Our happy retreat ended, the flame of love ascending, every innocent heart beating. Those who had communed before, preparing and desiring as if for the first time; and the meltings of love going from mother to children, and from children to mother. At half-past eleven she called them from their short slumber, or, rather, found most of them watching for her. Come! gratitude and love resounded in a moment through all the dormitories, from young and old; even dear Annina, lying in her fever, joined the loud chorus. The altar dressed by our truly angelic sacristans Véronique and Betsey, adorned with the purest taste, and blazing with lights made by their virgin hands. Oh! my Father, words have but little meaning. You can understand. All we wanted was the *vere dignum et justum est*,[2] we were so often delighted with in former days. Peace to memory—let all be hushed in the darling babe.

The year 1812 is a blessed one in the "simple annals" of St. Joseph. So long before as 1809 the Rev. Benedict

Written soon after Christmas, 1811.
Of the Preface in the Mass sung with the majestic Gregorian chant.

Flaget, a Sulpitian appointed to the see of Bardstown, and who was on the point of leaving the United States for a time, had been requested to bring back with him from France a copy of the constitution and rules of the Daughters of Charity. The desired document was received at St. Joseph's in the month of August, 1810, and its directions were at once carried out in an informal and a temporary manner. In the mean while the ecclesiastical superiors took them into consideration.

After a careful revision of the Vincentian rule, heed to the conditions of the country and the circumstances of the persons whom it was expected to bind, rendered some modifications necessary, and particularly was provision made that Mrs. Seton, as an exceptional case, should be left at liberty to watch over the welfare of her children, and act for them as though she were free from conventual restraint. In the month of January, 1812, it received in its modified form the approval of Archbishop Carroll, and was definitively applied to the community at Emmitsburg. At the same time the first election of persons to fill the different stations as appointed by the rule was held, and Elizabeth chosen Mother Superior. She was periodically re-elected to this position as long as she lived. The following note, jotted down on a scrap of paper, alludes to the first appointment: "Mother, what a celestial commission intrusted! Mother of the Daughters of Charity, by whom so much is to do for God through their short lives."

ELIZABETH TO FATHER BABAD.

Saturday Evening, 1812.

A moment caught from pain and suffering, close by the sick-bed. The choir resounding with the litany of our Virgin Mother from thirty or forty virgin voices, a thin partition dividing from the tabernacle. My father, pray, beg, implore that He will not reject the humble, broken heart—broken of its perverse and obstinate resistance to His will. The peace and safety of a mortified spirit is my daily lesson. Now pray for a generous, aspiring heart for me. I repeat it, you know not my miseries. No love of vocation, no pure charity, no assimilation with holy poverty, no pliancy of spirit. Oh, my father, hold up your sacred hands for us all.—L. J. C.

E. A. SETON.

TO MRS. SCOTT.

18th February, 1812.

MY JULIA MOST DEAR,—Your letter containing your boundless bounty came at a moment I would have given much to have had you by my side. Anna bathed in cold sweat, gasping for breath hour after hour, unable to utter any word but *my mother, my Saviour*, yet with such looks of love and contentment at the expectation of her departure, that nature itself was obliged to resign her. From her bedside I write. She is so quiet and so exhausted I know not how soon the moment will come. Dear and lovely, to be sure, is my darling; but much rather would I see her go in her innocence, than wait to take my load of sin and sorrow. She will not allow any of us to shed a tear around her. When she saw your letter in my hand she said: "Dear Aunt Scott, dear Maria, if I could take Aunt Scott with me! but I must leave all, and *you too*, dearest mother: His blessed will be done." But you worldly ladies look upon all our faith and hope with quite another eye. At least, my own friend, acknowledge the hour may be near—there is no saying wait—and will you not use your beautiful soul in considering what you would wish in that hour? My Julia, my friend, dear and truest friend, I must be silent; but my life would not be worth a thought if it could contribute by its sacrifice to the happiness I desire for you. Ever yours.

ELIZABETH'S JOURNAL OF ANNINA'S LAST ILLNESS AND DEATH.

When we first found her complaint obstinate, speaking of her danger, she said: "I can never believe that after all our dear Lord has done for me in this house, and attaching me so much to it, He will ever let me leave it. He knows I always will be His and His alone." Well, but, dear Anna, if poor mother should die, if strangers should fill her place, could you have courage to stay? "Why, dearest mother, if others were in your place, they would not hinder me from serving our Lord when they saw I did my best; but if our dearest will take me, I am sure I am very willing. But, oh, how I have abused His graces! If only I had made use of the opportunities He has given me here. If the girls did but know how sorry I am for every vexation I have given the Sisters, and every fault I have committed against the rule of silence, and every other bad example. Oh! if I get better, I will be different in every respect." Sometimes, when taking her powders, she would say: "My mother, why would you keep me; if my life is prolonged a little, it must be over at last." She wrote her former companions: "I am suffering now in earnest, not as we used to do on our knees when meditating the passion of our dearest Lord, we used to wish to suffer with Him; but when called to prove the wish, how different is the reality from the imagination! Let my weakness be a lesson to you." Half reproaching her for the little care of her health: "Ah, dear mother," she replied, coloring deeply, as if her humility were wounded, "if our Lord called me up to meditate, was I wrong to go? If I ate what I did not like, was it not proper, since it is but a common Christian act to control my taste? Besides, what would my example have been to my Decury[1] if I did otherwise in these cases? Indeed, I have given too much bad example without that. Dearest Lord, pardon me." Again: "Poor clay! I see myself dead upon that bed; but how short will be our separation, how soon you will follow me, *my mother!*" Sister Cecilia pitying her burning fever, she said: "In the woods I shall be cold enough, but wait till the flowers spring up." Looking down from the window: "Hard earth! my body must be laid in you." Then raising her eyes—"Oh! beautiful heavens, how high you are; when will my soul reach you? hasten, hasten, happy hour." On the festival of the Holy Name, being unusually dejected, she said: "When I think how soon I shall depart, I can not excite myself to that interior joy: my

[1] A band of ten girls over whom she watched like a little mother.

sins, my sins! but I am resigned that His will be done. I confide in Him—my dear Lord." At every cough through the night and day, that expression: "*Oh, my dear Lord.*"

Friday, St. Peter Nolascus (31 *Jan.*).—Our departing darling's consecration. She said: "Dear mother, I could not but be amused to hear Mr. Dubois say so much about consecration, having been accustomed long before my illness to perform this act, and since, continually repeating it. But now it is to be done, that I may become a Sister, and be numbered among the children of blessed St. Vincent." What a communion between the child and the mother!

Saturday.—Poor William came. How deeply affected by the admonition of the dear sufferer: "Be good, be good; oh, when you come to your death-bed as I am come, how you will wish you had been good, that you never had offended our dear Lord. Oh, if I had never offended Him!"

Purification.—At the feet of our happy mother, listening to dear Simeon prophesying on the darling babe, when He entered our chamber.[1] The sweet half-hour of love and peace with Jesus, as she sits on her bed of pain, and I kneel beside her. Covering her when she lay down, and giving her the usual cross on the forehead, she said with the most endearing smile: "Yet a little while you see me; again a little while you shall not see me, be-

[1] That is, our Lord in the blessed sacrament was brought for Annina's communion.

cause I go to my Father;" then, as if she feared it was too much to use such sacred words, she added: "So says my dear Lord." In her sleep even she cried out: "O eternity, eternity!" and seeing some writing of Rev. Mr. Babad in my hand, she said: "O eternity! it seems connected with the thought of him!" Lying on the bed with her crucifix in her hand, talking to Him of His dear head resting on thorns, of the thousand souls who would not come to Him: "Dearest Lord, I did not come when You called me, and You came and brought me. Oh, how I wish I were good to help them! but poor strayed sheep—here I am at the foot of Your cross. Death will come, and I shall hold so fast to the cross and to Your sacred feet. You shall be with me wherever I go. Oh, the poor souls, see how they fall into eternity: how I wish I could help them!" To the little ones who came to see her she said: "You come to look at what will soon be turned to dust; remember how short a time it is since I was playing with you all. Consider how soon you may die. Love our Lord."

Friday Afternoon, 17*th*.—Obliged to remain with my darling who seemed to be entering her agony. What anguish! what unremitting pains! "O my Jesus!" was all she could say, with her eyes continually on the large crucifix at the foot of her bed. Poor mother, what a meditation.

Saturday Morning.—All suffering—all patience. "If our dearest Lord did not hold me, how could I bear so many pains?" What a smile was on her face all that long hard trial. Telling her that Mr. Bruté was much pleased she was now a *Sister of Charity*, "Yes," she said, "I have somehow had to check a rising wish to live ever since that day." Why, darling, I answered; it seems you would rather have reason to fear, if you should live, the danger of not keeping to your engagements. "Oh, to be sure, mother, if it depended on me; but our Lord is so good, and has so long kept that thought in my mind, that supposing I lived the longest life, it would be but one moment to eternity, and short enough in which to serve Him; and I do not believe there can be a better way in this world to serve Him than as a Sister of Charity. This has long been my thought. Oh, our Jesus, how boundless is your goodness!"

Sunday, 20th.—After I had read the meditation to the Sisters, she begged me to leave her no more. Her pains so excessive, so many little prayers, so much reading must be done every day. At eight o'clock in the evening, after reading many of her favorite hymns to her, she appeared to enter her agony, and said: "Oh, my mother, what does this mean?" I told her, my darling, be ready. She saw some tears—"Oh, my mother, it is not for me you should shed tears; no, Kitty; no, Rebecca; rejoice for me." Looking on her crucifix, and kissing the dear feet: "My Jesus, you know my only hope is in you: never, never shall I be confounded." Then such acts of faith, love, and desire, with looks of joyful anticipation. In the litany of the Blessed Virgin, at *refuge of sinners*, she showed great emotion, and said as the litany ended: "Oh, refuge of sinners, pity me; I am a miserable one. What! all my idle words, my silly thoughts, and careless actions to be accounted for *this night*." I presented the feet of the crucifix again to her lips: "Yes," she added, with great affection, "my sweet Lord, your sacred wounds are my hope. Oh, my mother, oh, my sisters, call to our Jesus for me; say Jesus all around my bed, say Jesus everywhere." We said the litany of Jesus, while she pronounced His name with us in a manner not to be described; and coming to *Jesus, Infinite Goodness*, her transport glowed on her countenance, and it seemed as if her soul must go with the heavings of her poor little breast. Now her desire for the Holy Oil seemed almost to disturb her; but our dearest was so good as to hasten our wish. The Rev. Superior arrived: what a moment for her! He must wait for a book, and she kept her eyes on a crucifix. When the book was brought, she presented her hands the moment they were wanted, and with such a look of joy! Oh, happy, happy mother, in that moment. But now the trial was to come, for after extreme unction the alarming symptoms subsided, and she must wait. What delight in the morning to receive our Adored, what dear contentment, what peace when He came to her; and poor mother, too, kneeling beside her, received Him. It was an hour of happiness such as they alone can know who understand.[1] Through the following week, every minute of the night and day she was looking for the summons, but our Jesus said, *not yet.* Who could count the acts of faith, submission, love, confidence, desire, and abandonment expressed by this dear soul in so hard a trial of pains, deadly coldness, unceasing cough, choking, and heaving of the chest; every hour suffering more, apparently, than the many dear ones I have seen in their departing agony, and

[1] "The mysteries of the kingdom of heaven," which God has hidden "from the wise and prudent," and revealed "to little ones."—*Matthew.*

with no other words but "*Jesus, sweet Jesus, amiable Jesus!*" to which she seemed to attach some special meaning, as she always said it with a smile, even when distress was ever so great. "Tears for me, my mother? No, no, you see I am obliged to be willing to part even from you, from *you*, my mother. Yes, my dearest Lord, your will forever, not mine." What a spirit in her look when she added: "Yet, my mother, but for a little while: we will be united. What a thought—to part with you no more! to live and love in our Jesus for eternity!"

✣ *St. John of God* (*8th March*).—At break of day Annina told me she could not, dare not, go to communion, her anguish was so great, she was sure she would groan aloud. The whole night she had not slept one hour, or been able to remain five minutes in the same posture. I told her the confessor should decide. He brought her the Adored before mass, and from the moment she received Him she was as still as an infant in its mother's arms. A little while after, going to her we found her breast was purple in the center and near the heart—"My mother, what does this mean?" It means, dearest darling, that you have received Him, and He is now going to receive you. Oh! the ascensions from that heart, the looks to her crucifix, the accents of joy. After again inquiring if it were so, she told some Sisters around her the most animating things, and to me: "will you let me say something to all the dear girls this morning, my mother? Let my last breath be for Him." She called first for her *community*, which consisted of the highest class, who had among themselves certain regulations and practices of piety; secondly, for her decury children; and finally, all came in companies. What a sight for angels! with looks of the sweetest affection (and to a mother more than human loveliness), smiling on all with that peaceful ex. pression which comes from within, she spoke to each band short but most moving words of love to Jesus—peace in Jesus, and reminding the community girls how short a time ago she had been even more healthy than many of them, and of their united resolution to prepare daily for death; then showing her poor breast, so discolored, she said: "See how vain and foolish is all that is not for Jesus—how it passes!—but in the Resurrection!!!" lifting her eyes fixed on heaven in silence, and they departed with sobs and sighs they were unable to control. Her little decury children then came forward: "Oh, yes," she said, "come, my little ones, how often I have told you to be good, and to love our Jesus; now look at me—what would I be without Him? You see, dear mother, He knows how I love her, but what is mother now? what can she do for me, except strengthen me in the love of our Jesus, in whom we hope to be united forever? Now I must leave her, everybody—every thing, all alone I must go; be good, love Jesus, love Him." To a little favorite, whom she told to kneel by her side, she said much, admonishing her to be faithful to her first communion, and representing the scruples and the examinations made about communion when on the bed of death. To some new girls who had come since her sickness, she said, with great simplicity: "I do not know you, but I love you in Jesus; be good, love Him." When the Sisters came she looked on them with inexpressible tenderness, and pronouncing *My Sisters*, burst into tears. After awhile she told Sister K—— she feared she had been a cause of much trouble to her, but begged her, again, to pardon, and asked the general pardon of all the dear Sisters for the scandals she had given, entreating, also, their prayers. When all were gone: "alone," she said, "with my Jesus and my mother.' In the evening the community and the decury children sent to beg their little mother for a last penance. To the first she sent the prayer of union with Jesus dying on the cross, to be said when the clock strikes; to the little ones, "Remember, O most pious Virgin Mary," which she herself always said in the middle of her painful nights, with an expression of confidence and love for her which none of us could resist. Many of the Sisters asked for a penance, to whom she said very gayly: "To be sure, for His glory; whenever you enter the mountain church, thank our Virgin Mother for all the favors she obtained for me there. I never can tell half of them—all, I am persuaded, by her intercession; and ask pardon for my abuse of them." When we were alone she added: "Now, my mother, your penance is to remind our Sisters, every day you live, to pray for me; you know the judgments of God—remember." She sat up in her bed and sang vespers with the choir. The *Magnificat* (which she always said with the *Miserere* to counterbalance) seemed to lift her soul to heaven. In the night finding no efforts of ours, no change of position could obtain the least relief from her incredible pains, she looked firmly at the crucifix, and, "O now, my Jesus," she said, "I will bear it with your grace, but I must talk to you. O! my God! my all! my Jesus, you know how I fear to displease you, you know how I dread my enemy; hide me, my Jesus, hide me in your open side. You know I have been trying daily to purify this poor heart from every earthly affection, that it may be pleasing in your sight, and yours alone. Oh, now have mercy, save me from my enemy; will you leave me when I have no other help but you? If I looked only to your justice, I know I am lost; but your mercy, your dear mercy is all my confidence. You will save me from my enemy, you will not reject so poor a soul! My cruel enemy! but I renounce him, my Jesus; I renounce a thousand times whatever he may say to me, I renounce him." She had spoken so long a while with so much agony, I did my best to stop her, but she could not cease until quite exhausted, saying things of that kind which I can ever remember, with an expression, too, and a countenance almost supernatural. Some hours after, I asked: Why, dearest, did you say so often, "I renounce him?" "Because, mother, he tried even then to make me think of something else but what I was doing, and because I know I may, even in my last hour, be lost." This she also repeated the last night when she was dying: "My mother, remember the enemy,—let all pray for me in my last hour; yet I do not fear hell, our Jesus is *so good,—so good,*—infinite goodness. Say for me the prayer to the blessed sacrament: *Soul of Jesus sanctify me,*" and this with the prayer to Jesus dying and "Jesus, Mary, and Joseph: I give you my heart, my soul, and my life," she repeated every few minutes; in the intervals, echoing the name of Jesus from the lips of our dear Sister Rose, until Mr. Bruté came. Her desire to receive our Lord, she expressed in every way, and had begged for preparation prayers. He told her he would say mass for her,—suggested many things for the moment; to which she replied with all her soul, although a little before he came she had appeared somewhat to wander. When Mr. Bruté left her for the altar, she called after him, and earnestly repeated, she prayed for all, all her dear Sisters, for the seminary, and for all, as he had suggested. Her efforts were so great I tried to compose her, saying, as I knelt before her, and held high the crucifix: "Unite yourself to your suffering Jesus in the divine sacrifice." After mass how many, many most fervent acts and aspirations to Jesus! what cheerfulness of her dying countenance! how sweetly she applied her now speechless mouth to the crucifix! what a cry of joy to all around her! Amidst so many precious signs I will ever remember this act of gratitude and thanks to Jesus; the arms stretched towards heaven with inexpressible energy, and a look piercing even to Him on high, and an effort of the breast to cry and to express—what is known only in eternity.

Oh, mother, mother, give a thousand thanks all your life—every day of this life, until you meet with her again.—*March 12th.*

Spirit, leave thy house of clay,
Lingering dust resign thy breath;
Spirit, cast thy chains away,
Dust, be thou dissolved in death.

Thus the Guardian Angel spoke
As he watched the dying-bed,
As the bonds of life he broke
And the ransomed captive fled.

Prisoner! long detained below,
Prisoner! now with freedom blest,
Welcome! from a world of woe,
Welcome! to eternal rest.

Thus the Guardian Angel sang
As he bore the soul on high,
While with alleluias rang
All the regions of the sky.

ELIZABETH TO MRS. SADLER.

March 18*th*, 1812.

The dear, beloved soul is gone. I left her with Harriet and Cecilia in the sacred wood Friday last at one o'clock. As I sit by my chamber window, I look at the white palings which inclose them—who can tell the silent solitude of the mother's heart? its peace and rest in God. The countenances of Kitty and Rebecca reflect it, and have the same expression now as when, at her request, supported opposite the open window, her hands clasped and eyes fixed steadily on the clouds as if she could pierce them—they sang her favorite hymns while she departed. She took leave of all with such sweet affection, saying a word to every different band of our fifty boarders, who have a boundless attachment to her. Whatever she said, whatever she has written, all her papers, turned to one point: to be ready for death.

A MEMORANDUM OF ELIZABETH'S.

3*d* *May*, 1812.—Annina's birthday seventeen years ago. Eternity was her darling word: I find it written in every thing that belonged to her—music, books, copies,—everywhere that word marked with the pen or needle.

Elizabeth, although loving very sincerely the quiet and religious retirement so proper to her state of life, was not afraid to have Protestants come to see her, hoping that by their visits some prejudice—if not against her own person, against her misunderstood religion—

might be dispelled. Several of her relatives went to St. Joseph's at different times to call upon her. In May she saw her sister Mary, Mrs. Post, who, writing in June following, mentions one who is already known in this Memoir.

She says: "I met Bishop Hobart yesterday in the street. After *How do you do,* I told him I had lately seen one he had once esteemed a dear friend, and that she had inquired particularly after him. The abstractedness of his address was so contrary to what I had expected, that I mentioned it to Mr. Bowen in the evening, during a call that he gave. He said it had been his manner ever since this, I could almost say, impious controversy; that all affections of mind and heart require to be roused on any other subject. I involuntarily exclaimed: What a pity! He says that Bishop Hobart and others have spoken to him in such terms of Mrs. Seton as to give him the highest respect possible for her. . . . . . ." In the course of a few more years the bishop of the Protestant Episcopal Church in New York appears not only to have risen superior to prejudice, but to have entertained even a benign opinion of Mrs. Seton, for the same sister, writing in the month of April, 1817, says: "Do not be dissatisfied with me, if I tell you that in a late visit from your old friends, Bishop and Mrs. Hobart, after many inquiries after you, I showed them your last letter to me. I felt a conviction that the sensible, candid, and amiable exposition of your feelings and motives in regard to religious impressions must gratify every good heart, therefore, particularly one which I believed knew how to appreciate them. I was not mistaken: the high encomiums he bestowed on you, convinced me you have his former friendship with increased approbation—admiration I think more appropriate."

Towards the end of September, 1812, a French clergyman, who has already appeared at the closing hours of Annina's life, became permanently established at the Mountain. This was the Rev. Simon-Gabriel Bruté, who had come to the United States in 1810 with the Bishop-elect of Bardstown, when this one returned from France, after his ineffectual attempt to get relieved from the burden of a diocese. While at the college, Mr. Bruté taught Latin, French, Natural Philosophy, and assisted Father Dubois in missionary work and in the spiritual direction of the Sisterhood in the Valley. He will be frequently mentioned in these pages until the end; and, although such few (hitherto unpublished) writings of his own as will appear in this connection, would of themselves bear witness to the elevated character of the man, I give at once the testimony of his biographer. "Mr. Bruté's humility, piety, and learning, made him a model of the Christian priest, and the impression his virtues made upon both ecclesiastical and lay students, surpassed all oral instruction. . . . . The Sisters of Charity in this country also owe a debt of gratitude to him. Mother Seton found in him an enlightened director and friend, and his advice and influence was most beneficial to her young community at St. Joseph's."[1]

On the 15th of October, 1812, occurred the fourth death at St. Joseph's. It was Sister Maria Murphy who was now called to receive the reward of a life truly hidden with Christ in God. She was remarkable for a very mortified spirit, besides exactly practicing the other virtues of a good religious. On one occasion she showed great recollection and presence of mind in the house of God. It was a Thursday afternoon that with the mother she had gone up to the Mountain church to make the evening adoration, and while preparing to kneel saw a large snake at her feet. With much simplicity she made the sign of the cross over the reptile, and then taking it up fearlessly by the tip of the tail, carried it out of the sacred edifice into the woods and let it go in peace.—*Serpentes tollent:* "They shall take up serpents."—*Mark* xvi. 18.

FROM ELIZABETH'S NOTE-BOOK.

—— Maria.—Departed St. Theresa's day. Useless to make your eulogium to those who so well knew you, to name your virtues to those who witnessed a thousand acts of them daily. I seek before God a lasting and useful conclusion—to serve for our eternity! and rather from this amiable view of death, of eternity, of the gates of heaven, turn towards this life in which we are still de-

[1] *Memoirs of Simon W. G. Bruté, First Bishop of Vincennes, etc.* By the Right Rev. J. R. Bayley, Bishop of Newark.

tained. Few will be blessed with a death so premature; if some, few; the greater number are, rather, to serve. For the first intentions are enough. How immense and charitable those of Maria were! But for those who remain intentions will be tried; and let us be courageous with love and zeal to fulfill the will and order of Providence, nor refuse to live the longest life—a nothing to eternity. The most generous saints desired to remain: courage! *Sisters of Charity*, your admirable name must excite in you every preparation to do justice to your vocation. Go, Maria, go to your blessed abode; to your friends who wait for you: Annina, Cecilia, Harriet will receive you. Go, Maria, you have delivered very faithfully to your last breath your charge to be for others a model of charity also. Fear not, Maria, to be forgotten by your sisters; we follow, now, alas! to the cold grave, but we will follow also to heaven, yes, to heaven. O heaven! eternity! To see face to face! to praise with angels! to love incessantly, eternally with God.

She is gone to praise our Lord in the land of the living.

Here we contemplate a last time our blessed sister. Her soul has been carried above by angels. This cold and inanimate form, from which she departed triumphantly, is left for its momentary destruction in the grave. Momentary: so often it was united with the glorified body of our Saviour, it will receive also the glorious restoration which must take place for the just in the last day. O day! happy day, the last of all; after which eternity alone! but eternity even now—eternity takes its endless course for the soul—a delightful, an inexpressibly delightful course for the blessed soul that watched so well for it during its short time of trial. But as the angels even are not pure in His sight, our Mother, the Church, tenderly entreats us to put up our prayers for departed friends, that through the communion of saints, the merits of our Redeemer may still be applied, if necessary, to them. We will pray for Maria as we did for Annina. We will pray, not only in this solemn moment when Maria (as did here Annina) calls on us herself for our most tender duties, but we will follow her also to her cold abode, where, with her loved companions already preceded, she will await her glorious transformation; where pious thoughts, impressive views, eternity anticipated, will soothe our exile, and prepare our way to the land of the living—of eternal reunion.

1813.—Rebecca Seton.—Extracts from Elizabeth's Note-Book.—Dear Remembrances.

On the 25th of December, 1812, Rebecca Seton, who was then between ten and eleven, made her first communion, for which she had been preparing during several months. On the 10th of July preceding, her mother writes to a friend: "My little child of the cross, the darling Rebecca, is praying much and preparing for communion at Christmas." Elizabeth applies to her daughter the expression, *child of the cross*, on account of her intense sufferings from an accident on the ice the previous year, by which she injured her hip. Behind St. Joseph's house, between it and the stream, there is a lakelet that in summer nestles its crystal surface in the grass and flowers of the field; fine trees are around it, and at the foot of one, more spreading than the rest, wells up a source of water called Mother's Fountain, because Elizabeth used often to sit there and watch the children frolic; but in winter it freezes over and becomes a spot to slide upon. One time Rebecca was so giddy with play, that she ran down a little hill above the water and slid off on the ice, then suddenly fell, and was taken up a piteous cripple. Her pains were very sharp, but an excellent physician of Baltimore, a friend of her mother, afforded some temporary relief, and prolonged her life for several years. She could go about, however, on crutches only, living at St. Joseph's an object, partly from her helpless state, and partly on account of the infantile sweetness of her disposition, of the most charitable attentions, and every one's little pet.

A MEMORANDUM OF REBECCA'S.

February, 1813.

I received my dearest Lord for the first time in my life on Christmas-day, at six o'clock in the morning. I offered up my intention for all my dear friends, at least for as many as I could remember, and particularly for those poor souls that do not know our dear Lord's will. Jesus—Mary. My second communion was on Tuesday, the second of February, Feast of the Purification. I offered up my intention for all my dear friends and companions, and particularly for all at St. Joseph's house. My resolutions were to try and think of our dear Lord often in the course of the day, and particularly to bear my sufferings with patience. Jesus—Mary.

FROM ELIZABETH'S NOTE-BOOK.

Thoughts on the First Communion at St. Mary's Mount, 2d February, 1813.—He who perseveres to the end shall be saved. Piety must be habitual, not by fits. It must be persevering, because temptations continue all our life, and perseverance alone obtains the crown. Its means are: the presence of God, good reading, prayer, the sacraments, good resolutions often renewed, the remembrance of our last end; and its advantages: habits which secure our predestination—making our life equal, peaceable, and consoling—leading to the heavenly crown—to where our perseverance will be eternal!!! St. Paul, 2 Cor., chap. vi.: *And we helping do exhort you, that you receive not the Grace of God in vain . . . . . behold, now is the day of salvation.*

When the father[1] of a family rejoices with his children on a day of festivity, *they* remember not the daily misery. A good fire, the covered table and best garments, make them forget it will not always be the same. But the father foresees, anticipates the future with a sigh of anxiety; the paternal heart pierces the veil, and beholds!!! Oh, our Jesus! the hunger, want, and misery which may succeed. The lesson of perseverance, how necessary on this day—for you a day of anticipated heaven—for the poor father of the family—of death and judgment. Jesus—Mary—our angels—renewal of fidelity.

[1] She means the priest who has prepared the children to receive this bread of angels.

On the Fifth Sunday after Epiphany. Admirable epistle.[1] Gospel:[2] good seed and cockle. The Lord sows by His ministers, preaching, the tribunal, conversations, good parents, good friends, good books. Immense numbers of these different seeds. He has sown from the beginning of the world. He sows everywhere; but more abundantly in certain places. The enemy sows: by false friends, bad example, false doctrine, bad books, etc.

Present as a figure *one ear of corn.* Behold the work of our Heavenly Father—what was its first beginning? Look at this separate grain—recollect the time when it was first planted in the earth and covered with the frost and snows of winter, or trampled over in mire and mud, and afterwards behold the fields covered with green and gradually adorned with these beautiful plants. They rise to the height of eight or ten feet, thousands of shocks appear at one view in shining verdure delightful to the eye, spreading their long, broad leaves on bending stalks. On the very summit of the plant the towering plume appears, containing within it the fruitful ear, wrapt round in silken folds, which produces the multiplied grains pressed close together on every side. From whence did they proceed? from one single grain: and by what power? our Heavenly Father. What, then, must be His seed of faith, of His word, of His blood, of His cross, of His flesh in the Eucharist, deposited in our hearts through the winter of life? What must be the fruit in the harvest of eternity, whose echoing vaults and ever-verdant fields

[1] Coloss. iii. 12-18. [2] Matt. xiii. 24-31.

shall resound with praise and love forever! Oh, exulting, —oh, delightful prospect! joyful anticipations. How endearingly should we cherish this precious *faith*, this ineffable hope, this first seed of love now shooting in our hearts during the trial of patience and winter of life which will so soon pass away and bring us to the harvest of delights in eternity!!!

Oh, food of Heaven, how my soul longs for you with desire! seed of Heaven, pledge of its immortality, of that eternity it pants for. Come, come, my Jesus, bury yourself within this heart. It shall do its best to preserve that warmth which will bring forth the fruits of eternity. Oh, amen. Our Jesus.

TO MRS. SCOTT.

12*th March*, 1813.

. . . . . This day, one year ago, my darling, every day more and more beloved by her poor mother in our separation, gave her last long look out of this very window I sit by. She had, all her illness through, that propensity to look upwards poor mother has: *then*, what a look! She had told the children so earnestly just before, "Oh, love Him, love Him. What would I do now if I did not love Him? Mother can not go with me; I go alone. Dear mother! you know how I love her, but I must leave her. Oh, love Him who will be your all in death."

Dear Anna, was ever the beauty of the soul so pictured as on that dying face? How faithfully represented by memory. You would not believe the love of a mother could increase as mine has since she is gone. . . . .

BRUTE TO ELIZABETH.[1]

10 *o'clock—The Mountain.*

In a moment more—here on this mountain—for this good people—scorched, tormented all the week. The refreshing coolness—the copious waters—the gentle calmness of the word of God—then Jesus himself—Jesus on our altar. O Divine Master! O Infinite Goodness!

This morning, octave of Saints Peter and Paul, at a quarter-past five, at Annina's grave. A white rose ✣ peace—repose—eternal happiness—Jesus, Mary, Joseph: her soul in your blessed company for ever and ever. May I die the death of the just. May my last end be like unto theirs. Let these be our final resolutions: peace—patience—humility—meekness—conformity to the Divine will—fidelity unbroken in daily duties. Jesus! Mary! Joseph! Eternity—the holy sacrifice—communion—the tabernacle—our minds fixed on heaven.

FROM ELIZABETH'S NOTE-BOOK.

Mount St. Mary's, 23d May, 1813.—Thoughts on the burying of Picot de Clorivière. In presence of the corpse.

In what strange apparel does our Joseph Picot appear among us this day! Why the silence of that voice which used to join with us to praise our Lord? Why this motionless and lifeless corpse among his lively friends? Why

[1] The original is in French.

are these eyes closed to the light of day? Why is this cold countenance unmoved by our expressions and our love for him? Ah! Picot no more enjoys the life of this world. And are there no better hopes for him? There are. Oh, my young friends, there are, and the most happy, the most exalted hopes. No voice is here to be raised in judgment against this innocent boy; not one reproach to arrest the merciful sentence at the hand of his God. Our dear Picot was harmless. Not even in the trouble of his last and long delirium did he betray the least wickedness from his secret heart. Ah, no; when disordered nature was incapable of disguise (and in the confused speeches of sickness could not have concealed the propensities of a bad soul), what were the ravings of Picot, day after day? To repeat again and again his prayers,—to express in impotent efforts his gratitude to his attendants; to bless them and love them, to call for his uncle, his masters, and companions, has been the only train of his discourse.

To call many times a day for the precious image of his dying Saviour; to kiss and fix his eyes upon His hands, His feet and side, and cling his lips to the sacred wounds one after the other was his continual exercise, doing all he could to answer every call on his piety, often expressing his desire to receive his first communion. Yes, such the last day of his short life, now transferred to eternity. O eternity! the only word to speak this moment—eternity!

Picot! we shall see you no more,—speak to you no more; you leave us! descending into the grave now opened to receive you in its deep asylum; you will rest with our Delany, we will return to this altar and back to our dwelling, but you will return with us no more. Go! yet fear not one hair of your head could fall unnoticed when passing through the shades of death and the trial of your dissolution. All were counted, the whole of this body is but a sacred deposit for the grave, which must restore the whole by the *irresistible command.* But long before, your soul will have enjoyed, while we remain to hope and strive. Happy child, taken from the dangers amidst which we remain; happy child, to make the port so soon. Ah, should expiations remain for earthly frailties, the piety of so many friends will not abandon. We will unite in the same prayer for you and dear Delany; your common silence will be most eloquent to us, telling us so plainly our life is but a vapor, the world a passing scene, its dearest hopes illusive; that God and eternity is our all and all forever.

Thoughts on the B. V. M.—In returning to the valley from Mt. St. Mary's, on the Feast of the Assumption, 1813. —The glory and happiness of the Catholic Church to sing the praises of Mary. The striking proof she is the true spouse of Christ, since she best loves, honors, and cherishes her whom Jesus Christ himself so much honors, loves, and cherishes.

1. The glory and happiness of Mary—her predestination—was loved with an eternal love—what then the delight of the Holy Trinity in her!

2. Her immaculate conception—one soul again coming in innocence—what a sight for angels! If we beheld a soul with the eyes of faith after baptism—angels taking their watch around it.

3. Mary's presentation.

4. Her obscure life: humble, poor, retired, modest, a model to young virgins—gloriously hidden in God.

5. The annunciation! What glory! Embassy of an archangel. God taking flesh from her. The same which we now adore in our Jesus, in Jesus our Redeemer, in Jesus glorified at the right hand, in Jesus received in the Eucharist.

Oh, Anna, mother of Mary! how glorious! how dear a delight to be so closely related to Mary!

6. Jesus nine months in Mary's womb.—Oh, Mary! these nine months.

7. Jesus on the breast of Mary feeding on her milk.[1] How long she must have delayed the weaning of such a child!!!!

8. The infancy of Jesus—in her lap—on her knees as on His throne, while the rolling earth adorned with mountains, trees, and flowers, is the throne of Mary and her blessed Infant caressing, playing in her arms. Oh, Mary, how weak these words!

9. The youth, the obscure life, the public life of Jesus. Mary always, everywhere, at every moment, day and night, conscious she was His mother. Oh, glorious, happy mother, even through the sufferings and ignominies of her Son. Her full conformity to His will—Oh, virtues of Mary—the constant delight of the blessed Trinity—she alone giving more glory than all heaven together. Mother of God! Mary! Oh, the purity of Mary! the humility, patience, love of Mary! to imitate at humblest distance.

10. Mary at the foot of the cross. The piercing sword. The last word. The last look of Jesus to Mary.

11. The delight of the Holy Ghost descending at Whitsuntide on Mary.

[1] As (after Sedulius) sings our holy mother the Church in her sweet Christmas hymn: *Et lacte modico pastus est*, per quem nec ales esurit.

12. How happy this earth to possess her so long. A secret blessing to the rising church. The perfect praise arising from earth to the blessed Trinity so long as she remained. How darkened in the sight of angels when she was removed from it. Glory of Mary since her assumption. Rejoicing of the angels on her arrival in heaven. Her passing through the different hierarchies of angels and saints. Jesus crowning her. Her continual praise to God and intercession for us. The beginning of her eternity.

Conclusion.—Joy to be Catholics. Zeal for the honor of Mary. Pleasing Jesus much by pleasing her. Faithful service of praise, love, and homage to her; and especially by continual remembrance and imitation of her virtues. Vain to wear the outward sign of her children on the heart, without the virtues of meekness, purity, and charity so dear to her, within. Happiness of those gone to Mary—face to face with her. Aspirations to follow them in our own happy assumption. Amen!

Dear Remembrances.—It would be such ingratitude to die without noting them.

At four years of age—sitting alone on a step of the doorway looking at the clouds, while my little sister Catharine, two years old, lay in her coffin; they asked me: did I not cry when little Kitty was dead? No, because Kitty is gone up to heaven. I wish I could go too with mamma.

At six—taking my little sister Emma up to the highest window, and showing her the setting sun, told her God lived up in heaven, and good children would go up there. Teaching her her prayers. My poor mother-in-law, then in great affliction, taught me the 22d Psalm: *The Lord is my Shepherd, the Lord ruleth me. . . . Though I walk in the midst of the shadow of death, I will fear no evil, for thou art with me;* and all through life it has been the favorite one.

New Rochelle—Miss Molly B.'s—at eight years of age.—Girls taking birds' eggs, I gathering up the young ones on a leaf, seeing them palpitate, hoping the poor little mother, hopping from bough to bough, would come and bring them to life. Cried because the girls would destroy them, and afterwards always loved to play and walk alone. Admiration of the clouds. Delight to gaze at them: always with the look for my mother and little Kitty in heaven. Delight to sit alone by the water-side, wandering hours on the shore, singing and gathering shells. Every little leaf, and flower, or insect, animal, shades of clouds, or waving trees: objects of vacant, unconnected thoughts of God and heaven. Pleasure in learning any thing pious. Delight in being with old people.

Twelve years old.—Foolish, ignorant, childish heart. Home again at my father's. Pleasure in reading prayers. Love to nurse the children and sing little hymns over the cradle. A night passed in terror, saying all the while, *our Father.*

Fourteen years of age.—At uncle B.'s, New Rochelle, again. The Bible so enjoyed, and Thomson and Milton. Hymns said on the rocks, surrounded with ice, in transports of first pure enthusiasm. Gazings at the stars—Orion. Walks among cedars singing hymns. Pleasure in every thing, coarse, rough, smooth, or easy, always gay. Spring *there.* Joy in God that He was my Father. Insisting that He should not forsake me. My father away, perhaps dead; but God was my Father, and I quite independent of whatever might happen. Delight of sitting in the fields with Thomson, surrounded by lambs and sheep, or drinking the sap of the birch, or gathering colored stones on the shore. At home. Methodist spinning girls. Their continual hymn, "And am I only born to die," made deep impression; yet, when I would be my own mistress, I intended to be a Quaker, because they wore such pretty plain hats (excellent reason!).

Sixteen years of age.—Family disagreement. Could not guess why, when I spoke kindly to relations, they did not speak to me. Could not even guess how any one could be an enemy to another. Folly, sorrows, romance, miserable friendships; but all turned to good -- and thoughts of how silly to love any thing in this world.

At eighteen—fine plans of a little country home; to gather all the children around and teach them their prayers, and keep them clean, and teach them to be good. Then passionate wishes that there were such places in America as I read of in novels, where people could be shut up from the world, and pray, and be always good. Many thoughts of running away to such places over the sea, in disguise, working for a living. Astonished at people's care in dress, in the world, etc. Thousand reflections after being at public places why I could not say my prayers and have good thoughts as if I had been at home. Wishing to philosophize and give every thing its place, not able though to do both. Preferred going to my room to any amusement out of it. Alas, alas, alas, *tears of blood.* My God! horrid subversion of every good promise in the boldest presumption. God had created me. I was very miserable. He was too good to condemn so poor a creature made of dust—driven by misery (this the wretched reasoning). Laudanum. The praise and thanks of excessive joy not to have done the horrid deed. The thousand promises of eternal gratitude.

My own home at twenty.—The world and heaven too, quite impossible! so every moment clouded with that fear: My God, if I enjoy this I lose you. Yet no true thought of who I would lose; rather fear of hell and of being shut out from heaven. Annina a thousand times offered and given up while in her innocence, fearing so much she would live and be lost. Daily entreaties to God to take whom He pleased, or *all* if He pleased, only not to lose Him. Widows' society. Delight in the continual contrast of all my blessings with the miseries I saw; yet always resigning them. Evenings alone: writing—Bible—Psalms in burning desires of heaven. Continual offering up my sweet Anna, and William, and Richard, and Catharine, and little Rebecca from their first entrance into the world. Fear of their *eternal loss* the prevailing care through all the pains and pleasures of a mother. Midnight Te Deums hushing them. United soul with Rebecca, Harriet, and Cecilia. Confidence in God through all the varieties of our pains and trials.

At twenty-nine.—Faith in our Leghorn voyage. Reliance that *all* would turn to good. Delight in packing up all our valuables to be sold: enjoying the *adieu* to each article to be mine no more. Thousand secret hopes in God of separation from the world. Poor fool—no sacrament Sunday. Most reverently drank, on my knees behind the library door, the little cup of wine and tears to represent what I so much desired. Kissing of the little gold cross, my father had given me, on my watch chain. Unions and resolutions, while loving it as the mark of my Captain and Master whom I was so valiantly to follow. Four o'clock risings. Thoughts in the clouds. Glowing heart at rising of the sun. Te Deums. Rebecca's tears and mine over our picture of the crucifixion. Our midnight prayers. Sunset hymn and silent tears of longing for true life. Parting. So full of hope in God, and looks at our heavenly home. Liberty and enjoyment of the soul at sea through every pain and sorrow. Te Deum on the vessel's deck. Gazing at the moon and stars.

Dream in the Bay of Gibraltar of the angel on the green hill waiting for me over the black, steep mountains.

Ave Maria bells as we entered the port of Leghorn while the sun was setting. Full confidence in God. Annina's first question in the Lazaretto when her dear father took his first sleep—"Mother, is not God with us here?" (clasping her arms round my neck as we knelt)—"Mother, if papa dies will not God take care of us?" Her delight to read the Psalms and Testament with us. Her little word about Herodias, who she said, "thought to do great things by beheading the Baptist, but she only let him out of prison and sent him to heaven." Her terrors—dreaming some one was stabbing her, and awakening in my arms she said: "So it will be with me when I die; I will awaken from all my fears and be with God." Her fearful sobbing heart to mine, while kneeling in each other's arms by the death-bed of her father. Our earnest prayers for him after his departure. Our first night of rest alone in Leghorn; our prayers and hope in God. The Filicchis' love for her and her sweet behavior. Little pious heart seen in every thing. Her passion for visiting the churches, and pressing questions were there any Catholics in our New York, and could we not be Catholics ?

My first entrance into the church of the blessed Virgin Mary of Montenero, at Leghorn. At the elevation a young Englishman near me, forgetting decency, whispered, "this is their *real presence*." The shame I felt at his interruption, and the quick thought: If our Lord is not there, why did the Apostle threaten? How can he blame for not discerning the Lord's body if it is not there? How should they, for whom He has died, eat and drink their damnation (as says the Protestant text), if the blessed sacrament is but a *piece of bread?*

The anguish of heart, when the blessed sacrament would be passing through the street, at the thought, Was I the only one *He* did not bless? In particular the day He passed my window, when prostrate on the floor I looked up to the blessed Virgin, appealing to her that as the mother of God, she *must* pity me, and obtain from Him that blessed faith of these happy souls around me. Rising after many sighs and tears, the little prayer-book Mrs. Amabilia had given Annina was under my eye, which fell on St. Bernard's prayer to the blessed Virgin—*Memorare*. How earnestly I said it; how many thoughts on the happiness of those who possessed this, the blessed faith of Jesus still on earth with them, and how I should enjoy to encounter every misery of life with the heavenly consolation of speaking heart to heart with Him in His tabernacles, and the security of finding Him in His churches. The reverence and love for Mrs. Amabilia Filicchi when she came home from communion. Impressions of awful reverence at the mass of Nicholas Baragazzi in the private chapel, and full continuance of it when he visited our chamber (Annina sick) in his robe of ceremony after the marriage of his brother and sister.

The heavenly words and instructions of Anthony Filicchi teaching me the sign of the cross, and with what spirit to use it. His Amabilia teaching me why she used it in the petition, "Lead us not into temptation," and why Giannina used it when unwilling to fulfill her orders. New and delightful secrets to me. Strong desire to take holy water, and fear to profane it. First entrance in the Church of the Annunciation at Florence. Oh, my God, you only can know.

Annina's sweet love, and prayers, and delight to be alone with me. Thousand, thousand thoughts of our God, our Father, and Father of my darlings at home so far, far away. First impressions on reading St. Francis de Sales' *Devout Life.* His chapter on widows. Delight in reading and kneeling at every page of *that*, and a book called *Unerring authority of the Catholic Church.*

Philip Filicchi's last words: "I meet you at the day of judgment." So firm a heart that I would try to do the will of God. Last mass in Leghorn, at four in the morning: lost in the indescribable reverence and impressions, kneeling in a little confessional, perceived not the ear was waiting for me till the friar came out to ask Mrs. Filicchi "why I did not begin?" Sunrise on her balcony as I bade her a last adieu; the embrace of my little angel Giorgino and her beloved children; our Lord and our God!

Sunset over the island of Ivica. Thoughts of hell as an immense ocean of fire; waves lost in waves of everlasting anguish.

New York, *June 4th,* 1804.—There the points of remembrance. Rebecca, my own Rebecca, dying. Waiting, she said, to "die with sister." No home now; but all my lovely children. The pure heavens above, and God *there*, and the heart of hope and trust in all turning to good, stronger than ever. Saw myself now in the moment of life when I had with my dear ones a full claim on every promise to the *fatherless and widow*. And every hour and day that passed confirmed the most cheerful reliance on our God—our *all*.

A thousand pages could not tell the sweet hours now with my departing Rebecca. The wonder at the few lines I could point out (in her continually fainting and exhausted condition) of the true faith and service of our God. She could only repeat: "Your people are my people, your God my God," and every day the delight to see her eagerness to read our spiritual mass together until the Sunday morning of our last Te Deum, at the sight of the glowing purple clouds in which the sun was rising, and her most tender thanksgiving that we had known and loved each other so closely here, to be reunited a moment after in our dear eternity. Purest joy to see her released from the thousand pains and trials I must pass through, not one of which but she would have made her own.

Now my entrance with my darlings in our little dear humble dwelling. Their tender doating on their own mother. My Annina, my William, my Richard, my Kit, and sweetest Bec—at this hour yet, with what delight I look back at the hours of love around our fire, or little table, or at the piano; our stories every evening, lively airs, and thousand endearments after the lessons and work of the day, when each one helped dear mother. Our first Hail Mary in our little closet at night prayers, when Annina said, "Oh, ma, let us say Hail Mary,"—"Do, ma," said Willy, and Hail Mary we all said; little Bec looking in my face to catch the words she could not pronounce, but in a manner that would have made all laugh if mother's tears had not fixed their attention. The thousand prayers, and tears, and cries from the uncertain soul which now succeeded until Ash Wednesday, 14th March, 1805, it entered the Ark of St. Peter with its beloved ones. Now the crowding remembrances, from that day to the 25th, of a first communion in the Church of God. Hours counted—the watch of the heart panting for the supreme happiness it had so long desired. The secret—the mystery of benediction—heavenly delight—bliss inconceivable to angels. No words for that. Faith burning. Watching for morning's dawn through broken slumbers—at last saw the first rays of the sun on the cross of St. Peter's steeple, burnished so bright it seemed *that morning*. Every step of the two miles counted; so unworthy to enter that street,—the door of the church—finally to approach the altar. The lively hope that since He had done so much, He would at last admit so poor a creature to Himself *for-ever*. The walk back with the treasure of my soul. First kiss and blessings on my five darlings bringing *such a master* to our little dwelling. Now the quiet, satisfied heart, in the thousand encounters of the cross embraced so cordially; but so watchful to preserve peace with all. Most painful remembrances now. Yet grateful for them; the order of our grace so evident through *all*.

1808.—The last sound of the bells in New York when the vessel left the wharf and we sailed for Baltimore. Dear friends left; but I an object of pain and mortification to the dearest. .

Arrival at Baltimore, at the door of St. Mary's Chapel:

the rolling organ—kyrie eleison—awful ceremonies seen for the first time. Josephine and Rebecca so accustomed to be in my arms in church (crowded at New York), still hanging on mother in mute amazement and delight. Annina's frequent stolen glance of surprise and pleasure this Corpus Christi day of wonders to us, and consecration of St. Mary's.

First charities of Mr. Dubourg and of his excellent sister, Madame Fournier, to the stranger and orphans! My lovely, good, sweet boys at Georgetown. After two years' absence in their mother's arms. Let the children of prosperity rejoice: yet can they never guess the least of our joys who possessed nothing but in each other. The first meeting of my five in our beautiful little home so near the chapel for our daily mass. Round, round the wheel now of daily blessing. But how little improved, and how often perverted! Now the thought of the good Mr. Cooper of a school for poor children. Mr. Dubourg's incessant exertions to accomplish it. Blessed Cecilia sent, and Maria; our ever dear Susan next, and little Mary-Ann. Now our Cecily from New York, and beloved Harriet *to nurse her*. Their first impressions and pleasures: how delightful to poor sister! Our set out for the mountain. Our kind, kind friend Weise. Mr. Dubois's kind reception. Pure and innocent Ellen; dear Sally; excellent Mrs. Thompson. Woods, rocks, walks. Harriet's first anxieties to go to mass, to evening adoration. Our visit at eleven to the church, the bright moonlight night of St. Mary Magdalen. The evening I ran from the woods to meet Annina, Josephine, and Rebecca; oh, oh, how sweet! Then William and Richard arrived with sister Rose, Kitty, Cecilia, Maria, Susan, Mary.

A thousand pains. A thousand, thousand pleasures. Order of grace.

My William anointed and so well prepared for death. His quiet and silence from the frenzy of his fever, while his Aunt Harriet and mother said the litanies for him. Harriet's first communion on the Feast of the B. V. M. of Mercy, Sept. 24th. Her last communion the Feast of the Expectation, 18th Dec., 1809. "All peace and love," she said. "Hear the beating of His heart in the garden of Gethsemane. See how they scourge Him! Oh, my Jesus, I suffer with you. Why will you not bring Him to me? My Jesus, you know that I believe in you, I hope in you, I love you."

Cecilia's gentle death the 29th of April, 1810. Her burial. The children gathering wild flowers.

Anniversary of St. Vincent, 1811. Kempis. 118th Psalm in the choir.

Evening before Annina's death. Her singing:—

"Though all the powers of hell surround,
No evil will I fear;
For while my Jesus is my friend,
No danger can come near."

Her "*Jésus, Marie, Joseph,*" all the night.

The last clasp of her hands and look to heaven when she was asked "*if she was not grateful for all the goodness of our Lord to her?*"

A rose, a budding rose,
Blasted before its bloom;
Whose innocence did sweets disclose
Beyond a flower's perfume.
From pain and sorrow now relieved,
Immortal blooms in heaven.

1814.—REBECCA SETON.—LETTERS.—EXTRACTS FROM THE NOTE-BOOK.—DETACHED PIECES.—SISTERS SENT TO PHILADELPHIA.—LETTERS.

Rebecca had a young companion at St. Joseph's, with whom she contracted a spiritual friendship, of which some charming indications remain in a little note-book that once belonged to Annina. Her mother copied them with her own hand from the originals. She would appear, from the style of which a child of her daughter's age is hardly capable, to have retouched them also; so that, as they now read, they are the sentiments and generally the exact words of Rebecca, but revised by Elizabeth.[1]

A PRAYER OF CONSECRATION TO OUR BLESSED MOTHER BY REBECCA AND MARY-STANISLAUS.

February 5th, 1814.

Oh, our blessed mother, we now consecrate our poor little hearts to you. Oh, receive our offering. From this day we will begin, and with your assistance continue to try our very best to love and serve you faithfully. Oh! our dear, dearest mother, intercede for your poor little

[1] It is with a certain diffidence that I give these little particulars of Rebecca, as they will perhaps have a local interest only. There are many in the United States, whose early (peradventure and whose happiest) days were passed amidst the hallowed memories of the Mountain and the Valley, who will read them with pleasure. To these I offer no apology: indeed, they would not forgive me the omission. It is of the general public that I ask indulgence; and what is here said, I wish understood of several other things in this book.

children before the throne of your Divine Son, for He will not deny you, His *dear mother*, any thing; and, therefore, we beg of you to ask the dear virtue of purity of heart which is so very pleasing to you and your Divine Son, and that of modesty and love. But above all, our blessed mother, obtain for us a *happy death*, that we may reign forever in the blessed mansions of peace and love, which is our true country and home. Amen.

The rules and resolutions which these pious young associates had agreed to follow were: "To renew the consecration every feast of the Blessed Virgin. To keep strict silence from nine to ten, and in that hour to say prayers for the souls in purgatory. To say for one another every day the prayer of St. Bernard: *Remember, O most pious Virgin Mary.* Never to listen to detraction. Whenever any of the girls did or said any thing mortifying, to try and bear it patiently. To be kind to all. To obey the Sisters in every thing."

It was by such practices of religion that Elizabeth fostered in her daughter a spirit of piety which alone could turn her thoughts away from the sufferings she had to bear, and make her resigned to the adorable will of God. Writing to a friend about this time, she says of Rebecca: "Poor darling! her life, and spirits, and piety would delight you; yet she feels deeply the distress of her situation."

In the month of April Rebecca was sent to Baltimore to receive confirmation, which was given her on the

24th.[1] While there she was a guest in the house of a lady who treated her as one of her own children. Elizabeth was very grateful for this kindness. Writing to some one in Philadelphia about Rebecca, she says that she was then with "Mrs. Chatard, the wife of Dr. Pierre Chatard, in Saratoga Street (same one the archbishop lives in), who is my particular friend, and the first French physician in Baltimore. She is a most dear woman, and the kindest friend I ever found since I left you."

ELIZABETH TO REBECCA IN BALTIMORE.

Tuesday.

My soul's little darling—more and more beloved since the sacred gift has been bestowed on you. Oh! keep it carefully, and watch every thought and word. My darling, your tender Baltimore mother, Madame Chatard, will regulate all for you; only be obedient and good, and you will be happy. The boys send you much love. Josephine also. All would write to you, but they think you will so soon return. Jesus, Mary, and Joseph, bless my darling. Your own

MOTHER.

REBECCA'S THOUGHTS ON ANNINA'S BIRTHDAY.

3*d May*, 1814.

Mother's room close to the chapel. My Annina, the morning is beautiful, the sky serene, the sun shining, the

[1] I keep her little confirmation picture in my breviary, just as my father did in his prayer-book given him by Bishop Dubois. He received it from the Rev. Thomas A. McCaffrey, that true priest of God, who, long pastor at Emmitsburg, fell a victim

birds warbling their sweet notes, and my Annina lies cold in the solitary woods. She sees no beautiful sky, she sees no sunshine, she hears none of the sweet notes of the little birds around her; no, oh no, my Annina lies cold and stiff in the silence of the grave. Cecilia and our dear Harriet the same: all there, cold and stiff, their faces pale, their eyes closed in death. Oh, my Jesus, what an awful sight! Those whom we once so dearly loved, who once were so gay, who once listened with delight to the song of the lark now singing on the tree, its notes unheeded echoing through the wood. My Annina hears it not, my Harriet hears it not, my Cecily hears it not; all is silent to them. And shall we see you again? If you do with Jesus live, remember those you loved so well, who shed so many tears for you. Oh! pray for us, dearest ones, pray for us. How does my heart sigh and long to be united to you!

REBECCA TO MARY-STANISLAUS.

May 3d.

My Own Dear Stans,—My heart is very full, thinking about our beloved Annina. You know how I loved her, and how much more I love her now. I knew not my love until we were separated. Many a thought of regret and repentance I have for having ever given her any trouble. My beloved, dearest Anna, how does my heart long to be again united to you!

May 29th, Whitsunday.

My Most Dear Stanislaus,—To day we both had the happiness of receiving our only Beloved, through whom

to charity during the cholera visitation, and to whom it was given (as says a note on the back) by Sister Helena, Oct. 31st, 1841.

we hope to receive the blessed Spirit, as He sent it on the disciples. You know how tenderly our dear Lord speaks to them in the Holy Gospel of to-day, where He so sweetly tells them to give them comfort: "Let not your hearts be troubled." Then let us trust in His dear mercy, and let not our hearts be so much troubled about our sins as to forget to trust in Him. Oh, no. How could He call Himself our tender and dear Father, if He had not compassion on His children. I was reading to-day about those who are in trouble of mind. It says that when we are troubled, we forget how good our Jesus is; we do not think how merciful He has been to us. Ah, let us not be so. I told my Jesus this morning when I had the happiness of receiving Him: "Ah, could I say with St. Paul, *it is not I who lives, but it is Jesus lives in me.*" My Stanislaus, peace.

June 3d.

May my dear Mary-Stanislaus be blessed. All day I have been expecting a few lines from one I love so tenderly. Ah, shall we have the happiness of receiving our Jesus next Thursday? I fear not; but do not let us give up the dear hope of again having the happiness of being united to our only Beloved by His happy coming. Oh, may our hearts which have once been united to Him, their good Shepherd, like poor little lost sheep, brought back to the happy fold, and compelled, as it were, to stay among the happy flock; ah, may they never go astray again, may they, as it were, be chained with the chains of Divine love to their only refuge. Oh, those hearts which were, and will be, I hope again and again, consecrated and devoted to Him forever, may He protect them from every danger, and keep them under the shadow of His wing, bless, sanctify, and make them His for ever and ever, for all eternity. The bell rings my own dear Stans.

June 21st.

MY DEAR MARY-STANISLAUS, — I salute you in the Sacred Hearts. You know one of our little rules is the sweet virtue of modesty which the blessed Saint Aloysius practiced so much. It is one of the ways to prepare our hearts for the happy day so fast approaching. You can not think what I felt when I read the sweet meditation this morning, on the grace and love of our Jesus for us in the divine communion. Oh, my Stanislaus, how sweet it is to go and talk to our Dearest in the Tabernacle. Go, my darling, throw yourself at His dear feet, speak and open your heart to Him, tell Him all your wants and all your sufferings. I went to Him this morning and told Him all my little wants and desires, and how much I wished to please Him. I know you wish the same most sincerely. Your ever loving little friend.

Mrs. Seton once lent Annina's note-book to the Rev. Mr. Bruté, and before returning it he wrote something in it himself; some little thoughts so sweet, so full of true charity, so fragrant of the good odor of Jesus Christ, that they must have their place here. They are given in the original, in his unconnected French, mixed so quaintly with English, of which he knew not very much as yet. No translation could render the unction of his native language. Every sentiment is worthy of him who was called "the good Bruté," and is remembered at Emmitsburg as "the Angel of the Mountain."

BRUTE'S THOUGHTS ON THE EVE OF CORPUS CHRISTI, AND ON THE SOLEMNITY ITSELF.

Veille, Corpus Christi, 1814. — Jour pluvieux. Mes larmes en torrent pour les calamités de mon pays. Je revenais à travers les bois de tourmenter de nouveau un pécheur de vieille date que rien n'ébranle. J'étois triste. J'entends trotter légèrement derrière moi ; puis *hem, hem* à demi voix. Je me retourne, c'étoit le pauvre petit nègre de Mme McCatee qui a l'air d'un arbrisseau à demi froissé dont rien ne chérit le développement : tout jeune et un air vieux—mais l'œil si bon, si simple. Il me regardait d'un terrain plus bas, son morceau de chapeau à la main et tirant le pied derrière lui, mais avec un air ! J'aurais ri sans que j'ai pensé au grand Abraham qui regardait, je pense, ainsi le Seigneur quand il vint prier pour Sodome. Il se souvenait de notre autre dimanche soir ensemble, et la vache. "Mon enfant, avez-vous fait votre prière ce matin ?" "Oui, monsieur." "De tout votre cœur ?" "Oui, monsieur." "Il faut faire comme cela tous les matins et tous les soirs." "Oui, monsieur." Je continuais ma route. Il a couru plus légèrement qu'avant ; et cette fois j'ai entendu sa petite voix : "I go to church every Sunday." "C'est bien—c'est bien." Et je continuais marchant avec mes pensées. "Every Sunday, sir, I go to church." "Oh, bien, mon enfant, il faut bien aimer le bon Dieu ;" et j'ai tiré une médaille et je la lui ai donné ! et il a tiré le pied derrière avec un regard et une inclination ! Je me suis retourné—à quatre pas de là il baisait sa médaille ! Il a couru tout le chemin après moi. J'arrivais à la maison avec la pensée du commencement, mes yeux prêts à répandre leurs grosses larmes : c'était me disais-je comme Abraham avant le Seigneur ! Pauvre petit, il Lui est plus agréable que moi ! J'aurais du m'arrêter d'avantage et lui faire un peu de catéchisme. Pauvre enfant ! nud pieds, en rags, et un morceau de chapeau—noir—ignorant—sans mère, sans père, sans ami, personne qui chérisse sa pauvre tige froissée, abandonnée ; dormant sur le floor dans une guenille, courant le matin et le soir après la vache—voilà tout. Mais il est baptisé, son Père céleste est infiniment bon, le ciel s'ouvrira pour lui ! Se fermera—hélas ! pour tant de riches, de savants, d'opulants maîtres de nègres. O le ciel ! *ce petit enfant.* Coulez mes larmes.

Dix June, 1814,—Anniversary of ordination sacerdotal, dix Juin, 1808.—O my God ! J'ai dit la messe. Mon divin Maître—à l'oraison—à la prière des enfans. Au bas du saint autel comme vous étiez avec moi. Ah, jour si mémorable pour mon eternité—et pour celle de tant d'autres. Vous étiez avec moi, mon Maître, au *Gloria in Excelsis*—à ce touchant *lauda Sion* dont pas un mot ce semble n'a pu s'échapper à mon cœur. A *memento :* moment redoutable et délicieux—je désirais ardemment qu'on vous reconnut et honorât en mes faibles mains. Ah, que j'étais bien avec vous à la communion et encore plus quand je vous ai présenté ainsi dès 5½ du matin à cinq âmes vertueuses. O le frémissement de plaisir en les approchant—(four names illegible, women)—Mrs. Thompson et ses lunettes—je le revois à ce moment. Mon Maître ! Je vous ai pris avec moi sur ma poitrine. J'ai descendu la montagne vers Aloysius Elder. Le souvenir vif de ma France m'a saisi et de la première fois que je vous portai ainsi dans la campagne. Ah, nous chantions; et j'ai commencé à chanter tout seul *Adoro te supplex* comme si cela vous eût plu. Vous avez fait couler en abondance les larmes si délicieuses, O mon Maître. Je l'ai chanté tout entier jusqu'à la maison de pauvre B——. Personne—quatre petites chênes (?). J'ai résolu de le chanter aux Sœurs. Ah, si j'avais de la voix! Je me suis souvenu que je chantais aux convents—chagrins plutôt pour moi et ma pauvre mère qui y consentit peut-être par tendresse et nous vous déplûmes.

Arrivé, mon cœur s'est gonflé en vous déposant sur la petite table. Les pleurs ont coulé tout le temps que je confessais et exhortais. Puis un enfant sur le lit que je baptisai il y a un mois. On voulait l'enlever. Oh! non—oh non, c'est l'ange et la louange parfaite. J'ai parlé sur la pensée que vous avez si longtems eu votre divin sacrifice et votre tabernacle dans cette maison même. Je me suis retiré et ai commencé mon office entre les ondulations du blé que je traversais. Les pleurs en abondance redoublé en levant les regards vers l'église suspendue au dessus des arbres et Mr. Duhamel à ce moment à l'autel. Ah, me suis-je dit, je jouis donc du bonheur le plus pure—le plus exquis qui soit sur la terre! Et alors seulement la pensée de l'anniversaire de mon sacerdoce m'est revenue et m'a roulé vaguement et doucement pendant le retour. O matineé belle et pure! O mon Dieu si bon, si bon—que vous rendrai-je! Appelez-moi au ciel. J'ai résolu en simplicité (?). Cette pensée a encore charmé de plus en plus mon cœur enivré. Soit béni—et—et—et. Mon Dieu bénissez notre terre! L'âme spirituel de mon cœur.

Elizabeth used frequently to jot down her reveries, reflections, soliloquies, the aspirations of her soul, etc., but as she usually did so on any fragment of paper, on the backs of letters, on blank pages of her books of devotion, it has been impossible, fifty years afterwards, to collect many of these scraps.[1] The following are a few, and it may be said in the words of Bruté, writing on the cover of a little packet of her papers: "All picture *that* soul."

Poor old Mrs. Lindsey! She must see the mother. "Come, show me your rooms," she says, "and your pictures—it will tender my heart." Here is our Redeemer. "The Lord be merciful! is it He?" dropping her courtesy; "but where is the Holy Queen?" There, with our little Jesus. "O! O! O!" And here is the Pope. "Oh, bless him. I pray for him—look what he sent me," pulling out her *Agnus Dei.* Poor old Mrs. Lindsey! yet she likes not to be thought old, nor near to death. Oh, our Jesus! But I will see only the good when tempted to *construction.*

Most precious communion—preceded by alarm and thoughts of fear, but all settled in one thought: *how He loves and welcomes the poor and desolate.* He said, while the soul was preparing: "See the blood I shed for you: it is at this very time invoked upon you by My priests.

[1] The ones here given are all written, as indeed might easily be observed only from the spirit they breathe, since becoming a Catholic, and most of them belong to 1814, and the three next years.

They prepare and you will thank. Peace, silence, the garden, My will, My will forever." Oh, yes—Adored, Your will, Your will forever. In all my late communions this abandonment and misery has given a mixture of sorrow, and peace, and love, which is made a part of the daily bread—though so many other bad ingredients are added.[1]

Souls destined to partake His eternal inheritance—the dear objects of His love. Go to Him with faith, confidence, and love—He will help. Fill yourself with His spirit and He will govern. He wills you to be to them as a tutelar angel.[2] To guide them in His love, defend them from their enemy. He uses you as Pharaoh made use of Joseph, to watch over His house. And forget not *the account to be given*, if through your fault of vigilance, of goodness, of firmness! Your punishment will be proportioned to the dignity of those souls, to God's love for them, to the glory they might have given, to the *recompense reserved for them*.

To do violence to self on a thousand occasions. Renounce all satisfactions in particular. Endure the weakness of some, the murmurings of others, the delicacy of a third, yet forgetting no one! But graces will be proportioned to wants and duties, and the recompense proportioned also.

[1] By herself.
[2] It will be borne in mind that she was Mother-superior of the community.

Eternity.—In what light shall we view it? What shall we think of the trials and cares, pains and sorrows, we had once upon earth? Oh! what a mere nothing! Let then they who weep be as though they wept not; they who rejoice as though they rejoiced not; they who obtain as though they possess not. This world passes away. ETERNITY! that voice to be everywhere understood. ETERNITY! to love and serve Him only who is to be loved and eternally served and praised in heaven.

The loss of God.—Let us represent to ourselves a lost soul plunged in the depths of despair, saying incessantly to itself, *I have lost God,* lost Him through my own fault; I have *lost Him forever.* I have lost my Creator, my Saviour, the source of all my happiness. He destined me to glory, created me for Himself, placed me awhile upon earth to prepare me for heaven, where I ought now to be reigning with Him. But I have lost Him, and through my own free will.

Sunday.—Just now I come from asking when I shall die, when shall I sin no more; when look well to my own in silence and peace—not going out of myself like a feather on the wind, for, at last, how much more good can be done by staying within with God, than by the most zealous speculations. Plenty of people in this world to mind planning and opinions, but how few to build in God and be silent like our own Jesus!

Nothing in our state of clouds and veils can I see so plainly as how the saints died of love and joy, since I, so wretched and truly miserable, can only read word after word of the blessed 41st and 83d Psalms in unutterable feelings to our God, through the thousand pressings and overflowings. God, God, God; *that* the supreme delight that He is God, and to open wide the mouth and heart that He may fill it; but to be patient, gentle, humble—how little of that through my torrents of daily tears and affections so delightful and enrapturing over the old black book of this octave divine.

Our God!—A novice of the most simple and least outward polish says to me, with hands on her face, as she kneels before me: "All my actions, then, will be eternal in their consequence? Oh, my mother!" "so says one of your meditations." To her heart quite lost in the thought: "What, then, should mine be!"

Sunday of Good Shepherd.—Watching night and cramp in the breast made a heavy head for communion. As the Tabernacle door opened, the pressing thought: *This bread should not be given to a dog, Lord.* Immediately, as the eyes closed, a white old shepherd-dog feeding from the shepherd's hand in the midst of the flock, as I have seen in the fields between Florence and Pisa, came before me. Yes, my Saviour, you feed your poor dog, who at first sight can hardly be distinguished from the sheep; but the canine qualities *you* see.

Principal Impressions.—1. To die with Him—then to see all things in the little world of St. Joseph as they are, so good in intention and faithful in accomplishment by the best souls. 2. Why care for any thing personal? If it *is* or is *not*, *so* or *not* so? The little remaining moment *all* too little, indeed, for penance, much less for reparation of love. 3. Why not enjoy the interior cell with sweet peace and expectation, since He has arranged exterior things so evidently for that end? 4. The Judge who will show mercy in proportion as *we* show it. 5. The moment of judgment so uncertain, the punishment already for forty years deserved so certain. 6. The treasury so empty, the occasions to heap it so continual, the eternal regret if neglected. 7. A gloomy and constrained penance so unworthy to the Beloved and unedifying to His dear ones. 8. Perseverance: a gratuitous grace, yet forfeited so often! 9. Not the least even momentary event but by His dear permission or appointment.

I see nothing now in this world but the blue sky and our altars: all the rest is so plainly not to be looked at, but to be left to Him, with tears only for sin. We now talk all day long of my death, and how it would be just like the rest of the housework. What is it else? What came in the world for? Why in it so long? But this last great *eternal* end. It seems to me so simple; when I look up at the crucifix, simpler still. To-morrow, *first Friday* in the month, and Saturday, is my own day. Visitation: Magnificat at sunset this evening.

Sunday.—This morning our *adored harp* pressed close on the aching heart. Swept every chord of praise and thanksgiving; then weeping under the willows of that horrid Babylon,[1] whose waters are drunk so eagerly while

[1] Ps. 136.—"By the rivers of Babylon, there we sat and wept when we remembered Sion. On the willows in the midst thereof we hung up our instruments."

our heavenly streams pass by unheeded. The silent harp is pressed closer and closer. I see the door of my eternity so wide open that I turn too wild sometimes. Oh, if all goes well for me, what will I not do for those I love? But, alas! Yet if I am not one of His elect, it is I only to be blamed; and when *going down*, I must still lift the hands to the very last look in praise and gratitude for what He has done to save me. What more could He have done? That thought stops all.

Link by link the blessed chain:
One Body in Christ—He the head, we the members.
One Faith—by His word and His church.
One Baptism—and participation of His sacraments.
One Hope—Him in heaven and eternity.
One Spirit—diffused through the Holy Ghost in us all.
One God—our dear Lord.
One Father—we His children.
He above all, through all, and in all. Oh, my soul, be fastened link by link, strong as death.

The sleep and dreams of life. The horizon of futurity. The awakening to another life: dawning of eternity. Rising sun of immortality, beauty, splendor, angelic singing, views immense. Jesus—infinity itself, boundless light, all delight, all bliss, all GOD. All this may be to-morrow, if only from the sleep and dreams of life I may, through penance and innocence, truly awaken in Jesus. My Rebecca! *Chère Benoni:* child of sorrow, we will awaken in Jesus together, forever; no more His children of sorrow, but of everlasting joy unspeakable.

Annunciation.— Anniversary of my first communion. One day of my poor life without a cloud. The most singular peace from the vespers of Mary. When drawing up a meditation for our vows the very soul melted before Him. Then this morning's awakening at half-past four with *Ave* sung to arouse the dormitories. Our meditation, office of the Blessed Virgin Mary for preparation, mass. Vows so peaceable.[1] Then all day so sweetly, so gently, amidst the little duties of hearing, reading, speaking, singing. Vespers and hymns; and my dear old Holy Court,[2] making many extracts. Surely the little clouds that pass over such a sun have not a name. Sin, sin, and sinners, the poor, blind, misled souls that know not, love not; *that* the only grief and sadness.

Brain and heart burning this day of St. Stephen, who saw heaven open. Our poor Miss M——'s questions on faith! I pour out the soul to God, hoping He will put the right words in my mouth. But how dangerous for me should I only darken by my mixture of words and feelings! Poor girl! she has to combat the horrid impressions of the deriders and mockers of religion, as well as the rest of her oppositions. Yet such good dispositions;

[1] The Sisters of Charity renew their vows from year to year on the 25th March, feast of the annunciation, because it is the day upon which *Mademoiselle* Legras consecrated herself to God, becoming after the death of her husband, in 1625, under the direction of (Saint) Vincent of Paul, and conjointly with him, the foundress of the Gray Sisters, better known as Daughters of Charity.

[2] *La Cour Sainte*, by Father Nicholas Caussin, a holy French Jesuit, and at one time confessor to Louis XIII. It is a quaintly devout book, full of good reflections and historical examples: these, though, sometimes wanting in criticalness.

esteeming herself in this house a *wretch*, as I did myself in Leghorn.

✠

Oh, my Jesus! No one, no one ever wronged me. All have done too much, and thought less evil than there was. But oh, how many *I* have grieved, troubled, and scandalized! Let me then mount to Thee on the steps of humility, on which Thou camest down to me. Let me kiss the path of Calvary sprinkled with Thy blood, since it is that path alone which leads me to Thee.

The promotion of the heavenly kingdom among souls, the grand object of our whole life.

God—the Lord and Father of all.

God—incarnate for all.

God—to be believed by all unto salvation.

God—to be manifested to the whole earth.

His Cross—pointed out on Calvary.

His Sacred Body—on our altars.

Such multitudes in spiritual distress and desolation! Oh, what motives for prayer and exertions of every loving soul!

The interest of the heavenly and everlasting kingdom in the true spirit of faith and hope.

St. Lazarus.[1]—Communion. Directed such of the Sisters to thanks for the blessed missioners sent to enlighten our savage land.

[1] 17th December. A disciple of our Lord, and (as is commonly supposed) first Bishop of Marseilles—Apostle of Provence.

This day of manifestation! How many melting remembrances when, in 1805, alone with God. The desperate resolve to remain till the moment of death of no religion at all, since I could not find out the right one. With what ardor I would stretch out my arms to Him and cry, I will hold to you in life and in death, and hope to the last breath. Then, on this very Epiphany day, taking a volume of our Bourdaloue, I open the very festival, and at the words: "Oh, you who have lost the star of Faith!" The torrents of distress and anguish again overwhelming. To see a Catholic priest; oh, it was the only supreme desire on earth; but that impossible, so wrote immediately to (Bishop) Cheverus in Boston. His beautiful answer.

After Communion.—Now, my God, O God! Immense God! will your atom ever forget this Epiphany, 1815? The gratitude of a thousand years' penance would be little after it. My Jesus, our Jesus; oh, His kingdom! But poor souls, unconscious; *there* the point of points.

18*th August*, 1817.

Went down the chapel steps holding the fainting heart in the hand to our God, to meet a carriage, supposing William[1] there—but Mrs. Montgomery. Very well, and a Protestant lady with her. When I see all these people so various, my head and heart go wild with joy that He is God and *our* God, and we His poorest creatures. Served, indeed, so badly; yet He sees the poor heart, and, I hope,

[1] Her eldest son, returned from Italy.

the constant fear of offending, and the thirst to see Him better served and loved.

After passing a day with this poor Mrs. W——,[1] and hearing her sentiments on her family affairs and affections, I see plainly why so many souls remain in their deep darkness; why the light shines so full in darkness, yet is not perceived. Our God! They think they know Him, but have not the least idea of what spirit He is, or of their direct contradiction to it. Oh, the deep, sad impression to my soul. But we must pray, pray.

This lady declares the Catholic faith is the true faith; but I see plainly she has obstacles to grace, which our God alone can remove. Oh, then, to pray, pray, is all I see. She kept my heart so well under the press, showing all her oppositions to the reign of our Jesus (herself obstinately bent on supporting them), that I spent a day of tears and interior cry to Him. To see how they bind His blessed hands, pervert His word, and yet hold up the head in boast that they are true Christians! How my heart recoils from the *human* details she makes while it presses our Lord's. She insists even that He will pity hers—the most completely blind of any I have yet seen: not for faith, indeed, since she has enough to condemn her; but the absolute ignorance of the common principle: "Forgive as we forgive." Such obstacles to grace in one who values herself on *piety!* Oh, our good God! Incredible, if she did not herself speak it. Such is the religion of Protestants the most enlightened. Our poorest, coarsest Catholic sees so clear, compared with them, on these essential points of charity.

[1] The Protestant accompanying Mrs. Montgomery.

Not even little arts for obtaining fear or anxiety about this death can move the stronghold of peace, thanksgiving, and abandon of every atom of life and its belonging to Him. Even William I can see but in the great whole. What life, indeed! A gray-headed carpenter whistling over the plank he measures for Ellen's[1] coffin; just beyond, the ground plowing to plant some sort of seed; just beyond again, good Joe (I believe) digging the grave to plant Ellen for her glorious resurrection. Beautiful life! The whole delight in God. Oh, what relish in that word!

The tender interior look through sorrow at eternal joy—through the look of our Jesus, who wept for what you now weep, and must weep for to the last moment of life with loving bitterness and boundless exertions of penance—penance united to the only penance of our Jesus suffering, naked, and dying in obedience and payment for your fault. Penance, yes; life is so short, eternity so long. Let every fiber of the heart now suffer with Him that eternity may be most glorious, pure, serene, and loving. Oh, dear, dear eternity, come, take from this earth.

Beware of the disgust and tediousness of life proceeding from nature rather than Divine love. Keep on with hard earned, but eternal, blissful merit. Try to love, yes,

[1] Sister Ellen Brady (died on the 21st of April, 1818), the fourteenth who was buried in St. Joseph's cemetery.

to love your trial as from the *Will*;[1] try to love the dear, good, trying one.[2]

Through piety and gratitude come to the deepest recess of peace, and love, and true contentment of your heart, and let the little, whistling, chilling wind blow above your head, and blast nothing of your dear interior cheerfulness, your bright and hopeful look at eternity.

A night-storm at St. Joseph's.—I think I can form some idea of what death must be to one in full possession of his faculties, without the preceding weakness of nature which weighs so much on the soul. The beautiful serenity of last night at nine o'clock, when I was enjoying the brightest moon and clearest sky that can be imagined, was suddenly darkened over the whole mountain, which, overhung with black, threatening clouds riven by streaks of lightning, looked too awful; and I turned to the moon in her gentle majesty over our plain with inconceivable delight, thinking to my God: The soul that looks only on you goes quietly on, and the awful storm can come so far and no farther (for then it seemed to be going round to the East). Dropping asleep with my crucifix under my pillow, and the blessed Virgin's picture pressed on the heart, Kit and Rebecca fast asleep near me—what a contrast! to waken with the sharpest lightning and loudest peals of thunder, succeeding each other so rapidly that they seemed to stop but a few seconds between to give time for a sense of the danger. Every part of the house seemed struck in an instant, and the roaring of the winds from the mountain and the torrents of rain so impetuous, that it seemed they

[1] Of God. [2] Trial.

must destroy if the lightning spared. Oh, our God, what a moment! I had no power to rise or remember I was a sinner, or give a thought to the horrors of death or the safety of the children. God, my Father, in that moment so pressing, and the plunge (as I thought) into eternity the next. Oh, Mary! how tightly I held my little picture as a mark of confidence in her prayers, who must be tenderly interested for souls so dearly purchased by her Son; and the crucifix, held up for a silent prayer, which offers all His sufferings and merits as our only hope. The storm abating, I recovered my self-possession, and really felt (I suppose) like one who is drawn back from the door of eternity; then going gently to the choir window and looking out to see what had become of my peaceable little queen, I saw her wrapped in clouds lit up as they passed over her with so much brightness that, at first sight, they appeared like balls of light hastening towards us, while she was taking her quiet course above them to disappear behind the mountain. There again I found the soul that fastens on God: storms and tempests rage around, but can not stop it one instant. How good it would have been to have died then, if it had been the right time! but since it was not, here I am, very happy to meet all the countenances of terror and surprise this morning, and hear the repeated exclamation: "Oh, mother! what a night."

REV. MR. BABAD TO REBECCA.[1]

✣

J. M. J. L. J. C.

28th Sept., 1814.

DEAR CHILD,—I thought you were in my debt, not I in yours, for I had not received any answer to the letter I wrote to you by my dear child Henrietta Bedford, but you may rest assured that you are never absent from father's mind. I send you the blessing of the altar every day, and twice on Sundays, at mass and at vespers, when I have the happiness to give the benediction of the blessed sacrament, and whenever anybody asks my blessing, which on account of my children of St. Joseph's, I always give in the plural number.

These days past brought precious and dear remembrances of the year 1809, when I went to receive dear Harriet Magdalen[2] into the church. May St. Michael whisper to you his favorite motto: Who is like God? great, powerful, just, holy, dreadful, magnificent in promises, and faithful, bounteous and merciful, loving, amiable, adorable, etc.? Next Monday we will invoke our good guardian angels.[3] Ask your mamma what is the standard St. Michael bears in the battles of the Lord to rally all those who fight under him. Pray incessantly for the peace,[4] for Congress and the President, for this city,[5] the head of the Catholic religion in the United States, and be more and more every day the blessed child of the Heavenly Father.

[1] The original is in English. [2] Seton. [3] Feast on 2d October.
[4] The United States were at war with Great Britain. [5] Baltimore.

ELIZABETH TO WILLIAM.[1]

✠

25th Nov., 1814.

MY OWN DEAREST CHILD,—Your birthday! You know your mother's heart; it had a dear communion for you—for our eternity, my William.

Be blessed a thousand, thousand times. Take a few little moments in the church to-day in union with your mother's heart, to place yourself again and again in the hands of God. Do, my dearest one. Josephine sends you a little picture, and *both* their warmest love you may depend.

Love to my Richard,

YOUR OWN MOTHER.

In the month of September this year, a small colony of Sisters was sent from St. Joseph's to Philadelphia to take charge of an orphan asylum, which had been established there in 1797, to shelter children whose parents had died of the yellow fever.

ELIZABETH TO MRS. SCOTT.

Dec. 1st, 1814.

. . . . . There is one of the dearest souls gone to Philadelphia from this house, who has lived in my very heart, and been more than an own sister to me ever since I have been here. She has nursed Harriet, Cecily, Anna,

[1] At the Mountain College.

Rebecca, through all their sufferings with inconceivable tenderness. She has the care of the poor orphans belonging to our church with our good Sister White, who has the little institution in her charge. If ever you have a wish to find a piece of myself, it will be in this dear Susan Clofsey, who is one of the assistants. If you ever see them, love them for me; for they love me most tenderly, as I justly do them.

FATHER BRUTE TO ELIZABETH.—TWO NOTES.

6 o'clock in the Evening.

I am just from benediction. My Mother!!! I have thought of all,—thoughts unbounded. The *Adoremus in Æternum*,—the *Gloria Patri: Sicut erat*, 1, *in principio;*
2, *nunc;*
3, *semper*.

Oh, what a life, if only we made a proper use of it! Courage, my soul: "Magnify the Lord" with Mary. Oh, simplicity! simplicity! Pure abandon, purest intentions, fervor in little things, daily watchfulness, till the great cry: "Lo! the Spouse." The cross and the altar—communion and eternity.

At 10 read the Epistle. Oh, fullness of suffering and devotedness! How ashamed in reading it! even in America, and so far away from all I love. Alas, ashamed. What do I? All around, what an empire of sin! But I, how comfortable and easy-minded indeed, in the midst of these ruins of souls. A fine little spot! Yet all over the country does not heresy, Catholic ignorance, and sin reign abundantly. What left? the ——[1]? No! a tender, calm abandon. His holy will alone.

Read that epistle, O mother! and be a mother to your good foundation, but pray also for the poor useless priest.[2]

Read the gospel word by word: mysteries: adore, bless, love. An abyss of delight, a world of instruction. Jesus in each word, seen and felt; but how to make Him manifest! Yet this must have been and ought to be the whole of my offering and consecration to Him and His Church. Oh, pray, pray ye all.

NOTE FROM ELIZABETH TO THE JUNIOR CLASS AT SAINT JOSEPH'S.

Innocents, 28*th Dec.*

This your day, my children. To imitate through life these innocent, simple, unconscious babes, the first victims for our Jesus. Their mothers' anguish; even a little murmur, perhaps, that Mary and Joseph left them to suffer all, and brought on them this bloodshed and murder. The spiritual view so different! The little bodies cut down—the little souls joyfully flying up. Happy, blessed troop entering limbo, so welcome to the holy fathers, and expecting souls to whom they give the news that He who was to come, is come, and oh! that their lives had been given for His.

[1] One word illegible.

[2] Mr. Bruté was noted for his exceeding great humility. He was probably the most useful priest whom the French clergy—that noblest body of men in the world—have ever sent to the United States.

My children, mind, the soldiers of Herod, for you are the ministers of the Prince of darkness—worse far than they who could only touch the body, the soldiers of Satan kill and destroy your little souls. As a last thought: yourselves kill not each others' soul by scandal. Say of her who gives the bad example: There! a soldier of Herod.

1815.—Letters of Elizabeth.—Of Mr. Brute.—Of William.—Of Rebecca.

REBECCA TO MARY-STANISLAUS.

January, 1815.

Dearest Stanislaus,—The day on which we are to renew our consecration draws nigh—the purification of our blessed Mother. I renewed mine on All Saints' day, also, with my whole heart. Here is another begun; let us try and make amends for all the faults we have committed the week before. I will try my very best, and with our dearest Lord's grace I hope to fulfill my good resolutions. Let us try to do our dearest's will in every thing, then how happy will we be! Pray for me who prayed so hard for you this morning.

Good-bye. I must go into the chapel, for I think it is time.

Mr. Bruté went to Europe in the spring of this year, and as Mrs. Seton wished to send her eldest son to Leghorn, that he might acquire a knowledge of business in the counting-house of the Messrs. Filicchi, who had offered[1] to receive him as their own child, he volunteered to take him in his company as far as they could go together.

Writing at this time of William's departure with Mr. Bruté, she says "she feels as secure as good old Tobias felt;" and, indeed, her reverend friend was worthy of all the confidence of a mother's heart.

ELIZABETH TO WILLIAM.

March, 1815.

. . . . . If you should be received by Mr. Filicchi, it would only be to try if you could engage your mind in the career pointed out to you, and you would, I am sure, conduct yourself as you have always done, with attention and good will to every one. However, as I think that in such houses, order and exactness are of the greatest necessity, I point them out to you as of the first importance. Your kindly and attentive behavior, also, to that family most kind and friendly to us, I need not recommend.

My own William, let nothing be hurried. Be assured that you have the tenderest friends. Be as polite as possible to our ever kind, excellent Madame Chatard.[2] Never will you meet with truer friends than in her and the one I first committed you to; and although you will probably soon be separated from him, ever preserve for him the

[1] Some years before.

[2] She had invited William, with the kind-hearted delicacy of French politeness, to stay at her house the days that he and Mr. Bruté stopped in Baltimore on their way to Europe.

heart of gratitude for the unbounded goodness of his intentions towards you, and show it on every occasion in your power.

They sailed from New York in the *Tontine*, on the 6th of April, bound for Bordeaux.

As the Rev. Mr. Bruté intended, if his time would allow, to visit Italy before returning to the United States, Elizabeth gave him a letter of introduction to one of her old friends at Leghorn.

TO ANTHONY FILICCHI.

My Dear Sir,—This letter will introduce to you the Rev. Mr. Bruté, a most distinguished soul, as you will know in a moment if you have ever the happiness of a personal acquaintance.

There is no possible recommendation I could give him which would not be ratified by our Most Rev. Archbishop and the blessed Cheverus, by whom he is most highly beloved and esteemed. Our archbishop, indeed, values him as an inestimable treasure in the church, and you will find, if you have the happiness to know him yourself, that his uncommon piety, learning, and excellent qualifications (and even his family, since you Europeans take that into account), entitle him to the distinguished friendship and regard of Mr. Philip and of yourself. He has adopted the *great*[1] interest of my William so generously that, with

[1] *i. e.*, The *spiritual* one.

yourselves, I consider him our truest friend in God. What more can I say to interest you? Judge for yourself.

REV. MR. BRUTE TO THE MESSRS. FILICCHI.[1]

BORDEAUX, *24th May*, 1815.

GENTLEMEN,—Having been asked by your estimable friend, Mrs. Seton, Superioress of the Sisters of Charity in St. Joseph's Valley, near Emmitsburg, in the State of Maryland, to bring her eldest son, William, with me to France, and thence to put him on his way to you at Leghorn, I have yesterday seen him off for Marseilles with a passport and letters from the American consul here to the one there. My first intention was to accompany him some distance myself, but unforeseen changes which will hasten my return to the establishment in Baltimore, have obliged me to see good William on his way to you as soon as possible. You will find him simplicity and innocence itself, inexperienced, timid, a little too reserved, but full of good sense and intelligence, and at heart a person of the most delicate feelings, although hidden under such a cold exterior. I love him very dearly, and hope that he will be happy where he is going, and will give you all the satisfaction which your kindness to his excellent mother calls for. This incomparable woman, whose views are of the most elevated order, sends you letters by her son; I only add the expression of my regret at not being able myself to go with him to Leghorn. Mrs. Seton's two little girls, Josephine and Rebecca, live with her; they are so good, so amiable, like two angels of paradise; and,

[1] Original is in French.

indeed, the holy house they dwell in is paradise on earth. How a visit from you would be welcome! How pleased I should be to learn that one of you intended to visit our Continent again.

I expect to remain in France until the end of July, and hope to have a letter from you to present to Mrs. Seton, and will deliver any answer you may have relating to the things mentioned in the letters William bears. Please address me under cover to MM. Caduc & Cie., *rue des Fossés de l'Intendance, N.* 6, *à Bordeaux.* Good-bye, gentlemen, *à Dieu et au ciel,* is the well wish of your most obedient humble servant,

S. Brute,

Priest of the Seminary of Baltimore in the United States.

William Seton, after considerable difficulty in getting through the lines of the armies in the South of France, arrived at Leghorn in the month of July, and was very cordially received by the Filicchis.

ELIZABETH TO WILLIAM.

Trinity Sunday, 21*st May,* 1815.

My Own William,—Your two dear letters from New York came safe, and your last word opposite the Battery. Oh, my William, tears will overpower and my soul cries for our eternity. My dear, dear one, if the world should draw you from our God and me! not meet there! That thought I can not bear. I will hope, I do hope. My God, who knows a mother's love, sees and will pity.

I can write you but few lines at a time, the heart

is so full, but you will write to us as often as possible; you will never think it a task to write to beings so dear as your Bec, Josephine, and mother. For us it will be always like a renovation of life, for it is almost unaccountable how tenderly we love you.

This was written before the last news. You can easily suppose what our anxiety will be till we hear from you; but you know my old and confident rule, that those who most want the protection of Heaven are surest of obtaining it. My very soul cleaves to you day and night and night and day; the one look of my heart to our God for you, is unceasing except in sleep, and often even then. My full confidence that whatever changing events you may pass through, you will act as a man and a Christian, and will keep in view our true home and eternal reunion is my sweetest consolation; and that confidence is even extraordinary since you are so young, and may have so many trials to pass through. Dearest, dear, dear William, we are all taking care of one another, that we may live to see you again. While I calculate what o'clock it is in France, where we must hope you are arrived, Rebecca says: "One more day gone of Willy's absence." Many think the *Tontine* will return if you should meet the last accounts half way; for me, I can but look up and dare not even *wish*, knowing so little what is best: all to God alone in His dear providence. But do take every care of yourself, soul and body, and write, write; but I know your blessed mentor will take care of that as far as depends on him; and for your heart, I am sure it will not be wanting. I have the globe our blessed Bruté made for the Mountain standing in my room, and even at night, by the light of the lamp, often look at France as the spot on earth containing my dearest treasure. Oh, how often I kneel in spirit by your bedside. You understand, my own dear one. I would be as faithful to you as your good angel if I could. Richard is as you left him. He makes the Wednesday visit, sometimes in a lonely mood, since you are gone, and really does not seem as if he would ever get accustomed to the separation. I could not have guessed how great was his attachment to you if you had not been parted.

Guard well, my dear one, that pure heart which will be the charm of our reunion. Oh, if our God should be forgotten in that heart and it should become ——! No, no, no; never, never; let me die and be gone before that insupportable sorrow comes. I pray for you incessantly.

My dear one, I must repeat to you the earnest recommendation to show a most grateful heart to your blessed guide and friend. Do, do write, and love and pray for your own MOTHER.

With this letter went the following most sisterly lines from Rebecca.

MY OWN DEAR, DEAREST BROTHER,—Our separation was truly painful, but yet we have a continual comfort in our hearts that you have not gone to the Navy. We were very lonesome after mass that morning with Dick only. I expect and know that dear Mr. Bruté is very kind to you. Oh, my William! if you knew the wishes and prayers you receive from us, and dear Mr. Bruté also, both for your happiness and safety. Do not forget to pray on your way for your Kit, your Bec, your Dick, your own dearest doating mother. Sure, my Willy, if you do not go to heaven, it will not be for want of her prayers. I hope you will go to communion frequently, at least as often as you can. I expect it will be very convenient on board of ship, as perhaps Mr. Bruté will say mass, and you can go whenever you wish to. I believe all mother's wish and anxiety is for us all to meet in heaven; indeed, on this earth again, but more especially in the next world, as we can never feel the pain of separation there. That is all we wish to live for now to see you again.

When you went away that Sunday, I felt so heavy about you; but I could picture you to myself riding in the sleigh quite merrily and happy—that would cheer me up directly; but I know you suppress your feelings, as you are among others and can not express the feelings of your heart as we can ours. The letters have to go. My own dear William, I must stop. Our remembrance to our reverend dear Mr. Bruté, and beg his blessing for us.

I am still your ever dear little sister,

BEC.

MR. PREUDHOMME DE BORRE TO MR. BRUTE.[1]

MARSEILLES, *June* 16*th*, 1815, *Rue Pastoret, No.* 10.

DEAR SIR AND RESPECTED FRIEND,—Your pupil, Mr. William Seton, having given you an account of our journey since our arrival here, I have postponed to write until his departure from here, which has taken place yesterday morning; not by sea as you expected, but by land. We had almost assured his passage on a *xhebeck*, under the Sardinian flag, when we were told at our consul's that it was not safe, the sea being infested at present by Alge-

[1] The original is in English—not the writer's native language.

rines, who are in perpetual war with the Sardinians; whereupon it was concluded that he should go by land to Nice, thence to Genoa, thence to Leghorn. He goes with the mail for expedition and safety; he has been procured good letters of recommendation for Nice and Genoa, and provided with all the necessary advice for a young man who travels for the first time alone. I hope he will arrive safe at the place of his destination. As long as he has been with us he has behaved exceedingly well, and as a good pattern for my own sons; we considered him as one of them; he has been received and treated as such in my sister's house. In the necessary steps to be taken for his departure I have found great assistance in a gentleman who has resided many years in New York, and who was well acquainted with Mr. Seton's father. His name is Parangue, and you may mention to Mrs. Seton that he has given himself as much trouble as if he had been his own son. We have regulated with Mr. Seton the account of his journey, it amounted to 210 francs and 18 sols, and he has paid me the balance of 48 francs and 18 sols, which with the 162 francs I received from you at Bordeaux, make the said amount. Having now discharged my trust as well as I could, and I hope as you expected from me, permit me to add a few words concerning my family, for which you have shown so kind an interest. We enjoy here as much tranquillity and satisfaction as circumstances admit of. My good and tender sister considers my children as hers, and we form but one family. Mrs. Preudhomme's health is as it has been for many years, very unsteady. She finds herself very much at a loss, finding almost nobody who understands her language: there is but one ecclesiastic here that speaks English. Oh, that your zeal, instead of the New World, would direct your steps towards this city! Besides our satisfaction, it would find sufficient employment. We did find neither Mr. McCarty nor Mr. Miguel at Toulouse, and the other gentleman, who received us very kindly, had no acquaintance in Marseilles where we expect to remain at least a certain time, unless the European troubles should drive us back to peaceful America. My health is much improved, and my children have resumed their studies, and I am well pleased with both; the bad impressions, if any, received while at sea, have totally disappeared in Francis. Please to present our best compliments to Messrs. La Tavière and De Lor; tell also to the latter that I regret much not to have had more time to cultivate his acquaintance, and that if I was not afraid of appearing an intruder, I would open a correspondence with him. As he is now applying himself to the Greek language, perhaps I could communicate to him some ideas which would facilitate his study of it. Please, also, my respectable friend, to accept the expression of my grateful sentiments, as well as those of my whole family. Your friend and servant,

L. PREUDHOMME DE BORRE.

I hope you will gratify us with an answer.

MR. BRUTE TO WILLIAM.[1]

✣

RENNES,[2] *Sunday, July 17th*, 1815.

DEAR FRIEND,—Bonaparte's return made me look to myself, and I was even afraid that I would be arrested at

[1] Original is in French.

[2] His native town. He was born there on the 20th of March, 1779.

Bordeaux as a priest; but, thank God, the white flag has been raised again, and we breathe freely. You will share with us this joy, and my only regret is not to be able to write to your mother that you were with me on such an occasion; but we were forced to separate, and I am now very glad that we did, for I have lived amidst alarms ever since we were together in Bordeaux. I even felt some apprehension for your safety, my good friend, until I learned by your letter that you were out of Marseilles; although I would not have felt perfectly easy until I had heard of your arrival at Leghorn, because you told me that you would go by sea, and that route is not without danger. But Mr. Preudhomme writes me that you went by land, and I feel more hopeful that your journey was without accident. Give me the details of it, and do not refer me to those which you will not fail to write to your good mother. I shall give her all the news concerning you that I may know, for we can not let her hear too much about you. Write to her every opportunity.

Dear William, far away from your mother, thrown back upon yourself, this is the time to show that you are all that such good principles as you have been brought up in require of you, all that your previous conduct warrants us in expecting. Good friend, how willingly I would once more go over our many conversations touching this point, but I almost fear to have spoken too often on the same subject, and, perhaps, to have tired you a little. Ah, dear William, you know that your mother lives only that she may know you to be good and virtuous. That is enough, you will not disappoint her.

I have written to Mr. Preudhomme, thanking him for his attentions to you. Give my respects to your friends, and say how pleased I would feel could I for a moment be with them to join you in speaking of such a worthy friend of theirs as your mother is, a friend for heaven and eternity, and whose constant delight is to recall all that they have done for her in that direction.

My good William, remember your poor Bruté: he has felt very miserable not to have been able to fulfill, towards you more satisfactorily, your mother's wishes when she intrusted you to his care. Love him as he loves you, and let us pray one for the other.

S. Brute.

P. S.—Write to me at Paris, at the Seminary of *St. Sulpice, rue Pot de Fer, No.* 17. Let me know what you may have learned from the Filicchis concerning Mr. Zocchi's[1] books, and the personal effects of Bishop Concanen. Read to them the part of this letter in which I speak of them, and although I am a stranger, there will be one more heart beating for them with yours and your mother's.

WILLIAM TO MR. BRUTE.

Leghorn, *Aug.* 26*th*, 1815.

My Dear Friend,—I yesterday received from Mr. Filicchi your esteemed favor of the 12th inst. I was surprised to see it dated Paris, as Mr. Dubourg,[2] who

[1] An Italian priest of Mrs. Seton's acquaintance, who was at one time on the mission at Taneytown, in Carroll County, Maryland, and had returned to his native country.

[2] He was on his way to Rome, to lay before the Sovereign Pontiff the case of the church in Louisiana. On the 24th of September, 1815, he was consecrated Bishop of New Orleans.

was here three days ago, told me you were at Rennes. At the time I received your letter I was writing my sixth or seventh to mamma. I have not yet received a letter, although a few days after my arrival a vessel came direct from Baltimore. It is a pleasure to write to so kind a friend and protector: indeed, I have always so considered you; and though during our long acquaintance I may have shown a cold disinterestedness, yet my outward deportment never spoke my inward sentiments. Believe me, my dear friend, I always loved you in my heart. Had I no other motive than the love of my dear mother, who certainly ranks you among the first of our dearest friends, that alone would be sufficient for me. I must confess you have justly accused me of diffidence or indifference, but I was never really insensible to the value of your friendship. I perceive, more sensibly since our separation, the many and great obligations I am under to you. I am happy to hear that you still intend returning, and I hope you will give a good account of me to mamma, though I am afraid I don't deserve it; but I am sure you will pardon the faults and indiscretions I have committed while under your charge. As to being grateful to MM. Filicchi for the great obligations we are under to them, my dear mamma need be under no apprehensions. I plainly perceive how much we are indebted to them, and I shall make it my study to show that I am grateful. I arrived here without any accident, although I was pretty often cheated on the road; indeed, I have been uncommonly fortunate. On arriving at Marseilles, Madame de St. Césaire, the sister of Mr. Preudhomme, received me into her house as her son as she was pleased to call me, and we parted with tears. The French marshal permitted me to cross the Var, although the same day he had refused other foreigners. From Genoa I traveled in company of an English gentleman to Leghorn, where I have been received with the utmost kindness by Mr. Filicchi.

REBECCA TO WILLIAM.

St. Joseph's, *27th Aug.*, 1815.

My own Dearest Brother,—I can not tell you how constantly you are in my mind, and how much I pray for you; but the thought of the happy day when we will meet again comforts all the pain of separation. You can not conceive, dearest brother, what joy it gave us to hear the news of your safe arrival at Bordeaux. I have felt so happy ever since, and returned so many thanks to our dear Lord. I never prayed more sincerely for you than on St. Vincent's day: I shall love it the more, as you took the name in your confirmation. Every evening I stand looking towards the East where the beautiful moon comes rising up; I stand and think of the happy home where we will meet to part no more.

Be assured I am and ever will be your most affectionate little sister,

Rebecca.

WILLIAM TO MR. BRUTE.

Leghorn, *Sept. 2d*, 1815.

My Dear, Dear Friend,—I have this moment, with pleasure, received a second letter; the first was dated Paris, 12th of August, which, as you may recollect, was inclosed and written upon the same sheet with that of the

Messrs. Filicchi, who now present me yours of the 19th August.

Just now Mr. Filicchi hands me another letter, dated the 17th of July, at Rennes. I have long ago rejoiced with you at the happy success of your new revolution, and congratulate you on the noble and loyal part which your own countrymen have borne in it, and hope they may be the first to reap the benefits of it.

It is now two months, less ten days, that I have been with the Messrs. Filicchi, enjoying, under their friendly roof, all the kindness and attention that it would be possible for me to receive from the nearest relation; indeed, he[1] acts as a father to me, supplying all my wants and making my situation with him as agreeable as possible. My heart, when I approached the house of our friend, beat very much, but a few moments' conversation quickly banished all uneasy feelings, the natural consequence of my peculiar situation. You must know, my dear friend, that in the first moments of my arrival here, the communication with France was interrupted, which put it out of my power to write either you or our good friend, Mr. Preudhomme. This difficulty continued near a month. Immediately after its removal I wrote to Mr. Preudhomme, but (as I told you in my letter of the 29th) have not yet heard from him. I could not write you as I had not your address, except for Paris, where I had every reason to think you would not go on account of the reigning disturbances; however, I shall now often have the pleasure of writing you, and hope as often to hear from you. I have nearly every week an opportunity for America, and never fail to

[1] Anthony F.

avail myself of it. Next week there is a vessel for Baltimore. I shall present your remembrance to all, and remain your affectionate friend,

WM. SETON.

MR. BRUTE TO WILLIAM.[1]

✠

J. M. J.

BORDEAUX, *on board the Blooming Rose,*
17th October, 1815.

MY DEAR WILLIAM,—I am once more on shipboard. Your heart bounds at the thought that I shall soon see your dear mother and tell her all about our voyage together. Oh, certainly, speak of it I shall. But pray to God that I arrive in America, for unless you do I may go down in the waters, and then you know all our fine talk is gone; but pray much more fervently that we may prepare a grand future for our holy religion in your native country. Oh, my good friend, the thoughts! The designs of God: how unfathomable! But yet I feel extreme pleasure in doing what little I can. I have three companions with me, all of them filled with the best intentions. Monseigneur Dubourg will surely return with a larger number. Once more, my dear friend, let me ask you to pray that I may see your mother and speak to her of you, and give her your letters and those the Filicchis have been so kind as to intrust to me. Now, my William, the entreaties that you strive for your eternal salvation. Take this as coming from your mother's heart rather than from

[1] Original in French.

mine. Hearken to her cry from far-off America, from her holy valley; hearken to the voice from Annina's grave: "*Be good.*" Oh, remember me always, as I shall ever you. Love God, serve Him, be a true and fervent Christian. The rest, all the rest, is nothing, yes, nothing; absolutely nothing without religion. Good-bye, William, to Jesus and Mary I commend you. Ponder eternity.

Your faithful friend,

S. BRUTÉ.

Mr. Bruté reached the United States safely in the month of November, and "was appointed President of St. Mary's College, at Baltimore, where he remained until 1818, when, on the death of Mr. Duhamel, he again returned to Emmitsburg and resumed his labors at the college and among the Catholics in the vicinity."[1]

In October Rebecca was sent to Philadelphia, to be under the treatment of an eminent surgeon there. Her mother's good friend, Mrs. Scott, asked to have the child in her own house, where she would assuredly have treated her to all the comforts and delicacies that wealth and a noble affectionate heart could provide, but Rebecca earnestly begged to go to Sister Rose and the other Sisters at the Orphan Asylum, and live among those who reminded her of St. Joseph's.

[1] Memoir of the Right Rev. S. W. Bruté, etc., p. 45.

REBECCA TO HER MOTHER.

Orphan Asylum.

As I soon expect to hear of an opportunity, I must write to my own mother to tell her with what joy I think of the day I shall once more be in her arms. I am sometimes almost lost in thought, and am as overjoyed as if I were actually with you; but I hope to see my thoughts soon come true. Oh, my mother, what a day that will be: my heart gets too full when I think of it. I must tell you, to comfort you, how much better I am than I was. . . . . I have been to "Aunt" Scott's twice; she took me riding in her carriage—I do not know how far—to the Museum, the Bank of Pennsylvania, Bank of the United States, the Water-works, and I do not know where else; but what was better than all, Sister Rose took me to the poor-house. You must know what a coward I am, as you have experienced me. I do not dare to think of my own sufferings after having seen theirs; though Sister Rose tells me I have seen but the least part of them. There is one poor woman up in the incurable ward named Peggy (ask Sister Susan, she will tell you whom I mean); she told Sister Rose: "Sister Rosy, I forgot to tell Mr. Roloff the main thing yesterday." Well, what was it? "That I had no tobacco" (speaking softly). However, I had happily just spent nineteen cents in getting tobacco and snuff to carry with me. But I wanted very much to get out of the place, for as we were going up-stairs we met a person who behaved very cross to us, which made me very much afraid for fear we should meet with another one. When we got out, believe me, my own mother, I really felt as if

I were in Paradise. There was another poor creature there who had three holes burnt with caustic in her side. She said that during the time it was burning her, she could think of nothing but the wounds of our Jesus, and actually did not feel the pain of it. I also saw old Queen Agnes, just woke out of a sleep, and quite loaded with old watch-seals, and beads, and chains, and I do not know what all. Sister Rose told her there was a great many people died nowadays. In great surprise she said, opening her eyes wide, "Has any died to-day?" No. Then Sister Rose says, "Agnes, are you afraid of death?" "No." But would you like to die? "No, that I wouldn't: I think it a terrible thing that a body must be put in a pit. I am afraid they would put me in alive." Oh, but Agnes, you know that does not hurt the soul. "I don't know." Then Sister Rose said, "Agnes, this little girl's mother knew you when you used to be in the hospital at New York. "Who is she? I don't remember her." Mrs. Seton. Then inquiring earnestly, "Is she dead?" No. Then looking at me full in the face—"She is a pretty girl." Sister Rose says, "She is going to be good." "She looks as if she would be." I thought to myself, you have a fine taste! They all appeared glad to see me. I believe I have told you all my things here but one. Agnes missing Sister Susan, asked Sister Fanny, "where was the pretty sister (meaning Sister Susan), not the religious one (meaning Sister Rose), is she gone home to get married?" Oh, no, Agnes, says Sister Fanny, we don't marry. "I don't like that at all," she answered. . . . . . Oh, my mother, how I long to be with you; but yet a little while. I think it is time to bid you farewell. Ever your own child. BEC.

ELIZABETH TO MRS. SCOTT.

10*th Nov.*, 1815.

MY DEAR JULIA,—Rebecca can not say enough about your kind attention. Little wild darling; it would take me a month to hear half her perpetual conversation. Imagine our meeting after "all dangers past," as she says, for the overset of the stage between New Castle and Frenchtown had given such a shock to her nerves that she thought every thing dangerous afterwards. Her fatigue from the journey makes it impossible to judge of the effect of what has been done for her by Dr. Physick,[1] but I have at least the consolation of knowing he has done all that could be done. Sister Rose has sent me many bills you have paid on Rebecca's account, amounting to at least sixty dollars. How happy you are to be able to do so charitable an act, and how happy we are that it is from you we receive it. It is all counted, Julia, where good interest is given, and where the fatherless are such good advocates. I believe you must have the greatest consolation in thinking of your invariable kindness and charity to us. I have again most pleasing news from William. Rebecca says she told you all that the first letters contained. He can not say enough of the continual kindness he has received from every one since he left us; and so many who knew his father and doubled their attention for his sake. Dear child, his expressions of affection to me and desire to fulfill all my wishes are almost extravagant. He

[1] Philip Syng Physick was a celebrated surgeon of Philadelphia. He had been a private pupil of John Hunter, in London.

says he would gladly exchange all he sees and enjoys for one walk with Kit and Rebecca in our valley.

Tell me, when you write, how you are and what you are doing. Now, Julia, be good, and do not think too hardly of your poor friend,—leave all to our God.

TO MRS. DUPLEX.

December, 1815.

My Own Dear Friend,—Some one going direct to New York gives me just time to say we are all well, your sweet Rebecca excepted. Poor darling, her fast rolling tears, at times, are the whole expression of her pain. Blessed child! she would hide them if she could, to keep me from suffering. Our God loves us; that is our comfort. We have every true consolation, and must leave all to Him. Sister Susan, again by, is an unspeakable delight to her, and eases me of half the care. Our letters from William are a pleasure it is useless to attempt to describe. Every thing my fondest heart could wish for his earthly prospects in the tender care and kindness he receives, and Mr. Filicchi's desire to advance him and Richard. Richard is all health and life, pushing on with his good and happy heart to gain as completely as he can the qualifications William points out to him as necessary. Yet such a lingering heart about *home*.[1] Never mind, all will go right, since we look to God alone.

If that good Mr. McCartey would but send you word, he so often knows of opportunities, and we could hear from you. Not a line from any one in New York since he

[1] He called St. Joseph's his home. This for him was wherever his mother and sisters lived.

left his daughter here, except once a letter from Sister Post by Mr. Bruté, who, however, told me all his kind heart could say about you and dear Eliza Sadler. We often hear from him, poor friend; but he suffers under his President's duties. How much he said of your George's kindness to him! Do write me a word about him, and if you have heard of your dear family.

Added to this letter are a few lines from her daughter, which evidence the grateful heart she had (as all Elizabeth's children) been taught to nourish.

Dear mother writes you I am suffering. I am, but I must still tell you how much I love you, and ever will. If Captain Duplex is with you, do remember me to him, though I almost forget his looks, it has been so long, yet I do not forget his kindness. I wish you would pay us another little visit.

YOUR OWN REBECCA.

1816.—LETTERS FROM ELIZABETH, MR. BRUTÉ, REBECCA, WILLIAM, FATHER BABAD, MR. DUBOIS.—NOTES AND JOURNAL OF REBECCA'S LAST ILLNESS AND DEATH.—VISIT OF BISHOP CHEVERUS TO ST. JOSEPH'S.

WILLIAM TO REBECCA.

LEGHORN, *January*, 1816.

MY DEAR SISTER,—I am almost afraid you will scold me in your next letter for not writing oftener, but you must never measure my love by my letters, it would be doing me an injustice. I have just been out to the door to see some Algerine slaves, for the Tuscans enslave them when they capture them. They were drawing a cart while two fellows were throwing the sweepings of the street into it. They were dressed in a green jacket and trousers, heads close shaven, and a green cap on. An iron chain they carried was locked by one end at the ankle, and the other drawn round the body to keep it from the ground. They seemed to bear their hard lot easily enough; one was laughing and singing while the boys were plaguing them. The merry one came to me when the cart stopped and asked a charity, but one of the clerks told me not to give him any thing, as the people would not like it. You can't imagine what fierce looks some of them have; they are almost black, with long curved noses, big mustaches, and dark eyes. I could not but pity them; though, at the same time, I thought their sentence quite just; indeed, they do not suffer half the misery of a Christian slave among them. My dear Bec, you must think your brother odd to write so much of slaves, but I looked on them, thinking their situation might have been mine in some town of Barbary, if they had fallen in with us at sea, but no doubt your prayers preserved me. Continue to pray for me, dear Bec; terra firma is not without its dangers. I am afraid I can not this time send your music; the ship will sail to-morrow. I love you with my whole heart.

REBECCA TO WILLIAM.

ST. JOSEPH'S, *February 4th*, 1816.

I am quite sorry to think, my dearest brother, that I shall not be able to tell you as much as Kit has,[1] but my heart is still the same, though I can not write as much as I would wish. We have received no letters from you since October or November, but we could not have expected them, since there are so few arrivals in winter. I have been more confined to the room this winter than I was last, therefore mother and I spend many hours together, and we amuse ourselves very often with thinking what Willy may be doing.

A great many deaths have happened at the Mountain since you have been away, and by your mentioning, in your letter to Dick, Egan senior, we suppose you have not received the letter of mother telling of his death. Yesterday good— (?) Green died, he left his dear little wife and sweet babe by a very quiet death. Mr. McElroy (?) dropped dead at the foot of the locust-tree by Mr. Duhamel's, while pulling off his hat to Dick. Poor old black Kate has also taken her departure. Our good Sister Kitty,[1] too, on Christmas-day, which was a high festival and her favorite one.

Elizabeth here took up her daughter's letter.

MY OWN WILLIAM,—Your Bec looks so pale and tired that I must finish. She is the dearest, sweetest creature,

[1] Who wrote on the first page

[2] Sister Catharine Mullen, the eighth on the death-roll of St. Joseph's.

and my greatest uneasiness in seeing her so weak and suffering, is lest you should not see her again before she goes to heaven. Poor darling! Her love for you, and desire of meeting you again seems to be the only wish or care she has. What a world of separations! but it must not be thought of; we must follow the line, if only to meet at last, *there* the point.

ELIZABETH TO REV. MR. BRUTÉ, IN BALTIMORE.

You would never believe the good your return does to this soul. To see you tearing yourself again from all that is dearest, giving up again the full liberty you justly and lawfully possessed, exchanging it for a heavy chain and the endless labyrinth of discussions and wearisome details (to use the softest expressions). In proportion as my pride in you increases, my own littleness and empty sacrifice to our Beloved is more evident, and I am ambitious (indeed, often with many tears) to get up with you a little by a generous *will* and more faithful service in the little I can do. I really take it as my most serious affair to pray well for you, and to get prayers from all that you may do well this hard work before you. Yes, dear President, you will; and you shall have plenty of prayers from these[1] most innocent hearts. Look up confidently; He will not abandon you who have left all for Him, nor leave you in weakness while loading yourself for His sake.

I will tell you in what I know American parents to be most difficult—*in hearing the faults of their children.* In

[1] The Sisters and children of St. Joseph's.

most instances, when you see the faults are not to be immediately corrected by the parents, but rather by good advice and education, it is best not to speak of them to papa and mamma, who feel as if you reflected on their very *self*, and while to you it will be, "Yes, sir," "I know, I perceive," in the heart they think it is not so much, and will soften and excuse to the child what they condemn to us, and our efforts afterwards avail very little, so that is a great point. . . . . .

TO MRS. SCOTT.

23d March, 1816.

. . . . Your fear that I should have any additional charge is groundless. I have none. Sister Rose has been so long away she does not know home as it is, but I assure you that six years' experience of our daily duties and way of life, has made many of our good Sisters as much old women as I am, though only two of them are as old in years. Their care and attention to save me every trouble would appear even ridiculous to others, who, not living with us, do not know the tie of affection which is formed by living in community. Perhaps you have no idea of the order and quiet which distinguish a regular way of life. Every thing meets its time and place in such a manner that a thing once done is understood by the simplest person as well as by the most intelligent.

TO REBECCA.[1]

Eternity.

MY REBECCA, my own darling, your poor mother does pray for you with the cries of *a mother's* heart. My soul's darling, bear all your pains with our Jesus, and commit your precious soul all to Him, and you must pray much for me that, at last, in our dear eternity we may rest in Him forever. Your mother blesses and prays for you now while you sleep so sweetly under the shadow of His wing. Oh, be blessed forever!

MY OWN CHILD OF ETERNITY,—With my little pen I answer my dear, every day dearer little darling, how much I desire she should go and unite still closer to our only Beloved. Go either Thursday or Sunday, as the others do, and make your careful preparation of the purest heart you can bring Him, that it may appear like a bright little star at the bottom of a fountain. Oh, my Rebecca! let peace and love stay with you in your pains, and they will lighten and sweeten them all. Oh, the love of your Mother in heaven! Oh, the delight of your good angel presenting every moment of suffering to your crucified Saviour, who counts your sufferings with His! My soul's darling, moments and hours pass so swiftly to our glorious, happy eternity. Trust all, indeed, to Him, my dear one; put all in His hands, and we will see, by and by, when we get home to our Jerusalem, how good and tender He has

[1] She was staying some time at the college with the Sisters who had charge of the infirmary.

been in giving you the thorny crown. Sufferings are the ties, the bands which fasten and unite us to our Dearest. Child of Calvary! child of the Cross! Of the past, nothing should remain but sorrow for sin; of the future, nothing anticipated but the hope of heaven; of the present, one sole and only aim to fulfill in every moment His adorable will.

My Own Rebecca,—Still only your mother's poor blessing. The disappointment is very great at St. Joseph's, but you know the only will of our dear Lord is so good. We will not be separated long. I will even go to you this afternoon if it should clear. Mr. Deidier[1] waits. Love and blessing to our dear Susan. Tell her she was my first thought at communion this morning, even before you. Love to good Miss Polly. Be good!

Well, my darling, again we are disappointed; but I hope to see you at least on Easter Sunday. I hope. Kiss my own Richard for his and your mother. Kit and I took our one hour in the garden with the girls and Sisters, who sat up from nine to ten. How often my eyes turned from my corner to Mr. Duhamel's, with a little prayer for my dear one! This is the anniversary of our separation from Willy. So goes the world. The girls enjoyed the Italian pictures and the *Ecce Homo.* Sister Cecilia fixed on a little altar in the choir for them; they were so good; and your little H. like an angel. Be good, too, my darling;

[1] This reverend gentleman was one of three priests whom Bishop Flaget had recruited in Auvergne for missionary service, when he visited France in 1810.

kind to all who are so kind to you. Love Sister Susan for me, and be attentive to all. Your own

MOTHER.

REBECCA TO WILLIAM.

ST. JOSEPH'S, *April 5th,* 1816.

MY DEAREST BROTHER,—We received last night your most dear letter of January, and could have cried together to think that you have not received our letters. But be assured, dearest Willy, we will write you every opportunity we can hear of. Last Sunday one year was the memorable day we parted with you, two o'clock it was as the bell rung for silence—silence it was with us. Mother can not speak of it to this day without starting tears which mine answer. The spring is so far advanced that we already hear the turtle-dove cooing, which sits on the tree over Annina's grave. We think, perhaps, it may be the one we bought from *Jim,* and mother let go off her hand.

Her mother here continued the letter:—

MY OWN WILLIAM,—I find this little word on the table. This morning I found myself praying for your confessor, so anxious that he should lead you well. I beg so hard you may be an "honest man," as you say, for you know an honest man gives to God his due, as well as to man. How you will be shocked to see Mr. Jefferson[1] turned to a John Gilpin in the papers! You must allow, it is something revolting to see a chief magistrate treated so. I do

[1] He was ex-President.

not understand politics or characters, but have a horror to find that our government can countenance such a freedom of the press. You, my son, reflect and be moderate. Take always the side of order, it is God's first law, says our true poet. Bless, bless you from the full heart of your own

MOTHER.

REBECCA TO WILLIAM.

ST. JOSEPH'S, *April 8th*, 1816.

MY OWN DARLING BROTHER,—We received two more letters from you again to-day, and are too sorry that you do not get ours. I think it impossible but you will some time or other receive them. I am going to Mr. Duhamel's as usual, but I would be twice as happy were you there. I have Dick, and that is a great deal. I anticipate much pleasure; Miss Polly so kind,—Sister Susan so kind. You would have laughed just now had you seen old Clem receive his new Easter coat. "A-ha!" he said, "my good Mother Seton!" So much pleased. I hope you will not fail to give us a little description of these times in Italy. Mamma tells us they are so beautiful. I would so much wish to join in your pleasures, which must be very great, never having been there before; but that great ocean between us, and Mediterranean Sea, put me out of all such thoughts, but I trust, my darling brother, we will meet in another land where there will be no seas and oceans to separate us. I think I am daily getting better, both as to my limb and health. I hope and trust, if it please God, I may live to embrace you once more. That is my earnest desire, it revives me to think of it. It seems almost like a dream to think I have a dear brother, and one who loves me so dearly, so far away. Farewell, my dear, dear Willy. I scarcely know where to stop. Ever your most loving and tenderly attached sister,

BEC.

P. S.—I pray for you and our best friends, the Filicchi family, every day in mass, and also when I go to communion. Pray, if it be our dear Lord's will, I may live to see you once more.

TO FATHER BABAD.[1]

June, 1816.

MY BLESSED FATHER,—My good angel has inspired me to continue to answer your precious letter. Oh, what a pleasure it is to obey you, ever dear and holy father; and oh! my blessed mother. I have begun to watch every action of hers, that I may imitate her. I spoke to her last night about correcting my defects, faults, and whatever she saw in me displeasing to our dear Lord or to her. And you, my dear father, tell me twice or thrice a week what displeases you, or what is displeasing to any one. Oh, my dear father, never have I passed such a week as this has been—it seems but a few moments. One day passed, another came, all alike in heavenly thoughts, all alike in that sweet repose which you know better than words can express. In the sacrifice of the mass my soul seemed to join yours and that of my sweet mother's, and adore our divine and heavenly Father. You know how the soul can be at such a time better than can be written.

[1] The first page of the letter is lost.

Let us join and invite heaven and earth to praise God for His adorable goodness, and make up in some measure for so many thousands who know not His adorable name. On Wednesday evening, after I received my poor, dear mamma's letter, I went to the chapel to our dear Lord to pour my soul out before the altar, and meditate on the sufferings of our divine Saviour. My soul seemed to follow our meek and humble Saviour every step. But yesterday morning I offered up my communion for the meditation of our dear and Adorable Saviour's passion, and to be united to His sacred heart. After mass my soul seemed to enter the room of the Last Supper, and then follow our Blessed Saviour every step of passion, and then to the sepulcher; and after, it seemed to see the Blessed Virgin without her Adorable Son. It seems as if the passion of our Divine Saviour was present to me every moment of the day. My dear father, I intended to have written you a very long letter, but time will not permit. J. M. J. Amen.

MR. BRUTÉ TO REBECCA.[1]

REBECCA, MY SISTER,—I thank you for your dear little note. I have pasted it on the last page of my Bible, the one that your mother gave me. I am just from the altar. To-day is the anniversary[2] of my first mass at the altar of the Blessed Virgin in the Seminary of *Saint Sulpice*, in my poor France. But I would not edify you in saying that I still have a country upon this earth, did I not beg you to remember that our Lord himself has given us the example of attachment to our native land: He who so

[1] The original is in French.

[2] He said his first mass on Trinity Sunday, which, in 1816, fell on June 9th.

much loved his dear Jerusalem.[1] Pray, then, for France—for France at every time so dear to the Church.

At the communion I took you in my heart and offered you to our Lord as completely as I could. I hope that your desire is to detract nothing from this offering, but to be entirely His with so much love, with such fidelity, that a little lamb could not show the like. Oh, suffer then in peace, for it is all on account of the infinite love He bears you that He makes you suffer. Suffer, my dear Rebecca, because it is *His will*—His who is your Father, your Redeemer, your Sanctifier for an eternity. None of us wish to oppose His will; but all unite their prayers to yours that He may support your weakness invincibly to persevere. "Love is stronger than death," heaven much more beautiful and greatly more delightsome than earth. To God I commend you; now pray as prays for you your poor brother,

S. BRUTÉ.[2]

[1] Mr. Bruté was a man of intense, but never fanatical patriotism. His devotion to country, like the friendship of the Roman of old, was *usque ad aram* only. He was most faithful, also, to the obligations entailed towards the government of the land he lived in, and which gave him protection for "life, liberty, and the pursuit of happiness." I have heard my father relate, in glowing terms, half a century afterwards, how Mr. Bruté, when many of his flock were leaving Emmitsburg to assist in the defense of Baltimore during the war of 1812, made an ADLOCUTIO, exhorting every man to do his duty.

[2] Mr. Bruté was very skillful in making pen-and-ink sketches. I have heard my father say that he has seen him dash off the cleverest little things in an exquisitely careless manner, without lifting hand from paper. This note, and almost all Mr. Bruté's other writings that I possess, have some drawing of the kind at the top or bottom, and often at both. They illustrate a mystery of religion, or recall to memory an occurrence that consoles or points out the hope of future happiness. Some of these pictures though, are of an entirely miscellaneous character, and more carefully worked, as for instance, one on a tolerably large scale, of St. Joseph's Sisterhood, taken October the 7th, 1818, another of *La tour de Cordouan*, 9th of May, 1815, a memorial of his visit to France: these speak the diligence of the man who "labored with all his art to make the resemblance in the best manner."—*Wisdom*,

FROM THE SAME.[1]

Bec, no rest last night. Then a standing or sitting posture, as the knights of old on the eve they were knighted. Ah, well might we take this whole life for the meritorious watch of our eternal knighthood. But where do I carry your fancy and mine. It is too odd to go any further that way. Come, then, my pen, seek for better, and since the hand has no rose to cull this morning for the beloved sufferer of my Jesus, we'll write her this name better to her sight than any rose or lily—JESUS. Then write the other she likes too so much, write quick—MARY. Write still the blessed Father of the house she lives or suffers in—for her life is now but suffering—write little pen, write quick and soft, her nursing father—JOSEPH. Well, now, dear Rebecca, be pleased, and when poor awkward creatures of this world try to soothe half a minute of your pains, look on high and be delighted that it is your Father, your God of love and salvation, your beautiful Beloved himself who bids any of His creatures to speak to your soul of His only goodness, only comfort. He, my dear Bec, not I, in any of these little black writing spots; He, not the flower you admire—the little food which feeds your spark of life—ah, more, He even in what only still truly pleases you and makes you yet so happy in your pains and faintings—your *mother*. He himself mostly seen in her smile, her maternal voice, her quickening and

xiv. 19. The present letter has *en tête* a trefoil amidst rays, with the name of a person of the Trinity written on each leaf. Around is the word *eternity;* at the point of the stem: "Mary, Joseph, etc., etc. Oh, that we may be in the list!" On the back are a little cross and a crutch.

[1] Original is in English.

animating look. He in all, my Rebecca; and let the storm roar around the walls and the grates of this transitory hard lazaretto of life; let sufferings, cruel and unrelenting, bid you stand and watch when the smallest bird enjoys his rest, let, let, let—the soul still knows how to cheer up, seeing and feeling her God, her Father, and Almighty lover in all. Ah, yes, if I know your faith and your love, they will be as unrelenting and pressing on as the sufferings can be, and more. One look to your bleeding Jesus will restore more strength and resolution than the most wearisome night would have taken away. He loved me and for me was patient upon His cross, so I love Him and will be patient too. Blessed be the short patience of this *douloureuse* life: this life is short, and the sweet fruit of that patience eternal.

YOUR BROTHER.

ELIZABETH TO MR. BRUTE.

Trinity Sunday.

Magnificent day for the soul!

Mr. Kerney, the old, buried at Emmitsburg this morning, and poor Joseph Elder at the Mount. Oh, I not buried yet!

Will you please to give or send this to Mr. Cooper if he is not gone, and if he is, will you please to open it and take out William's and Filicchi's letter and send them to Père Grassy if he is not gone.

Bless the happiest of women in the Holy Trinity this day (always excepting those who love better). Here is for your breviary a little St. Gabriel, fallen accidentally into the hands of Sœur Marguérite, who begs you to remember that Monday is St. Margaret's day, and that you will bless. I wish you much to have this St. Bernard.

E. A. S.

TO WILLIAM.

22*d July*, 1816.

MY OWN WILLIAM,—Although I have written you continually, by way of Baltimore and New York, I find you so seldom receive our letters. Still, every opportunity shall be improved in the hope that at last some may reach your dear hand. So I must give it up to our good God, and trust He will comfort you and make me stronger in this bitter separation, which I feel so much the more as you may sometimes be even tempted to think we neglect the only comfort we can give you in it; but my poor, doating, overflowing heart you ought not, can not doubt, my son, nor will you doubt it more than I yours.

Mr. Bruté is here on a little visit to us of a day or two. He speaks of you and of your dear, docile, amiable conduct to him as if it were only yesterday you were together. I write our Messrs. Filicchi continually, but trust all to the good angel. If only they could know my grateful heart, it would be no matter for the rest.

DEAR WILLIAM,—You will think it a profanation, but I can't help. Passing by from the Mountain, on my way to Baltimore, I see upon the table of your mother these three first words so precious to you, "My own William," and I ask to come within with two or three lines, for I remain as much as ever attached to you, and so anxious that you may be so kind as not to forget your poor Bruté.

I rejoice every time they receive (letters) from you, hearing how well Divine Providence brings on your prosperous ways, and, also, very particularly, ah, you know, most of all other things, I rejoice at your many little hints of your perseverance in your sacred duties; and you know enough how they delight your mother and sisters not to suppress them. God bless you. Pray for me. I for you.

S. BRUTE.

DEAREST WILLIAM,—Mr. Bruté would put his little word in, and I have but to add my earnest desire that you would keep your heart well resigned about Rebecca. He says that there are instances of recovery in her situation, but she is extremely weak and suffering. She sits up the greater part of the night with her head leaning on my bolster, but she is always so gay and has so much fortitude, it delights me and all around her. Often we say: "What is Willy doing now?" and my poor heart tries to hide. But, my dear one, we must take all in this world as it passes. If only you will cultivate the true spirit of a man, and give your noble soul its rights, and our God His rights, so immense and endearing. Oh, if I did not think you happy, I would be miserable indeed. But so much you have already said of every one's kindness to you, I hope the greatest pain of my William is his separation from *his own four*, and never can you guess how truly we share that. Bless you a thousand, thousand times. Oh, my son, keep your heart high with mine. Our God will turn all right for us, if only you will be faithful to Him. Every kind remembrance to our friends. My very soul wraps itself around yours is all I can say. Your own devoted MOTHER.

Mother and I are left alone while Miss Kate and Master Dick are enjoying themselves. Never mind, one of these days we will have our enjoyment too. We are truly sorry to hear that you receive so few letters from us after having written so many, but I tell mother I think you are now enjoying them while we are so uneasy. Ah, do, dearest Willy, try to meet me in the world where there are no separations, and where my soul will call for no one so much as you, next to mother; but I hope we may all meet. Pray for me as I pray earnestly for you and all our so kind friends. Ever truly your most loving sister,

BEC.

Excuse my little scrawl. I know you don't mind it.

MR. BRUTÉ TO REBECCA.[1]

Jesus.—Eve of His Transfiguration.

REBECCA, MY SISTER,—You have again been in great suffering this day, but your good angel was beside you. Mary, your tender mother, saw your pain; their prayers were wafted to the well-Beloved and called down upon you His graces. Ah, Rebecca, His grace! It is that gives you patience through the long hours of the day, and soothes the restlessness of tired nature. Poor nature! it is too blind and weak to prize the treasure of crosses and the happiness of such painful sufferings. But faith! Oh, Rebecca, what a brilliant light faith sheds upon your sufferings! Arrange the flowers,[2] it is a holy occupation;

[1] Original is in French.

[2] The sole amusement of this poor suffering child during the last summer of her life, was to make up nosegays from flowers spread out before her on a table, in which she used to show a great deal of taste.

dispose them to adorn the altar of your well-Beloved, while He favors your soul with His choicest and most precious graces. Dear child, the martyrs envied such happiness as you now possess. The saints of the desert voluntarily led a life of continual suffering as yours is. Oh!. courage, then; humble, loving courage. It is, I know, a faint heart, the most cowardly of hearts that cries out to you: have courage! But I do so in the name of your Divine Jesus, pierced, covered with blood, in agony for you. Oh, yes, dispose the flowers for His altar, and when you are so exhausted as to be unable to do any thing, even to pronounce your prayers, let your silence, your peaceful abandonment of every earthly desire, your complete resignation speak to His heart, to that heart so very tender, so infinitely loving. Oh, let us hide ourselves within it during this short moment of our mortal life. Bright eternity will soon open to us as it opened, a little earlier, to Annina. Eternity! Heaven! Does not the heart rejoice; is it not raised up at these words?

Deign to pray for my retreat. One of your sighs, one of your tears offered to God for me! To pray for others. Oh! what a satisfaction to you, and what sweet-smelling incense burnt upon your suffering heart to God, who is all charity. Pray then a great deal for others, for those whom you hold dear, for those who nurse you, for poor sinners, for the souls in purgatory. Make, the first thing in the morning, an offering to God of all that you will suffer in the course of the day as one unceasing prayer. You will thus be a real Daughter of Charity.

S. Bruté.

FATHER BABAD TO REBECCA.[1]

✠

J. M. J. L. J. C.

September 26*th*, 1816.

DEAR, DEAR REBECCA,—By your last I perceive that the fear of death and judgment has pierced through your flesh and soul. Thanks to God for such a favor. I hope you will now more safely work your salvation with that salutary fear, one of the most precious gifts of the Holy Ghost. The more we fear here, the less we shall have to fear there. Let humility make amends for the other virtues which are wanting, and you are striving to acquire. You are still but a child, our Lord loves you, and knows the infirmity and instability of mind to which your age makes you liable. Prepare yourself for the approaching feast of our good angels, and believe me forever,

Your loving father,

P. BABAD.

WILLIAM TO MR. BRUTE.

LEGHORN, *Aug.* 22*d*, 1816.

MY DEAREST FRIEND,—In pressing haste I wrote yesterday to my beloved mother, by a vessel going unexpectedly to Philadelphia. This morning I received two letters from mamma and one from Richard, *via* Rennes. Your tender heart will better conceive than I express my pleasure on receiving these pledges of affection.

[1] Original is in English.

Our beloved friend, Mr. Philip Filicchi, is in the agony of death; perhaps to-morrow thousands will bewail him. If virtue is a prize, they will lose indeed. The hundreds of poor fed at his hands, the orphans depending on his support, the prisoners relieved by his charity, will mourn a benefactor. But how tranquil must be the passage from this life to eternity of a soul unstained by crime; of one who has ever made his riches subservient to religion, and placed his honor, not in money, but in God! Mamma gives a distressing account of Bec's health. Dear, beloved sister, if I could only hold her once more in my arms, that moment would be worth more than years of pleasure. I can not bear the thought of losing her while I am so far away, but God's will be done. I am glad to hear that you have got Dick[1] so near you, and I hope all will be satisfied with him. . . . . . Present my kindest respects to Mr. and Mrs. Chatard, Mr. and Mrs. Barry, and our good friends the Tiernans. I conclude by assuring you of the unceasing love and gratitude of your friend and servant,

WILLIAM SETON.

The following letter, from the Reverend President of St. Mary's, illustrates his literary taste, and instances a zealous desire of forwarding the study of the classics in the institution over which he presided:—

[1] Richard was in Mr. Luke Tiernan's counting-house in Baltimore.

MR. BRUTE TO WILLIAM.[1]

BALTIMORE, *Oct.* 17*th*, 1816.

MY DEAR WILLIAM,—I request you most earnestly to present this *supplique* to the MM. Filicchi.

"Two editions of *newly discovered* manuscripts of classics have been given at Milan by F. Angelo Mayo,[2] consisting of the works of Fronto and Symmachus, together with a great many *pièces inédites*, letters, etc., of many of the most celebrated names of antiquity: Sallust, Ennius, Plautus, Cato, Pliny—the Emperors Antoninus Pius, Marcus Aurelius, Verus, the historian Appian."

To possess here these new literary treasures, to have them the first in our college, and perhaps be able immediately, by subscription, to give the first American edition, would be an honor for the Catholics—an honor which antiquity ought to yield rather to Catholics. May your zeal incline you, respected gentlemen, to procure and send us a copy of them. Such is the humble and confident

[1] The original is in English.

[2] The celebrated Maï (afterwards Librarian of the Vatican and Cardinal of Holy Roman Church), who had acquired his remarkably studious disposition in the learned Society of Jesus, was at this time engaged in exploring the Ambrosian library, in which he discovered, and brought to light many treasures latent in twice-written manuscripts (palimpsests). B. 1782, D. 1854.

I well remember the enthusiastic eulogy of this great man, which our professor of archæology, Baron Visconti, made to us one day that he took his scholars an excursion on the Palatine, and bid them remark that he who living had done so much for our knowledge of ancient Rome, illustrated its history even after death; for it happened that the workmen employed in clearing the foundation for the tomb which, before dying, he had designated for himself in his title of Santa Anastasia *Sub Palatio*, struck upon a portion of the very walls of Romulus.

"E'en in our ashes live their wonted fires."

prayer of the friend of William, who from this shore shares so sincerely in all his love for you.

S. BRUTE,
President of St. Mary's College.

DEAR SIR,—If there was any mode by which those books could be sent to me, I would pay their value, if a bill could be sold on me for the amount. If they were given to the captain of the ship *Scioto*, he would take charge of them. Yours, with regard,

LUKE TIERNAN.

Postscript by Mr. Bruté.

A letter which I received yesterday from our dear Mr. Cheverus, the bishop of Boston, has this paragraph, which I sent to-day to your ma. "*La veuve de M. John C. Seton, le frère du mari de Mme. Seton, se dispose en ce moment avec ses deux enfants à entrer dans l'Eglise. Elle vient assidument à l'Eglise catholique.*" Persevere, dear William, both in your principles and steady habits of piety.

REV. MR. DUBOIS TO WILLIAM.[1]

MT. ST. MARY'S.

OUR OWN DEAR WILLIAM,—Our Dick is here on a visit. I must profit by his return to write, if it is only a few lines to you. I would write a volume if I had time, but to my former almost excessive business is added the care of the parish, since good Mr. Bruté left us. Every account we receive of and from you would increase my affection for you, if possible; certainly it gives me always a new

[1] The original is in English.

pleasure. Continue, my beloved friend, by your steady, religious, and manly conduct and attention to business, to gladden the declining years of your excellent mother, to open the road to your affectionate brother, and to secure to your probably only surviving sister the respectability and protection which the good only can give.

Your mother is as well as her constant attendance on Rebecca can allow. Indeed, her health with such hardships is a miracle, up one-half of the night at least, for three months past; she does not quit her a moment in the day-time. This blessed little angel is melting away, but amidst the ruins of her little frame, the soul appears to shine brighter than ever. Her eyes, too, are clear and piercing yet. Cheerful, nay, playful, whenever pain leaves her a moment, she talks of her going to heaven just as you were talking of going to Italy. Last Friday, having felt uncommon pains, she expressed a desire to receive *extreme unction.* I could not but approve of so pious an intention, and although I saw no immediate danger, I thought she would receive this last sacrament with better dispositions by being more sensible. Accordingly, I went to her room to hear her confession, in order to give her extreme unction the next day. It is impossible to give you an idea of the composure of mind and heavenly resignation of this blessed angel. After her confession was over, "Father," said she, "is there any harm to hope that I will go to heaven as soon as I am dead?" No, my beloved child, said I, if the hope is grounded not on any confidence you have in your own merits, but in the mercy of God and the merits of our Jesus. "Oh!" said she, "it is so, I understand it; what merits such a child as I could have! but when I look at the cross, and consider that our

Lord has shed His blood to save me, then I hope that my sufferings will be accepted as my penance without going to purgatory. . . . .[1] Oh, how would I like to go to heaven! Then I would love God, and would not be afraid to lose Him." The next day she felt better. Richard, whom she wished very much to see, came, and finding her in a kind of fit of joy, I advised her to postpone extreme unction to a time when, suffering more, she would be in need of all the help of this sacrament.

. . . . . Our seminary is more numerous than ever. The garden will be finished this year, as well as the yard, which will be planted with trees this fall. I bought all the woodlands between us and the plantation which formerly belonged to Wyse. The dormitories are plastered. I built a corn-house and granary over the cave, and by building a good brick-wall round the spring, have succeeded in carrying the water to a milk-house which I have formed under the stone-house, then to a long trough near where the pump was, with twenty-four cocks for twenty-four boys to wash at the same time. The same trough conveys water under-ground into the kitchen, and still the spring has water enough to send into the garden through pipes, with a spout of water in the middle of it which rises from ten to fifteen feet. I tell you all that, my dearest friend, because it has been the spot of your infancy, and that it naturally recalls to your mind many sweet remembrances.

When you write to me again, let me know whether such urns as you remember we have for flower-pots on our altar can be had at Leghorn, and what is the price and

[1] These dots, marking something left out, are in the original.

the probable expense of carriage here; also, whether pictures, twelve feet high, and good copies of masters, could be had from students on reasonable terms. I should be glad to get half a dozen to complete our church; but I wish to have no pictures but such as should be edifying, and eight or ten urns for St. Joseph's and Mount St. Mary's. Do not say a word about any of the above articles to the good Messrs. Filicchi: enough has been already given by them. Poor as we are, I will muster all my resources. We may use the charity of our friends: we must not abuse of it.

Farewell, my beloved friend; that every blessing may attend is the daily prayer of everybody here, but particularly of your devoted friend and servant,

J. DUBOIS.

I send you a hasty scrawl begun at eleven o'clock at night; hence so many scratches, as you will remark. I had begun it this morning, but was called away to attend poor old Joseph Livers, who fell from his hay-loft down to the barn-floor, about twenty feet. Happily, he did not kill himself.

RELATING TO REBECCA.—NOTES AND JOURNAL BY HER MOTHER.

1816.—Rebecca at recreation says: "How can any one think of what our Lord has done for them and not love Him! That is such a mystery to me why everybody does not love Him. Sometimes I have such feelings—almost like despair—because I can not keep my good resolutions; but when I have these sorrowful thoughts, and

I can only look at a crucifix, I directly think : Be sure He will forgive after He has done all that for me."

✣

St. Joseph's Patronage, Sunday.—Our sea of sorrow a little past. Poor Bec, with blessed Sister Sarah holding her, can contain her misery a moment and be quiet after a conflict of five days and nights in groans, and tears, and agonies—out of my power to give any least idea of. Could not believe if I had not seen. Always saying: "My dear Lord, my dear mother," with incessant big rolling tears—unable to sit or lie. When she at last could remain a few moments in bed, and the excessive agony was suspended, I said : "Well, Bec, not a single little prayer these three nights and days!" "Indeed, but, dearest mother, for my part, every moment of the time I was praying." Poor darling, once she stared her large eyes, and said to us, as if in consultation : "I am almost tempted to beg our Lord to ease me, do you think it will displease Him?" and with such faith, when permitted, she begged Him to let her have only a moment to get into a posture, and actually was eased enough to get into bed, almost gone, though.

✣

Rogation Monday (*May 20th, that year*).—Poor darling! Telling her of our beautiful meditation on the love of God, she told me, as I knelt beside her: "Ah, dearest mother, I now hardly dare tell God I love Him, I prove it so badly; and it seems like a bold falsehood to say and not do any thing to prove it. Indeed, I think our Lord sent me this sickness for my neglect of my little practices of piety since the retreat; for when I have been out among the girls taking a little pleasure, it did go so hard with me to leave them and go to the chapel; yet when I am there, I seem never to have time to say enough. Yet you know, too, how negligent I have been these two weeks; still it is certain I prayed night and day, in continual aspiration since I have been so, for no one can help me but He." Dear, simple heart! these her exact words with such pure looks of sincere meaning. Oh! my God! how piercing to my cold, dead heart, so truly, without proof or effect. Dear, dear Rebecca, every day dearer and more resigned, I must hope she will be safe.

Opening her eyes with weary smiles at me, she says: "I must die, that is clear; how will you live without me, mother?" "Mother will soon wear away and follow, darling." We exchange so many rapturous looks of hope. Now she gets Mr. Bruté's picture. I would have put it away, but—"No, no," she cried, "nowhere but opposite my eyes, at the foot of my bed."

July 20th.—✠—Dear beloved Bec—obliged to give up her bed entirely; no change of position from continual sitting, but to kneel a little on one knee.

Softly she sings the little words:—

"Now another day is gone,
So much pain and sorrow over,
So much nearer our dear home;
There we'll praise Him, there we'll bless Him,
Ever, ever, ever more."

She leans so peacefully her darling head on mother's lap, and offers up, she says, "her poor body covered with the blood of our Jesus." In a peaceable evening moment she said: "Not only reconciled and willing, but my heart jumps for joy when I think of my crown; yet, also, I look the other side and I fear, but, indeed, I do try to be very sorry for all my sins."

To-day again we talked it all over. The darling beloved is determined to hope all. At sunset, her little heart melting into mine, she drew the picture of our love and her happiness in her own mother; and told with liveliest memory the sufferings she had seen in poor-house and hospital in Philadelphia, remembering all the poor people said to her; her delight in carrying them snuff and little articles, from her pocket money. Then made her comparison of the love of all around her, and her many comforts. I ask her, Can you say, with a true heart, *Thy will be done?* "Oh, that I can," she answered, brightening with joy, "if that is enough." Dear, dear darling, how she is wrapt in the very nerves of my soul.

Again, up night after night. And now the most simple but earnest preparation for communion, with long silent looks at the *Ecce Homo* opposite her, and though exhausted by restless pain, yet received at the choir door with white cap and cape. Such a dear, simple, recollected heart—running her little fingers under words in the prayers she delights in—full rest of the finger and long sigh on the words in the litany, *Cross of Jesus, support me.* Then said, with her whole soul, her favorite 102d Psalm.

Reading in a book, on sufferings, these words: "The little bark draws near to land; do not regret that it will so soon be safe, or desire again to try the boisterous ocean." She read my look, and answered: "Dearest mother, you think I am not willing to die, but I am, indeed, I am; all I fear are my sins. Oh, my Saviour, pity and pardon me."

Then, again, after a long silence on my breast, our tears so well mixed together: "Yet I can not think our Lord would send me so much suffering, if He did not mean it for my penance, and to save me; and I have, indeed, that comfort to remember I always prepared for confession carefully, and was very earnest to obtain the grace of good absolutions. Death, death! oh, mother, it seems so strange I shall be no more *here*. You will come back, my dearest mother (drawing her cheek to mine), you will come back alone. How lonesome you will be: no poor little Bec. But that is only one side. When I look at the other, I forget all that, for you hope my salvation is sure, don't you?"

Eve of St. Theresa.—So many times alluding to the terrors of death: tears rolling, arms clasped round my neck, yet looking on the crucifix with the frequent little smile and expression of hope and confidence, repeating: "My dear, dearest Lord," through every aching of the bones and tearing of her cough. . . . . .

St. Theresa's Day.—What a morning passed with the darling—her perspectives—the large, clear eyes raised up, and often streaming with tears, while she would wrap her arms around me so tenderly in silence. While I was covering her feet, she said: "Mother, the worst is, I will have to give an account of all the masses I have heard so badly. Oh, my carelessness!" and her tears redoubled; "and my first communion—yet surely I tried to make it well; and, finally, dearest mother, if I have so great a blessing as the last sacraments"—she looked earnestly at the crucifix and dried her tears, saying: "One drop of that blood would have done enough, yet He gave all to cover us with His merits." She then spoke of receiving extreme unction, of her last struggles. "There is something dreadful in death, my mother," and she turned again a strong look at the crucifix. After a while she added: "How I will beg our Lord to let me come and comfort you, and be near my William;" but the thousand, thousand endearments of her manner while saying these things can never be expressed. Waking through the night, she would be speaking of what was doing in heaven, where there was no dark night, no racking pains. In the morning, she asked for all her little papers. Some, she would say, "are foolish and simple indeed, but were written in good moments—these burn, and these, because they relate to my confessions (looking on one side, she burst into tears). Oh, I received absolution the day I wrote this;" and with a long look to the sky opposite our window, she added: "That absolution was written in heaven, I trust, my mother, and I shall have all the last sacraments, and be remembered so often at the altar when I am gone; and may I not now often go to communion, my mother, while I stay? I may have so much yet to go through."

17*th October.*—All resigned and cheerful, she told me: "Now if Dr. Chatard was to say, 'Rebecca, you will get well,' I would not wish it. Oh, no, my dear Saviour, I know now the happiness of an early death; and to sin no more, my mother, there is the point" (wrapping her arm around me). "Last night I seemed, in the midst of my misery, to be quite gone from my body, and I was somewhere summoning all the saints and angels to pray for me; but the Blessed Virgin, St. Joseph, my own angel,

St. Augustin, and St. Francis Xavier, whom you know I love so (St. Augustin's burning heart for our Lord, you know, too, mother), these I seemed to claim and insist on their defending me in judgment. Oh, my mother, that judgment!" Then, again, with eyes fixed on the crucifix, she would remain silent as long as pain would permit.

"Oh, mother, mother, how I suffer; do pray for me—so much I may have yet to go through. You see every day something is added of new warning how soon I am to go. Dear, dearest mother, yet I do not remember more than once or twice to have thought my sufferings too hard, or to have felt any bad impatience, so our Lord will pity me and give me a short purgatory, I hope, but His will in that too: at least, I will be safe *there*, and sin no more."

She will hear no more little amusing readings, nor play our little plays—"One only object, my mother—one alone *now*, all the rest is nothing." Yet she is the liveliest little soul in her worst pains. In the play of her heart she says: "I consent, dear Lord, to live till You are born," meaning until Christmas.

Poor little darling! she clasps her dear hands and bows the head over them in the gentlest manner, hiding the death-pale face so often wet with tears, saying: "I do wish so *His will* should be done, my mother." Our God! how dear to me to see His love in my little darling so above human nature, while she says, looking at her crucifix: "Not one moment would He let me suffer, but for my good—our compassionate Saviour."

. . . . . Richard come. She looks at the crucifix, and says: "I am so thankful since our Lord permits it—if my William—but I must resign," and fixing her eyes on the crucifix: "Yet," said she, "tell how I loved and blessed him to the last—oh, his precious soul!" "Ah, mother," she says, with her endearing look, "why so sad and sorrowful? If our dear Lord sends pains, He sends us comforts, too." Her dear, simple heart rests with such confidence in God. "I am covered with His own blood, I must hope." She sits up night and day in her chair, now leaning sometimes on my arm; yet laughs at being sleepy, and says: "I am so tired, and look how bright Annina's carpet is—my dear, dear home" (meaning the sky). All-Saints' Eve she felt herself much worse, and earnestly entreated for the last sacraments. In the afternoon I had read to her (not foreseeing the change, but by the happiest grace of the moment) different prayers and sentiments on receiving the holy viaticum and extreme unction, in a dear little French book of dialogues between our Lord and the soul, so that she was as fully prepared as depended on exterior help, and the interior force of faith gave her an avidity and comfort pictured in every feature and action. The superior being gone, she sat in the attitude of a person expecting some awful event; every motion or word seemed too much, every cough she thought her last; eyes to the crucifix or bent on mother in wistful questions, "Is *He* coming now?" (meaning our Lord). "Say this little prayer—that little prayer." So passed the night. In the morning the superior sent word he could not leave the congregation, and Mr. Hickey came to give the last plenary indulgence. Every one dreaded to tell her, knowing her extreme reserve and reluctance to see a stranger; but how far her heart of faith from that! She received him with the most pure look at God; thanked him, and begged his prayers in her broken voice, and expressed in every way she could how satisfied she was with his coming. . . . . Still, from hour to hour, waiting through the long day, looking at her first communion candle burning under the crucifix before her as at a clock, quite sure that when the little candle was burnt down she would go; and the pious thoughts from the little heart beating so short and quick—the aspirations about her first communion—her thanks for the graces now showered on her, until the candle dropped in the socket. Then a look at the crucifix of deep disappointment and tenderest submission to His will in union with His agony in the garden, expressed in the broken words her cough and choking permitted. Night came, and with it some rising fears of temptations and dread that her patience might fail. In infinite goodness He sent the superior, who, seeing the most pitiable situation of the dear sufferer, kindly offered to stay with her the night. Her joy and gratitude were inexpressible; the presence of a priest seemed a security to her against all the power of the enemy. She begged him even to say his office near her, keeping up the most cheerful smiles, and reminding me that Mr. Bruté used to call our little room "the Tabernacle of the Just." She would often look round at him, so pleased, though seeing only his back, and would express to me by signs and looks at the crucifix her peace and contentment. At midnight, not having slept or eaten for more than twenty-four hours, the superior told her to take something and try and sleep. "Well, I will not come back if I get asleep. Good-bye to you, sir; good-bye, Sister Susan, give my love to everybody; good-bye, dear Kit (kissing her most tenderly); and you, sweetest mother, good-bye." Her little heart filled as she hung her arms around me. The superior said, we will all sleep, too. "Oh, I hope not," said she, alarmed. I assured her mother would watch, and she composed herself, telling me: "I will give your love to all I meet on my journey." But no sleep or rest for her. . . . . .

All-Souls' day come, her hopes redoubled. Our God! our God! Rebecca's hours and agonies known to You alone. The meek, subdued, submissive look; the pure, artless appeals of sorrow and unutterable distress. Sink and faint, poor heart, while recalling them. The hundred little acts of piety that All-Souls' day so sad and awful; the fears of poor mother's bleeding heart for patience and perseverance, the silence. Oh, our God! the looks of that day. How often were the blood and wounds of our Jesus offered as our only appeal, no one daring to ask for her relief, for fear of anticipating Your will, or depriving her of the grace she so ardently desired of making her purgatory with her mother, or interfering in any way with the designs of Your infinite love. Yet the dread of our own weakness! Oh! that day, and night again, and following day. The bare remembrance, how agonizing. . . . . I must not even be out of sight a moment. "My love is so weak, so imperfect," she said, "I have proved it so little, I have been so unfaithful," and her poor heart seemed sinking, but her silent, expressive looks were on the crucifix. . . . The little crucifix round her neck so tenderly pressed and fastened to the dying lips or breast! The expression with which she said the words in the hymn, *Jesus, lover of my soul*, "hangs my helpless soul on Thee!" and again the cheerful union with the hymn: "Come, let us lift our joyful eyes." . . . . At night the superior came again, promising to stay with her to the last. So often she bowed her little agonizing head (in which all her misery seemed centered) to the holy water he signed her with; at last, near four in the morning, Sister Cecilia beside her, mother's arms lifting her, she sunk down between us, but the dear head fell on the well-known heart it loved so well. Think only of your Blessed Saviour now, my darling, I said. "To be sure, certainly," she answered, and said no more, dropping her head for the last time on her mother's breast.

Ever-memorable day for me. Rebecca laid so low beside Annina. Mother could think of nothing but *Te Deum* in the bitterest anguish, and hearing the loud sobs around. The heart is high above.

Eve of the Octave of ——.—Dear suffering Bec. Blessed child of the cross. Her hours seemed days, but our Jesus kept the register of them. Oh, Infinite Love! Eternal Love! Love for her in eternity of old and eternity to come: Jesus between these two eternities suffering for her, suffering for Rebecca. Happy little one whom the world so kindly pitied in its ignorance, seeing not behind the curtain of faith, seeing not the merits Rebecca was treasuring by her union with the passion of her Jesus, seeing not her suffering ardor to kiss with so many tears the Adorable Hand pressing the nails and thorns so sharp to nature, yet so dear as the dispensation of His grace and love. How continual was her look to her dying Saviour! Dearest Rebecca, now your sufferings are over, faith and hope are no more for you, but love enjoys and triumphs for eternity. So pure the sky over the dear graves, Rebecca's already well covered with greenest moss, and even a little violet in full flower on it. A long silence there—but communion to-morrow again, and next day, and next day.

ELIZABETH TO MRS. SCOTT.

Nov. 14*th*, 1816.

My Dear Friend,— . . . . . I know very well how you are pitying me, but if you had seen my little beloved's sufferings as I did, you would have been glad to see so good and innocent a little soul set free. No one could guess what Rebecca was who did not see her in her excessive sufferings. She was, you know, but a good-looking child; but the last months of her life she grew so lovely, soul and body, it would have delighted you to see her, even in death. But death, death, my Julia—what is death? and that long, long eternity? My little room has a window looking directly on the woods where my darlings sleep. It keeps up my heart to look there over twenty times a day—first thing in the morning, last at night, and think: No more pain now; up, up, the beautiful, joyous souls.

Remember me to those I so truly love around you, and always love your poor

E. A. Seton.

REV. MR. BRUTE TO WILLIAM.[1]

Baltimore, *November*, 1816.

My Dear William,—Though we can scarcely hold our correspondence very closely, yet this is too particular an occasion. I could not keep silent to one I love more tenderly than he can imagine, since, after our reserve of first

[1] The original is in English.

traveling acquaintance being over, those letters from Marseilles, from Leghorn these, reached well my inmost heart. It is for Rebecca I write, whom you so dearly loved, and, I dare say, I loved also as an aged brother—so charmed with that young, so innocent, so amiable little sister. My William, were you by me in this dark room of my lonely presidence, tears alone with yours would be the whole talk and expression at such a moment. But surely you say that I would but feel it is the brother of the womb, and a most fond brother, who beside me would shed his bitter tears, and you, that the tears of the poor priest are bound to flow only before his God, and with a full thought of his duty to Him and to the hearts He tries, and charges him to comfort and lift up to heaven. My William! how easy, indeed, this time to carry up these sorrows to heaven and follow such an angel with a kind of sad yet delightful exultation. I hope you will feel a powerful impression from such unspeakable comfort as has softened here, for all, the departure of our beloved child.

My William, be attentive to the voice of Grace on the occasion. Dwell in prayer on the best thoughts of the moment. You, a sensible and lofty soul, love to soar above in your good time of prayer. Prayer, ah, prayer! our speaking with God, our infinitely beloved! Prayer, my William; do give up your heart in time to it, and that often. Your heart is the best heart, made for the only true enjoyment of this life, religion. Oh, my William! Yet, as in that night likely to be our last on the high seas together, let me entreat you for religion, but heartfelt, practical religion. See that excellent Mr. Philip Filicchi, whom I never knew, yet have wept for with you and mother; see, as of Rebecca's, the triumph of that death.

Reflect on it, cherish for yourself the prospect; such be your end. Pray for your poor friend,

S. BRUTE.

The Right Reverend Bishop Cheverus went to Emmitsburg early in December, and cheered Elizabeth by his sympathy and the holy tone of his condolement for her recent loss. Before bidding farewell—it was the last time they ever saw one another on earth—he presented her with a little English prayer-book, as a souvenir of his visit to the Sisterhood. On the fly-leaf of it, he wrote:—

"Dear Sister, remember in your prayers your affectionate servant in the Lord. ✠ JOHN, Bp. of Boston."

ELIZABETH TO MRS. DUPLEX.[1]

MY EVER DEAR DUPLEX,—I hope the blessed Bishop Cheverus will take this letter to you himself, as there seems a spell on all I write to you by post. I wrote that our little beloved was gone. You can understand, and you only, her triumph and delight in the last sacraments, and dearest hopes even after death through the divine sacrifice of the altar. I could give you no possible idea of the peace, sweetness, fortitude, and piety of that beautiful soul which shone so well and so purely on her face. High, high up your heart, dearest friend; no sad and unavailing regrets. See her now, where she is, and that will silence all. Rebecca was so well convinced of the happi-

[1] She was singularly attached to Rebecca.

ness of an early death as an escape from the thousand temptations, as well as from the sorrows of life; so grateful to die surrounded by every help for her soul, and in the arms of her doating mother, that I can scarcely wish sweet Kit a better lot if the fondest desire of my heart could be granted. Dear Bec used to tell her: "You may depend, Kitty, I will pray you up." Sister Susan said: "You think yourself a great favorite, Miss Bec, to be heard so easily!" "No, I don't," she answered, solemnly, "but with all the sacraments, and covered with the blood of my Saviour, I do hope every thing." . . . . .

1817–18–19–20–21.—Letters.—William returns from Italy.—Sisters sent to New York.—Letters.—William a Midshipman.—Letters of the Mother and the Son.—Mr. Brute to a Nephew of Elizabeth.—Letters of the Mother and the Son.—The Mother's Death.

ELIZABETH TO MRS. SADLER.

January, 1817.

My cheek began to burn the moment I saw the well-known, long-loved writing of your hand; and, after reading, my quiet heart commenced to flutter at the thought that your first impression at my long silence was so far from the true cause; but I still it by an appealing look to the crucifix, so long the book of my dying Bec. So far from religion being a source of coldness or neglect towards you, it is that very point in my little compass of life that brings my thoughts and liveliest imaginations closest to you. . . . . . Yet that most delicate and sacred subject I have long since learned to leave to God, except where my duty is explicit.[1]

Since dearest Bec is gone, I am free from so many painful cares, and able to fulfill so many more duties in the service of our little world in St. Joseph's, that every thing seems to show a new color, and life has a charm for me which I often wondered could be found in it.

TO WILLIAM.

St. Valentine's (*14th Feb.*), 1817.

MY SOUL'S OWN WILLIAM,—The bitter, freezing wind is now always rattling, and they write me on every side —New York and Baltimore — that the ice will let no vessel go to you; yet my head and heart are so full of you that, though letters for you are waiting at both ports, I must write. If I wake in the night, I think it is your angel wakes me to pray for you; and last night I found myself actually dropping asleep repeating your name over and over, and appealing to our Lord, with the agony of a mother's love, for our long, and dear, and everlasting reunion.

TO THE SAME.

✠

April 4th, 1817.

MY OWN WILLIAM,—If any thing in this world could endear you more to the heart and soul of your mother, it

[1] She alludes to her faith, which she never *obtruded* upon friends or strangers.

would be your letters by the *Scioto*. Far, indeed, be it from me to hold so dear and generous a son by any tie of duty to me in a situation which does not meet the bent of his wishes; yet your own mother is obliged to entreat you to have still a little patience, that we may judge for the best with more safety. I wrote Mr. Filicchi earnestly some months ago on the subject of your future prospects in commerce, and twice since, most pressingly, on the situation of Richard, and now a letter accompanies this with a statement of your sentiments in your own words, which do you the greatest honor, my son, and fill your mother's heart through all our painful trials with inexpressible consolation; for by them I see well that integrity and filial love overrule all your youthful and natural feelings, and I can but be most grateful to our God and to you that they have so long held you under circumstances most painful to you. I have now gained my main object in parting with you, my beloved son, which was not so much to establish you with affluent friends, or set you on a tide of fortune, as to give you time to know yourself a little, to know the world a little, and to overcome your first ardent propensity for the navy, which I know is even now the passion of your heart; yet it would be unjust to our tender affection if I withheld my whole mind from you who have so well unfolded yours to me, and should conceal from you my fears, not for your dear person, my darling son, but for the dear immortal object which your Annina and your Bec would now solicit you for even more earnestly than your poor mother and Kitty. My soul's William, I need not tell you to rise above the clouds that surround us. You know well enough that we must pass our course of trials with the rest of human beings; those who have least of them are not the most enviable. For my part, I would think all the pains I ever endured fully rewarded by the sweet and unspeakable pleasure I received in reading your sentiments of love and duty contained in your last letters; and as to those of independence and honor, I see only what every honest man ought to feel, and glory in them instead of differing with you, quite sure that in your case I should feel *exactly* as you do. I would be too happy to inclose your letters to Mr. Filicchi, but fear you might not approve it, though every word speaks but gratitude and purest sentiments of virtue. If you could take confidence and open your mind to him freely, point out your consciousness of not "earning your bread" as you say, and even consult him on the change you would desire. All I can say is, that you will never want every nerve of my heart exerting itself for you, in whatever path you may enter. What more can your own mother add? If a mother's love could be a fortune to you, *you would be rich indeed;* alas, it is poor coin in this world; but be assured it will bear its interest in heaven, where it solicits, I may truly say day and night, for every blessing on you.

Dearest William, the more I think of it, the happier I am, you have spoken your dear heart out. Mr. Filicchi himself must surely be pleased, for how could you have passed almost two years in a way so unfruitful without his being sensible of it? I send this by way of New York. Oh, my William, if it was but I who could be so near you as this letter will, that I might tell you not to be fearful of making me unhappy, and hear from your own mouth what possible step I could take to make you happier. I can only repeat to you the desire of my heart. Here our second Good Friday of separation. Oh, the heart of a mother in that hour! Bless, bless you a thousand times.

TO THE SAME.

April, 1817.

How I shall long, long to hear from you again, but many a day must pass before. Richard is very busy, he says, this spring time, but his remaining or not at Mr. Tiernan's yet undecided. You two boys are the whole world to me. Sweet Kit, like a little dove in the ark,[1] but you two out on the wide ocean. What a difference.

My dearest one, I make you an extract of the page I wrote Mr. Filicchi, that you may know what I have said to him, and I hope and trust it will not give you more pain; you will know how to act in consequence.

"By the *Scioto* my William writes me, and opens his heart in a manner that would please you from a son, as it did me. After repeating, as in all his letters, the most generous treatment he has received from yourself and families[2] in strongest expressions of gratitude, he says that since he is in Leghorn he is conscious of not having saved you the least expense in the counting-house, his own words are: 'If I were only of sufficient use to spare one clerk, I might say that I earned my bread, though still under every obligation for kindness beyond what I could have hoped,'" etc. Bless you a thousand times. Love your own mother as she does you. Remember me always to our friends.

[1] At St. Joseph's. [2] His own and his brother Philip's.

WILLIAM TO HIS MOTHER.

LEGHORN, *May* 18*th*, 1817.

MY DEAREST MOTHER,—I avail myself with pleasure of an unexpected occasion for Baltimore again to address you. I believe it is more than a month since I last wrote by the *Heroine*, *via* Boston, no opportunity having since offered. About two weeks ago I received, by a vessel from New York to Genoa, your letter of January, inclosing lines from our dear Mr. Bruté and beloved Kitty. It is the only one since the loss of our little angel, though you mention having written repeatedly; indeed, I have received none from yourself mentioning the last moments of our dear one, and yet I hardly regret the circumstance. The thought is always painful. The touching letter of Mr. Dubois more than sufficed (though no incentive was necessary) to call forth all the tender feelings of a brother, and at the same time to inspire the most pleasing certainty of her future happiness. I find that many of my letters, also, have miscarried; so you see the misfortune is reciprocal, and we must be patient, though on such occasions it requires no small exertion to be so. However, I know your dear heart is ever the same, and of your love I am always sure, with or without letters, and you know me too well to think that I could neglect you for a moment. . . . .

Our good Mrs. Philip Filicchi resides entirely at Pisa. I saw her a fortnight or three weeks ago, and she was exceedingly well, better than I had ever seen her. Her health has since been confirmed to me by letters. Mr. Anthony and family now occupy the beautiful house in which Mr. Philip resided, and have very much improved it. All are quite well, and love you as much as ever. . . .

TO HIS BROTHER RICHARD.

LEGHORN, *May* 18*th*, 1817.

. . . . . I have laid open my mind to mamma with regard to my situation here. I am confident, my dearest mother and you will feel with me the inconvenience of being a burden to those who have in so high a degree extended their generosity to us. In no other light can I view my remaining in Leghorn. I sincerely hope that the explanation I have given may not in the least disturb her. Certainly, years of misery would be preferable to giving her a moment's pain; but she must be sensible that if a change is necessary at so critical a time of life, no time should be lost in effecting it. Perhaps I may long lament the two years already lost, but it is not too late to do something yet.

In the month of May Catharine Seton was at a friend's house in Baltimore. She had formed some of the younger girls at St. Joseph's into a decury, after the manner of her sister Annina, and used to watch over them with all the care of a little mother. The two following letters are from one of her children, and in their sweet simplicity may recall to some the memory of early years at the valley school of Emmitsburg.

TO MISS CATHARINE JOSEPHINE SETON.

St. Joseph's Valley, *May 28th*, 1817.

My own Dearest, dear Mother,—How long the time seems since you have left us! All your children are writing to you, and as we have to write on half sheets of paper, mine shall be full. My own precious mother, I hope you will return in better health than you left us (in). All your children say your sacred-heart beads for you every day. Oh! my dear mother, you do not know how much I love you. I feel so dull since you have been gone! Mother says she will not look at our letters, so we can write what we please. Dearest mother, when you write, tell me whose letter you open first, and mind, call me 'daughter' in your letter, for I love you to call me daughter; and do please write me as long a letter as you do Eliza and Jane, or I shall be jealous, for though you told me at the mountain never to admit so mean a passion, I do not know if I have not felt a slight stroke of it already. Dear mother, I hope you are very happy in Baltimore, where you see your dear brother and all those girls you love so much. Do not make yourself unhappy about our dearest mother,[1] as she is in good health, and contented, because she thinks you are happy. Write soon to us all, as we are impatient for a letter from our dear mother. I hope the ride did you some good, as it was such a pleasant time of the year for traveling. I take great care of your lily, and water it every evening. It grows very fast. How much I wish for the 29th of June, as mother says she

[1] Elizabeth.

expects you home on that day—such a happy day it will be! How I wish for it! I was at the mountain on Monday; I thought of your being then in St. Peter's church, and so far from me; but then if you were happy it was no matter. I could write a book full to you, and never grow tired. I forget you are gone, and look every day down the refectory for you, as I used to do when you were here, but then I see another girl occupying your place. We all go in to see mother every day, and to say something of you, as we all love to talk of you to dear mother. Give my love to Hammy, and C. and A. Nelson. We are in the music-room writing, Hammy's children at one side of the table, and yours at the other. Tell Hammy, Josephine would write to her, but is sick in the infirmary, and can not. I know my dearest mother will excuse my bad writing, as Sister Margaret wants the table to make bills out on. I believe this is locust year, for the mountain is covered with them. The locust-trees are all in blossom, and smell delightfully. I am afraid you will be tired reading this, as it is so long and foolish. I love you, as I always did, with all my heart, and I hope you love me a little more than a halfpenny. One of the girls said she would take my place in being your child, and made me very angry, but I won't tell her name, it would be detraction; but you don't love her very much. I hope you will soon be well enough to write to us. Precious mother, I love you ten thousand times better, if it were possible, than when you were here. Indeed, I can not tell you how much, but I can feel it. I liked to have been punished for going in the infirmary without leave, when I went up-stairs, but ignorance of the rule excused me. My own dearest mother, I must conclude; indeed, I am very sorry for it. Your affectionate, loving, and I wish I could say loved daughter,

BIDDY.

TO THE SAME.[1]

ST. JOSEPH'S VALLEY, *June 6th.*

MY OWN MOTHER,—I am now writing to you on your little desk, where you wrote last on in mother's room, and Jane and Maria are doing the same on the other side of the room. Eliza is gone to the mountain, or she would be very glad to write to her dearest mother, I know. Our garden comes on very pretty, only the weeds are so impudent that they will intrude, and Jane and we have got enough to do to pull them up and root them out. I hope, my dear mother Kitty never gets in the vapors when she thinks of being so far away from her own mother, as she is very well, and vapors are bad things to be sure. There is a great number of little bugs come on our rose-bush, particularly on the buds which are almost blown; but I hope they will have the manners to wait till you come back for us to have the pleasure of seeing you pull them. I thought Maria would compose a second Jierimias' Lamentation. I made a mistake in spelling Jeremias, but no matter, for I know you will excuse my bad writing and spelling, because my love is not placed in either, but in my dear little mother. I believe we are going to sing this afternoon, as it is Sunday, behind the Calvary in St. Joseph's garden. My dearest mother, indeed I wish I had

[1] The school and Sisterhood were at this period in a very flourishing condition. Elizabeth, writing to a friend a few months earlier (December, 1816), says they have at St. Joseph's, "sixty and more boarders, besides the country children, and treble the Sisters we had when you were here."

nothing to do all day long but write to you, for I could fill up a book in writing to you. I feel so lonesome since you have gone away, that I hardly know what to do with myself, if Jane did not cheer me up by telling me there are but three weeks and one day left for your return. We count every day you are away; it seems to us like an age. As I know my sweetest little mother will like to hear who received the medals, I must tell her. C. Clary (?) was to receive that of merit, and E. Pilch that of queen, but Josephine McDonnell happening to say that Sister Jane asked the Sisters to vote for Pilch, no medals were given. A great pity, to be sure. Don't forget your promise of writing to your children, we are so impatient to hear from you. Last Monday we proposed to make an excursion to the top of the mountain and take a survey of the country; accordingly we set out, and finding many blackberries on the way, we stopped to pick some. On a sudden, some of the girls began to scream out (you know they are apt enough to do that) that there was a snake around J. Fennell's leg. Sister Jane immediately jumped over the fence and ran to her. She found poor Fennell almost frightened to death, and upon examination found that she was only stung by wasps or bees, who, thinking themselves insulted by her approaching too near their nest, resolved to revenge themselves, and engaged the briers to help them by holding her fast. We left Fennell at Mrs. Brawner's, and proceeded on our travels. At length we arrived at the foot of the mountain, and soon began to climb up the rocks, but we met a snake on the way, to the no small terror of us all, particularly M. Stiegers, who, you know, is *very nervous*. However, we went on a good deal longer, till we thought we might chance to lose our supper, which we were not willing to do; we, therefore, sat down awhile on the rocks, and gathered a few berries, and then began to return home by another way. We had to run all the way down, and at last met with a road which we took, but as it happened a wrong one. After following it for some time, we found ourselves stopped by a swamp. We turned, crossed the fence, and got into a field. From one field we went into another; in some the grass was very deep; some of us were making the sign of the cross every step we took. At length, after wandering about a good deal, we met with the right road, and had to go half a mile back for Fennell, then arrived safe home and went straight to supper. We went to a field a great ways past 'Uncle'[1] Esau's last Saturday, for Skid got holiday for us to gather strawberries. We got a few, and when we came home supper was over, so we had a second table. Indeed, my dear mother, though I do not get into trouble so often as I used to, yet I have a share of it. One of the girls said that you did not love me, and that a great deal of love was lost on my side. It put me in the glooms, though she only said it to make me cry, but I would not before her, to give her that satisfaction; and another said she would ask you to let her be your child in my place, but I will not mind any of them, but always love you sincerely, whether you do me or not. Oh, my dear mother, if you only knew how much I love you. I could kiss the desk I write on a hundred times over and over. I had the happiness of going to communion on Corpus Christi, and then I begged our dear Lord, when I had Him in my breast, to let me die on the same day with my dear

[1] An ancient African.

mother Kitty, so I might be good enough, and both of us prepared to go to heaven. My dearest mother, I must conclude, as the bell is ringing.

Your affectionate and loving

BIDDY.

Write soon.

In the year 1817 the third colony of Sisters of Charity went out from St. Joseph's. The place to which they were sent was the largest field for Christian usefulness in the United States, the city of New York. A gentleman writes to Mrs. Seton from thence: "The good Sisters got here on the 28th (June) fatigued by the journey, particularly Sister Cecilia, who was much indisposed;" and on the 24th of August following, Elizabeth says, in a letter to her Protestant friend, Mrs. Sadler: "Will you tell our dearest Duplex for me, that the Sister Cecilia, who has been these eight years what she herself would have wished to have been in our sick-room and death-bed scenes, is with Sister Rose? I hope she will see them as soon as she can. Perhaps you, too, dearest Eliza, would call with her a moment, as they themselves can not call on you. You may suppose what both are to my heart after so many years, and cares, and pains, and comforts together."

William Seton returned to the United States after receiving his mother's answer to the letters in which he pointed out his dislike to the sort of life he was living, and a kind friend at Washington at once obtained for him a midshipman's warrant in the navy.[1] In the spring of 1818 he was ordered to report for duty on board the *Independence*, 74, then lying in Boston Harbor. Elizabeth's letters to him reveal her inmost heart and the beauty of a mother's love for a son exposed more to spiritual harm than to the dangers of a hard profession. Her tenderness recalls, in some degree, the extraordinary affection of Monica for Augustine, and like this blessed woman, model of Christian mothers, she put her hope in prayer. Writing to a friend of her son's departure, she says with sentiments of the most religious trust in Heaven: "This world of separations must have its course, and we must take its good and evil quietly as it passes. For my part, I am now so accustomed to look only to our God in all that happens, that it seems to me the most painful things in the order of His Providence can but increase our confidence and peace in Him, since all will draw us nearer to Himself, if only we kiss His hand as that of the best of Fathers."

[1] Some friend procured him a lieutenancy in the army even before he went to Italy, but through the most honorable sentiments of respect to his mother's wishes, who thought a military life might lead him astray from the practice of the duties of his religion, he gave up his own natural aspirations to set himself deliberately into a hateful position at Leghorn. In February, 1818, he was again offered a second lieutenancy (in the First U. S. Infantry), with orders, if the appointment should be accepted, to report to Gen. Ripley, at Pittsburg. In a letter to his mother about it, he writes: "I would not give up my warrant for a captaincy in the army; I would have no objection to the order, however," with allusion to the active duties a soldier might expect out West.

ELIZABETH TO WILLIAM.

Monday, February 16th, 1818.

My Soul's Darling,—You go, so adieu again. With how much more courage I say it now than in 1815! You must fill a station and take a part in our life of trial, and all your mother can beg is that you may keep well with your good Pilot; as Burns says: The correspondence fixed with Heaven will be your noble anchor. To go when you can to the sacraments, as a child to his father, will be a main point for that. You and I are too soft-hearted about our friendships and condescension to circumstances of the moment. Mind well the consequences, my beloved; in your situation they will go very far—but we have talked that over. Mind your health; be prudent in exposing it when you can not say duty is in question.

25th.

Now, my love, I must hope that you are safe in your berth. Your little ship left behind has had cloudy weather, and dragged scarce three knots an hour. Good Madam Reason argues and insists, shows so plainly our order of duty, that we must separate; yet, with all that she can say, I miss you to such a degree that it seems my own self remains but as a poor shadow, and its dearest part is gone. My best comfort is to be continually begging our God to bless you, and to be guessing and supposing where you may be. Your first letter is so longed for. You know there is no news here; those who were sick are better; every one speaking of you, the strain a mother loves.

Another most kind letter from Mr. Harper. Little White came to see me the other day, and told me that there was a little boy at the Mountain who said, now William Seton was gone he could never have any more pleasure, for he loved him better than any one in the world. I shall have him to see me, you may depend, as soon as the roads can be passed (they are deep, indeed). Write me if you see the good Bishop of Boston.

Unite your dearest heart well with mine every morning at least. This I earnestly beg: you don't know how much it will help in some of the peculiarities of your situation. Oh, my William, you know all I would say. Dearest child of my soul, mind we *must* be one day where we will part no more.

WILLIAM TO ELIZABETH.

INDEPENDENCE, *Friday, Feb. 27th*, 1818.

MY DEAR MAMMA,—I arrived here three days ago, after traveling night and day. The day before yesterday I reported myself to the commodore, and obtained permission to remain on shore for that evening. The next morning I reported to the fighting Captain Downs, and obtained permission to remain a day longer. To-day I have reported to our First Lieutenant Rose for duty. My introduction was rather unpleasant, for I was ushered into a court-martial sitting on a brother midshipman for disobedience of orders. At New York I heard of Uncle Wilkes's death. Charles is a midshipman in our ship. The commodore received me very kindly, also Mr. Sullivan, and Bishop Cheverus with the heart of a brother, or rather of a father. He desired me to tell you that Mrs. Wally had quite recovered of the fever, and also her daughter, who had been attacked by the same disorder. He asked me to remember him affectionately to you. Commodore Bainbridge said that he had known Grandpapa Seton and papa intimately. He is a fine man. I am so anxious to know what I have to do, that my head is quite confused. The post goes every day, so that I shall never want opportunities to write. For the present I conclude, as we are only allowed three candles and a half per week. We are twenty-two midshipmen on board, many of 1818. Remember me affectionately to Mr. Dubois, Mr. Bruté, Mr. Hickey, and all whom you know I love. Don't forget the boys, Charles, etc.

TO THE SAME.

BOSTON HARBOR, *March 4th*, 1818.

MY DEAREST MOTHER,—Again I attempt to write you from this noisy house. Indeed it is a very difficult thing to find a fit moment, surrounded by twenty-four midshipmen, each endeavoring to say, sing, and do what he can in order to beguile the tedious hours, for we are to all intents and purposes imprisoned about three hundred yards from the shore, which I have not visited since my arrival. Next Sunday, however, I hope to revisit our dear Bishop Cheverus, whose truly affectionate and tender kindness I shall ever gratefully feel. I forgot to tell you in my last that in passing through New York I could not see Sister Rose, she being out when I called; Sister Cecilia, however, and some of their little family,[1] I saw. . . . . . If I

[1] The orphans at the asylum in Prince Street.

could judge by myself, no earthly pleasure should take me from you: but our cases are widely different. At times my feelings so far overcome me that I can not restrain the outward expression of them; happily for me, our apartment is so dark that we can not see without candles at midday. Our duty is very easy. The drums beat up hammocks at half-past seven o'clock, and to quarters at nine. During the day we have our different watches: sometimes two, sometimes four hours. At night the same; but as there are many of us, we only keep a regular watch every third night; but we may be turned out at any hour, night or morning, to go ashore, and then must not leave the boats on any account. Last night was my second night watch; I kept from twelve to two.

ELIZABETH TO WILLIAM.

March, 1818.

My Own Dear Love,—I have just received your third letter, and finding mine has not yet reached you, it strikes me to inclose this to Bishop Cheverus, as I write him on a little business.

I never was so overpowered as by this sad parting. Reasoning is in vain. I look up a hundred times at the dear crucifix and resign; but too often with such agony of heart, that nothing stops it but the fear that it will break before you return, or that my death will make you unhappy. But this will not strengthen you whom I wish to strengthen. I should say: My son, go on as you have begun; our love will not settle you in life, will not give you an independence. Your mother ought to say many things, but can say nothing. Look up to the pure heavens in your night watch, my soul's beloved, and you will hear what that soul would say to you, what our dear ones gone would say, too. That watch is more in my mind at night than sleep, could you know the blessings invoked on you. But it is too great an indulgence to say so much of my poor heart, dearest one.

Aunt Post writes a loving letter about you. Such earnest requests, too, for dear Kit; but the robbing of the mail and treatment of the passengers last week makes me dread her going. Yet she will go, if Mrs. Scott goes, as was proposed. I wrote you, I fear, by the very mail which was lost, inclosing a very pleasing letter from our Richard, and telling you of Mr. Filicchi's good disposition towards him. Barry writes me he expects letters from Leghorn every day, so we will hear further. Mr. Harper[1] also writes the kindest letter, inclosing one from your commodore, with every fair promise for you, my beloved, speaking of his friendship, too, for your father. Oh, the goodness of our God in every thing!

[1] In one of her late letters Elizabeth mentions to a friend the uniform courtesy towards her of this illustrious Catholic, Mr. Robert G. Harper, and his delicate kindness to her only surviving daughter. When Mrs. Seton first arrived in Baltimore, in 1808, Mr. Harper called upon her and offered his services in any manner they might be useful. He then introduced his family, and when St. Joseph's was founded, proved by words and actions his interest in the institution, and sent his daughters there to be educated. It was very probably through him that the distinguished convert, Judge Gaston, of North Carolina, became acquainted with the establishment, and placed his daughters in it. Elizabeth speaks in a letter of the judge's zeal in making the house known in the South, and the high opinion he entertained of it, which she, however, modestly thinks to be above its merits.

Easter-Tuesday Morning.

The boys at the Mountain in retreat till to-morrow, their first communion. I have had your heart in mine so close in the many I have made these dear festivals. A letter from Sister Rose mentioned you were in church with Duplex the Sunday after you left me, so I had the sweet comfort to know that you enjoyed a moment longer in New York than you expected.

Heavy rains these past nights gave the strongest thoughts of the impossibility of your constitution resisting these night-watches, soaked through, perhaps. I repeat, however, "God is my hope," and to Him I incessantly commit you. Let the world go round, if only my William is happy, and remembers me in all his dangers, since he can not think of me but the first wish of my soul be remembered too. Every good heart here would say something to you. Your name never mentioned but with love. Sister Anastasia says, "Tell William I never forget the little prayer for him." Sister Martha says: "I am sure I remember him at my prayers as if he was my own brother." So we make a wall around you, my darling. Bless, bless you a thousand times.

WILLIAM TO HIS MOTHER.

Boston Harbor, *March 25th*, 1818.

Dearest Mother,—Just ashore on liberty. I received last Wednesday your first letter of the 10th of March, inclosing one from our Dick. I can not tell you with what pleasure I perused both; joy to know he was safe arrived and pleased with his situation, and delight in the love of my *dearest one.* Yet your gentle reproach was not unfelt; could you for a moment doubt my affection because I did not write as I promised from every city? You know my heart too well to think me indifferent. Could I ever be happy without your love? No, my beloved mother, this world would be a desert without you. Let me know something more of our darling Kit when you write again, and do let that be soon. Every day, when the purser brings on board the letters, I almost devour them with my eyes to see if there may be one for me; but alas, so often disappointed—one of your letters must have been lost when the mail was robbed. We have rigged our ship, but there is no prospect of getting to sea just now, except in one of the frigates. I have written to Washington to obtain a berth in any that goes. I have seen Uncle John's widow; she is very kind, and invited me to come there whenever I am ashore. Our good bishop and Charles Wilkes desire to be affectionately remembered to you. Remember me to Mr. Dubois and all at the Mountain; also to those around you, for you know I sincerely love all that love my mother.

ELIZABETH TO WILLIAM.

Friday, April 5th, 1818.

MY DEAR BELOVED,—Now do tell me what a mother can say to so bad a child. You love me, but not one word will you ever say about my idol—*yourself.* Oh, my, I never can put it into you, so it is in vain to plague you about it. I may go on quietly gazing at the clouds, where I can learn as much about your daily pains and pleasures, wants and comforts, as by your letters, which yet are so extravagantly dear to me that I carry them on my heart, read and read, weep and weep plentifully over them, be assured. I often ask—but what is this dear rover to me so much more than all the world? Why do the heart-strings all wind round him so? That I can not tell; let it pass, for it depends not on me. You seem, indeed, my William, to be more present to me than my own soul, and yours and its dear futurities are truly its very passion. Only think, our dear little Mary Harper received the last sacraments in January. Louisa writes me she was then like an angel, and no doubt she is one now. Her poor father, Mrs. McTavish writes me from Baltimore, is weighed down with sorrow, which I deeply share with him; but how much deeper with the parents of those two precious souls[1] belonging to the *Adams*, going, indeed, uncalled to their God. I tell you, my son, if *you* do so, you will also strike me dead. The very possibility that it may happen is an insupportable thought. The thousand dangers you are in seem all small compared with that one. I charge you to beg our God daily to keep you from it. Put yourself a moment in my place, who must look so far beyond the present scene, since the present scene can be but painful separation—that separation so unavoidable for this world, even if it should be ever again sweetened by a momentary meeting. My dear one, pity my anxiety, I can no more hinder it than I can stop my desires for our eternal reunion.

[1] Midshipmen killed outright in a duel.

Saturday, 6th.

I do not know if you hear of your Andreuze; from a word I heard dropped, he is not very well contented; but, as you say, he loves traveling. If I were a man, all the world should not stop me, I would go straight in Xavier's[1] footsteps, the waters of the abyss and the expanded sky should be well explored. But I must wait for liberty—must wait, as dear Bec used to say, until I get higher than seas or skies.

Soon as I know you are gone I shall put up my map of Boston, and care no more to look at its harbor now so dear, and always before my little table where I write. Remember my favorite Xavier's prayer when you are in the raging tempest: "Compassionate Lover of souls, save me," and never omit your *Ave Maris Stella*:—

> Star of the vast and howling main,
> When dark and lone is all the sky,
> And mountain waves o'er ocean's plain
> Erect their stormy heads on high,
> When mothers for their darlings sigh,
> They raise their weeping eyes to thee:
> The Star of Ocean heeds their cry
> And saves the found'ring bark at sea.

In the month of June a nephew of Elizabeth came from New York to see her, and met with an accident in getting out of the carriage at the Sisterhood, by which he sprained an ankle. Word was at once sent to the Mountain, and Mr. Bruté (who had been there since February) went himself to St. Joseph's and brought the sufferer to

[1] She had a very particular devotion to this great servant of God, whom she calls in one of her early letters, after becoming a Catholic, her *favorite saint.*

the college, where he received every kind attention that could be offered, and when he left, Mr. Bruté even accompanied him part of the way on his journey. The following paper explains itself. No other relative of Mrs. Seton found such a signal and truly providential opportunity of knowing the right faith. He rejected it, "Like the deaf asp that stoppeth her ears, which will not hear the voice of the charmers; nor of the wizard that charmeth wisely."—(Ps. lvii. 5–6.)[1]

THE REV. MR. BRUTE TO L—— P——.[2]

My Dear Sir,—It is too painful for a true heart to remain entirely shut up, hiding even his best thoughts from you. I love you sincerely, since I respect so much your good aunt here; and have received so much of the most affecting kindness, believe me, when I passed through your city, with little indeed to recommend me to it.

Now, then, you know that we are so attached to our happy Catholic faith, that it would rather appear strange to you if I said nothing at all to our good visitor. Yet to say any thing whilst under our roof, except some circumstance or desire of yours had called for it, would have seemed to trouble the charms of your kind trust of yourself to the poor priests; but this I will put in your hands in our way to Gettysburg, that you may know how truly we feel interested for you in that first line of all—that of your spiritual happiness.

[1] The young man died a year or two after—I believe very suddenly.
[2] Original in English.

My dear sir, that our Lord wished grace, truth, and blessing for us in religion is my own delightful impression so from my infancy, as I hope you from your own dear M. P——.[1] I try every means to enjoy religion above all, and we have really such particular comfort in our way, that my continual thought of affection and of gratitude, when kindness is shown to me, is: "Could I only make them sensible of the same!" I have sometimes heard then a Protestant friend tell me: "Yes, truly, you must be happy to believe so." See that we have not to doubt, and remain uncertain about such precious graces as I see so very much doubted of by some societies among our brethren, whilst, to be sure, others still think much of them : for example, baptism itself, or a Last Supper, strikes me. That we, like you, still do reverence our bishops as the true successors of the first ones appointed by our Lord, but we do, indeed, with faith itself; when, unhappily, private judgment, left alone, misleads the Presbyterians, for example, to deny that most excellent and beautiful order of things, and misleads the good Quakers still further from the genuine notions of that divine institution of an authorized church and ministry, without which Christianity itself —the gift of God to our earth—would have long ago been dissipated. This strikes me. Your line of bishops and their particular doctrine, since the unhappy separation of the sixteenth century, and our old line with other doctrines so particular and so important, stand together in my eyes; but how can I adhere to both together? The old one traced up so strictly to the former times, and acknowledging with great fidelity and simplicity that it has re-

[1] His mother. When Mr. Bruté and William were going to Europe, in 1815 she was very kind to them.

ceived promises of infallibility and unalterable preservation of the true sacraments and institutions of our Lord, whilst the English line was obliged in the very separation to renounce that only secure principle, and remain on a level of respective and equal fallibility with all the other branches of Protestantism, even the remotest from the better grounds you still maintain. This does strike me so much. Alas! my dearest sir, how painful it must be to so sincere a friend of Christ, so humble a disciple of His, to be provoked by the last ranks of Unitarianism when they disgrace His divine character, to have Him but a man and common prophet; how painful, I say, that they can say: "Why! is your private judgment any way more certain of the sense of Scripture and its literal meaning about the Divinity of Christ than, for example, about His real presence in the sacrament? You are exactly as fallible as we are, and if you think the Unitarians in an error not to believe Christ their Lord, so exactly can they think you are to believe He is. You acknowledge no divine mission of a church, no infallible promises for a certain teaching, you can then teach nothing more certain than we." So will say an Unitarian, and then he goes on turning into figures the literal expressions of the Divinity of Christ, etc., and calling other Protestants idolaters to worship the Man Jesus, as you formerly called the Catholics so for the Blessed Sacrament.

Alas, alas, dearest sir, that it might be granted to your church to come back to its only secure ground, unity with our Catholic one, from which, would to our Lord, Henry VIII. had never separated it! and all mutual wrongs of private persons, which, whether kings or popes, ministers or priests, ought never (to) have injured the church itself, faith itself, sacraments themselves, would be entirely forgotten, and still the unity so evidently made by our Lord the true ground be kept on. How soon would all the other wild sects which the Protestant principles have authorized, and will ever authorize, disappear, for our very French infidels have forcibly and logically demonstrated that to ruin Christianity they had really but the Catholics to contend with, all the others being self-destroyed for any consistent mind. This much to write is, may be, too much; yet you have it only to reflect on privately and at prayer—prayer, my dear sir, all to obtain the true light. And you may have in the same time our most friendly assurance that if you favor (us) again with your kind visit, not a word, no, no more than this time, not a word will intrude here on your peace except yourself may be pleased with it, for to possess you has been our delight, as well as to visit so good, so respectable an aunt, so amiable a cousin will again be yours; you promised it to us. No, dearest sir, not the least pain will be offered you. Our secret prayer only will ever be sent for your happiness, and every thing done to show you the true affection you so well personally deserve.

Yours so sincerely, S. BRUTE.

ELIZABETH TO MR. BRUTE.

Your letter[1] to sister admirable, if first the big stone of darkest ignorance and indifference were removed on the

[1] "A letter to try to convert Mrs. Post, her sister, to the Catholic faith—how useless she thought it. Most curious."—(Note by Mr. Bruté himself in one corner of the letter.)

point of prime necessity, *that there is any true Church or false Church, right faith or wrong faith.* But neither you nor any one who has not been in that ignorance and indifference can imagine the size and depth of it; and putting myself again a moment in the place of my sister (even with my great advantage of having been passionately attached to religion when a Protestant, which she is not), I imagine I read your letter, and looking up with vacant surprise, would say: "What does the man mean? Says he that all who believe in our Lord are not safe? or, if a poor Turk or savage does not believe, is he to be blamed for it? They make God a merciful being, indeed, if He would condemn souls of His own creation for their parents bringing them into the world on one side of it or the other." My brother Post once asked me so simply: "Sister Seton, they say you go to the Catholic Church, what is the difference?" It is the first church, my brother, the old church the apostles began, answered poor trembling Elizabeth Seton, always dreading to be pushed on a subject she could only feel, but never express to these cool reasoners. "*Church of the Apostles!*" said my brother, "why is not every church from the apostles?" Sister Post interrupted: "Well, apostles or no apostles, let me be any thing in the world but a Roman Catholic—a Methodist, Quaker, any thing—a Quaker, indeed, I should like extremely, they are so nice and orderly, and their dress so becoming; but Catholics—dirty, filthy, ragged, the church a horrid place of spits and pushing, etc., etc.," and whispering to me as a mystery: "They say, my sister, there is a great picture there of our Saviour, *all naked.*" It is a fact that a most pious, better-informed woman than my sister or poor Elizabeth Seton, found me kneeling before my crucifixion, and shrunk back with horror seeing a naked picture.[1] That very lady, Mrs. Livingston, quitted the Protestant Church for the Methodist meeting, and I said to those who laughed at her, "Why not? if she likes the Methodists;" forever accustomed to look only to little exterior attractions, as the dress and quiet of the Quakers, an enthusiastic preaching among the Methodists, or a music of low voices among Anabaptists, or any other such nonsense. The thought of a right faith or wrong faith, true church or false one, never enters the mind of one among a hundred. Oh, my God! my heart trembles and faints before Him in His little sacristy close to His Tabernacle while I ask *how am I here?* *I* taken, *they* left! . . . . .

ELIZABETH TO WILLIAM.

1st July, 1818.

. . . . . . Mr. Dubois always begs so many remembrances to you. A most interesting scene took place here last week. The Sulpitians of Baltimore (except Mr. Bruté) solicited of Mr. Dubois the suppression of the seminary, thinking he was getting rather in debt, and that the masters he employed would be more useful in Baltimore, and lo! our good Emmitsburghers came forward, offered Mr. Dubois eight or ten thousand dollars in hand, and to buy the seminary for him, if he chose, only not to leave them. The archbishop, seeing how hard it would go, has directed all to be left as it was before. So much for the good "country peeps," as Mr. Duhamel[2] calls them.

[1] This was before she became a Catholic.

[2] The Rev. Charles Duhamel was a French missionary, and having only an imperfect pronunciation of English, used to say country *peeps* for country *people*.

21st.

MY OWN BELOVED,—How I do long to hear from you. Sometimes I think perhaps good Mr. Brent succeeded and sent you an exchange as you wished, and you may even be gone in your *Guerrière* or some other warrior; at others I feel the whole weight of the thought that you are still between decks in harbor this hot weather. We have no news of the good Harpers,[1] which I am sorry for, because we have many reasons to be interested in them as our truly best friends. Mr. Fox is here, and says some gentleman arrived in the *Washington* told him that he saw Richard, and he is very well. Sister Rose is here, too, taking Charles to Baltimore College. He will be happy there, I hope. Dearest, dear William, I could fill all my paper with that so unavailing repetition. Good and dear son and child of my heart, be comforted. You never gave a pain to that heart but the pain of parting and separation.

WILLIAM TO HIS MOTHER.

U. S. S. "MACEDONIAN," BOSTON HARBOR,
July 21st, 1818.

MY BELOVED MOTHER,—Your letter of the 10th instant came the day after Mr. Barry's, and I am happy to tell you that I received my orders to the *Macedonian* frigate almost at the same moment your dear letter was handed me. My desire has been so great to get to sea that you can't wonder at my being rather elated at the prospect of so fine a voyage. . . . . . The ship will go round Cape

[1] They were in Europe.

Horn into the Pacific as high up as Columbia River, and higher if the captain chooses, but so far she is ordered. We will cruise in the Pacific two years, visiting all the important cities on the western coast of North and South America, together with the islands visited by Captain Porter, where we will see savage life in its true state. It will be, in fact, one of the most interesting voyages ever made from this country. . . . . . I long to hear that you have perfectly recovered from your late illness; if not, do, dearest mother, let me know it, and I will use every endeavor to come to you. It would be a great satisfaction to me, indeed, to pass a little time with you before so long a voyage. The ship will not sail before the last of September or the beginning of October, in order to meet the season for doubling the Cape; some say she will not sail till November. Charles Wilkes and several of my friends from the *Independence* have just been ordered to the *Guerrière*, which is expected to sail to-morrow, and several others to this ship. I am quite comfortable here, living in the wardroom of the *Java* until our ship is ready to receive us. If Andreuze returns, remember me affectionately to him, and also to all my friends, particularly to Mr. Dubois, Mr. Bruté, Michael Egan,[1] etc.

ELIZABETH TO WILLIAM.

1st August, 1818.

My Soul's Darling,—Here your so long desired letter dated from your *Macedonian* is just arrived. You must

[1] Later a holy priest. He was nephew to the first bishop of Philadelphia.

not think of coming, my beloved, even if your voyage is delayed to October or November. One only thing I can not stand in this world, that is taking leave of you. The little while, too, you could stay; the fear of its being noticed that you were absent[1] the very moment you might be wanting. We must be firm. This world, it is certain, is not the place you and I are to enjoy our love in. Don't be uneasy about my health; at my time of life nothing can be more uncertain. The sickness I had (inflammation of the lungs) leaves a long weakness; but there is nothing alarming, my love, I assure you, as to immediate consequence. I may live to welcome your joyful, happy return from many a cruise. Andreuze is not yet here, but coming. Doyle is at the Mount, but I have not seen him; only good little Michael[2] comes for mass-serving, and loves you so that his eyes glistened with tears when I showed him your remembrance of him.

In my "shady retreat" (the little willow grows so handsomely) how I sigh for you: above, where, happily, sighs go not in vain. We will see: all our hope is there. I seldom say a word to you of how everybody remembers and regrets you, and some unite their hearts with mine to love you as true sisters. We have letters, also, with affectionate inquiries about you from all that love us. Mr. Dubois never wearies speaking of you. His health is restored. My own William, remember how I love you.

[1] Even by permission.

[2] Egan.

WILLIAM TO HIS MOTHER.

BOSTON, *August 29th*, 1818.

MY DEAREST MOTHER,— . . . . . I should have written sooner, but we have had a very busy time of it fitting out ship. Now we have hauled her out into the stream and are almost ready for sea, wanting only our powder (of which we take one hundred and sixty barrels) and some small articles which we take on board in the course of next week, when we shall drop down near the light and wait for sailing orders, which the officers think we shall receive in two or three weeks. The *Macedonian* is a most beautiful frigate, pierced for fifty (carrying forty-eight) guns; more completely and handsomely fitted out than any ship that ever sailed from this or perhaps any other country. She has thirty midshipmen and eight lieutenants, all clever fellows; our captain,[1] a fine man, the same who was first-lieutenant of Captain Porter in the cruise of the *Essex*. Oh, my beloved mother, if God spares me to see you after my cruise, what a happy moment I anticipate! But, alas! it is so far off, and to think that I leave you unwell will cause me to quit port with a heavy heart; but He who directs all will bring this voyage to a happy end, and me to your dear arms. Tell Kitty to write me a long letter before I go, it will be such a time before I shall hear from you after we sail. Bishop Cheverus, I suppose, has written you; at least he said he would the last time I saw him. Doctor Matignon is dying.

[1] John Downs, one of the heroes of our gallant navy.

ELIZABETH TO WILLIAM.

✠

8th Sept., 1818.

MY SOUL'S WILLIAM,—After waiting so long and sending so often in vain for your dear August letter, here it is on the doating heart of your own mother, and by the uncertainty you were in what time you might sail I hasten this, thinking our good angel will not let it be lost. Oh, my William, now indeed is my true courage called for to see things as they are. Three years, three years—yet I protest to you that I could give you up to *duty* with a free heart, if the way was but clear for our dear *futurity;* but oh, who but our God can know my anguish at the thought of resigning you *there* also, and the thousand, thousand fears that *we meet no more*, because you well know that our meeting again has decided conditions which, in your situation, it is next to impossible to fulfill. We are ready enough to be led away when there is every help and support to keep us right, but when tyranny of custom, example, and every outward circumstance helps our own passions within, what becomes of the beloved soul? I have now, fixed at the foot of my bed, the crucifix which used to be at the Mountain—the one you said you would willingly carry to me even from that distance, if only I might see it. You understand well the thousand thoughts it brings. My soul's William! how strange to be *man*, and *God* but a secondary consideration, or no thought at all; to be a few years beating through this world after shadows, then enter an eternity of existence quite unprepared, though to prepare for it is the only end of our being here below. You know, beloved, I seldom say much of these things; but it would be concealing the sharp arrow in your own mother's soul from yours, into which I would wish to pour every thought of my heart. Long letters from Richard—all very cheerful. Kit is the very picture of health and cheerfulness. Do not be uneasy for her, my dear one. Mrs. Scott's affectionate letters to her would be a comfort to you in your anxiety about the poor darling. . . . . . At the end of the letter my heart would break out again; but it must not, will not give one pain to yours it can ever avoid. I know I should strengthen yours; but, my beloved, how little you can know what it cost me to part with *you*. Every thing else in this world has its place in my affections in measure, but my love for you has no bound or measure, and can never be satisfied but in our eternity. Oh! hear, then, the cry of a mother's soul, my beloved, and take care of what is dearer to her a thousand, thousand times than herself.

WILLIAM TO HIS MOTHER.

U. S. Ship "Macedonian," Boston,
Sept. 18*th*, 1818.

My Dearest Mother,—I received yesterday your dear letter just as the ship was preparing to get under way; all hands called to send up top-gallant yards, and unmoor ship, a stiff breeze blowing. Before night I must bid adieu to the United States. I think the most proper place to direct your letters will be to Valparaiso, in the province of Chili.

My beloved mother, could you see my heart you would find nothing but your dear self and those beloved beings who center in you. My heart is full, but I must endeavor not to let disheartening thoughts intrude at such a moment. I must be on deck at my station directly, so I can say no more. May God bless you, and grant we may meet again. I will write by every opportunity. The pilot takes this. Adieu. Your own

WILLIAM.

TO THE SAME.

VALPARAISO, *March 13th*, 1819.

MY DEAREST MOTHER,—I wrote you on our arrival here by an English brig bound to Rio Janiero, since which no opportunity has occurred. This goes by a Nantucket whaleman. God speed his passage, bring him safe home to his wife and little children, and this letter to my beloved mother. How much I envy the captain his prospect of a speedy return home! I do assure you that night and day my thoughts are constantly with you and my dear Kit. Sometimes in my night-watch I imagine the *Macedonian* safely arrived in the United States, and welcomed into Boston by the thundering guns of the old *Independence*. No delay, from Boston I post it to New York, shake hands with our friends there, then on to Philadelphia. Here I debate a moment whether to go by steamboat to Baltimore or take the stage through Lancaster to Gettysburg. The latter route is ever dear to me in my remembrance, having traveled it in such sweet company. At Gettysburg I take a private conveyance and arrive with a beating heart in Emmitsburg—then to St. Joseph's. The scene there may be *felt*, not described. Afterwards comes the meeting my dear companions at the Mountain: my friends Mr. Dubois, Mr. Bruté, Andreuze, Egan, etc., all are remembered and loved. Thus I pass many a tedious watch, or rather watches which would be otherwise tedious without these pleasing thoughts, glide away almost imperceptibly, and I rejoice to find myself four hours nearer to my happiness. Oh! my dearest mother, may God yet grant us the blessing to meet again and find you well. Don't be tired of life before I can see you once more; recollect the cruise will be half over by the time you receive this. I have been on shore very little since our arrival, and we are now about to sail again in a few days. It is said that we only wait the return of Judge Prevost, of New York, an American commissioner in these parts. He arrived here in the British frigate *Andromache* a few days ago, and went to the city of Santiago, about ninety miles from this place. We have passed our time here in scrubbing up the old ship and painting her. We exulted to find that the *Andromache* could not compare with us, either for neatness of rigging, decks, guns, etc., or beauty of model; so that we bear the bell in this harbor, as I fancy we can anywhere else. We have also given two splendid balls, which were attended by all the fair of Valparaiso, and our consul and Lady Cochrane have given several to our officers on shore. Upon the whole, we have passed our time rather agreeably in Valparaiso. We now sail for Callao, the seaport of Lima. The midshipmen of the *Andromache* tell us that there the fogs are very heavy morning and evening, and the middle of the day almost insupportably hot, so that I'm inclined to wish myself there and off again. From there I believe we shall go to the Galapagos islands, directly under the equator, uninhabited except by wild fowl, both of the land and sea species in immense numbers, together with seal, sea-lions, and other amphibious animals, also great numbers of land and sea turtle; the land tortoise weighing, many of them, from three to four hundred pounds, and will carry a man on their backs without any apparent exertion. One of them we had in our ship, given to us by the captain of a whaler who arrived shortly after we did. The tortoise was small of its kind, but I have frequently seen our little midshipman riding him about the gun-deck without the creature altering its pace in the least. They are all black, with feet resembling an elephant's, and rather a hideous appearance, but afford such delicious eating that green turtle are not looked at when these are to be met with. At these islands we shall remain some time to strip ship and have a complete overhaul of rigging, spars, etc., and to repair and refit every thing. They say that our going to Columbia River is now unnecessary, as Judge Prevost has already received possession of the settlement from the English for the United States. I forgot to tell you that we are going to California, but upon what business I can not exactly say. I hope to give you some day a full account of all our wanderings. I look forward to the end of this cruise with hope and anxiety; hoping to find all well, yet anxious, very anxious for the health of my dearest mother and sister. May God preserve you and grant us a happy meeting. As for myself, I have not known a moment's illness since I left you—thanks to Him who has protected me. I need not tell you to pray for me constantly. I often say a Hail Mary for you. When you write to Baltimore remember me to all our friends there, to Mr. Harper, Mr. Barry, the Chatards, and the rest who have been so kind to me. Don't forget to present my respects to Sisters Sarah, Ellen, and Rosaline; I can not now think of any one with indifference whom I have ever seen with you, those particularly whom I know you love. Remember me also to my friends at the Mountain if you have an opportunity—to Mr. Hickey, Doyle, G. Elder, E. Elder, Heyden, etc. I shall endeavor to write to Richard if I can by this occasion. I will begin a letter at any rate, if I have to finish it another time it will be the longer. Remember me most tenderly to him.

TO THE SAME.

U. S. S. "MACEDONIAN," VALPARAISO BAY,
April 12th, 1819.

MY DEAREST MOTHER,—I write you in haste by a ship bound to Rio Janeiro. We have made a short trip to Coquimbo in order to pass away time, and were very hospitably entertained by our consul and the inhabitants. The city lies about three degrees to the northward of Valparaiso, and is pleasantly situated on a plain at the foot of the Andes, about a mile and a half from the sea-shore. The port, or place of anchorage, which consists of a battery of three or four pieces of cannon and five or six huts, is nine miles from the city, and completely land-locked for small vessels, and affords excellent shelter. It is a pleasant ride from the port to the city, and the manner of riding still more pleasant, as the horses are always galloped. We entered into the custom with spirit, you may depend, and put them to their speed the whole way to the city, where we had been invited by our consul to a ball, which was attended by the governor and other distinguished persons of the place. The city is much handsomer than Valparaiso, and contains many churches and convents, and one or two fine squares. In point of cultivation it forms an agreeable contrast to the barren hills of this place. We remained there but three days, when we bent our course again for Valparaiso, where we are still. It is said we wait here to know the event of Lord Cochrane's attack on Callao, our captain, from motives of delicacy, not wishing to be present at the time it is made. I have had an opportunity of witnessing some of the extraordinary customs of the country in holy week. The day before yesterday being Maunday Thursday, all the Catholic ships in harbor wore their colors half-mast, and their yards a cock-bill or in a zigzag, careless position, expressive of mourning, and in the evening a stuffed effigy of Judas, with a sword by his side, was hung at the jib-boom ends. On Good Friday they amused themselves by keel-hauling, beating, shooting, ducking, and concluded at night by burning him. To-day, about ten o'clock, they squared yards, mast-headed their flags, and all fired salutes. To-morrow will be Easter. Oh, my beloved mother, what scenes does this happy day bring to mind! But, alas, they are past. Heaven grant they may return; we can only hope it. Do, my beloved mother, use every means to preserve your health and my dearest Kitty's. I know you will, it is only yourself I fear you may neglect; you know how much my happiness depends upon it. God bless you, and our dear Kit and Richard—a thousand loves. Remember me affectionately to all.

ELIZABETH TO WILLIAM.

29th September, 1819.

MY OWN WILLIAM,—I have written you every way I could devise,—New York, Baltimore, Boston, etc. The most welcome of all letters from Valparaiso we received the middle of July, and we hardly dare hope for another yet. The one for Richard was forwarded immediately. Our last from him, in June, said much of you, his longing to hear from you, etc. Your own Kitty is quite well—returned from her summer excursion at the manor.[1] How we think of you, delight to speak of you, listen to every wind as if it might reach you; our thousand fears and hopes, all so inexpressible, and counting the days and weeks as they pass in view of that dearest one which will bring you again to us. Oh, my dearest William, will it, can it be that once more you will come to your little valley? Every time the clock strikes, I so earnestly bless and call down blessings on you. This is but one word to go to the good, kind William Hickey, in Washington, to tell you we are well. He also wrote you the welcome word, and sent you papers, which, I trust, reached you. Oh, my love, dear love, *love me*,—you know how and by what proof. When you are passing Cape Horn again you may be sure my poor, wild mother's heart is always around, to shelter and cover with a mother's prayers—my only, only comfort, night and day, beloved. What could ever force me to live separated from you, but the One Adorable Will? I would

[1] The country seat of the Carrolls. Mr. Harper had married a daughter of the illustrious patriot Charles Carroll, of Carrollton.

go the world over in any disguise,—hidden even from yourself,—to be only in the same vessel and share the same dangers with my William. Oh, my soul's dearest, deny me not the only meeting where we will *never part.* You know, well, it depends on yourself. The agony of my heart, as I carry your beloved name before the Tabernacle, and repeat it in torrents of tears, which our God alone understands, is not for our present separation; it is our long eternal years which press on it beyond all expression. To lose you here a few years of so embittered a life, is but the common lot; but to love as I love you, and lose you *forever*—oh, unutterable anguish. A whole eternity miserable, a whole eternity the enemy of God—and such a God as He is to us.

TO THE SAME.

20th March, 1820.

MY OWN LOVED WILLIAM,—It can not be, I trust, that so many letters as your poor, faithful mother has written you should all be lost. Just now we have your dear one of January, which says you have not had a line from home since you left us, and that you had no prospects of return until next January. The two words, so painful, stupefied me, for my hopes had been different. Life is death, indeed, in this hard separation. What they call fortitude, I think I know something of in every case; but this one shakes my very soul; and you well know why, my beloved: not for our momentary separation, hard as it is, but—. How I hold you wrapt in my inmost heart it is impossible to describe, or give you the least idea of. Every sound of spring was a delight to me until your last letter; but as it will not bring you, all seasons are alike, and winter, if you come, will be the welcome one. You say "Tell all that's going;" but from one month to the other, I can say we deviate scarcely half a degree in any thing.

TO THE SAME.[1]

ST. JOSEPH'S, *May 27th*, 1820.

MY OWN LOVE,—Could I get a least idea if you have received any of our letters, I would know where to begin the little journal. My last was since the arrival of your young lieutenant.[2] . . . . . All here goes quite nicely. Mr. Dubois, like a prince on his mountain: full school, debts paid, improvements in all directions. Egan still there. They are cutting the mountain in terraces, to bring the garden up to Mr. Duhamel's house. Our Saint Joseph goes on so well; no building, though, this year. The long winter over, and a cheerful spring around us,—sweet roses, green fields; Kit just come from a pleasant walk to the river, and the dear old tree by the falls, where you have cut our names.

Your last received was dated January. No hope, then, of an earlier meeting than next winter. How sure we were, dear Kit and I, it would have been this spring; she would consent to go nowhere until your letter told us your delay. Oh, our talk and surmises, hopes and fears about you last winter, and the love and blessings poured on you from our doating hearts! Yet I often please myself with

[1] The last letter he received.

[2] Percival.

the thought that whatever hardships you go through, you do not suffer as I do the sharpness of the pains of separation. You find so many things to take your attention. It is too late, my beloved, not to doat on you with a tenderness proportioned to your dangers and my fear of losing you forever, for you know that the long, long day to come is all I care for. How often am I up on your deck with you! How often by your hammock! Every fresh breeze, every calm, the sighing of the wind through the trees over our dear graves, the creaking of the willow at the back porch—sounds so like the noise of masts in a gale—all speak of you. Oh, my love, my love, how my heart and soul hang continually around you. May I but once more hold you in these poor arms! Oh, may God bless you. My soul's darling, look up to the blue heavens and love Him. He is so good to us. Your own forever,

E. A. SETON.

REV. MR. SIBOURD TO ELIZABETH.[1]

PHILADELPHIA, 3*d February*, 1819.

You must not be astonished at my keeping so long the journal you sent me on the sufferings of your late dear Rebecca, which I perused most attentively, with uncommon emotion, shedding a flood of tears of joy, on reflecting on the courage and Christian resolution of that little angel, whom the depraved world we live in was not worthy to possess. If momentary sufferings give a right to an immense amount of glory, what are we to think of her who suffered so long, and with such resignation?

[1] Original is in English.

Indeed, I am ashamed of myself, when I consider I am at such a distance from her in my sufferings, that are but light, and of a very short continuance, when compared tc hers.

I was full three months without going through any operation, and overjoyed at the prospect of returning soon to my usual occupations, at New Orleans; but the day before yesterday my joy was checked, when Dr. Physick apprised me that he saw a new shooting of the polypus, and that I must submit to a new operation of it, and that a radical cure requires time and patience. God's will be done. What grieves me most is receiving letters from New Orleans, informing me that the American Catholics feel very much distressed at my long absence. I can tell you that I never complained of my sufferings, and that I never prayed to God for their discontinuance, knowing very well that my grievous sins deserve a thousand times more than what I suffer; so that my prayer is: O God, act with me as Thou seest most conducive to Thy glory and my salvation.

You need not, my dearest child, recommend your children to my prayers, which are due and paid, both to you and to them, either living or dead. Make yourself easy on the score of him who went round Cape Horn. Ask for the covering of grace, and he will be warm enough. I give my blessing and prayers to all who are dear to you, and be sure you have an affectionate father in

Ls. SIBOURD.

BISHOP CHEVERUS TO ELIZABETH.[1]

December 19*th*, 1820.

MA BIEN CHÈRE ET VÉNÉRABLE SŒUR,—Though it be better to be absent from the body and to be with Christ, still I can not help rejoicing that you remain in the flesh, and that your dear soul has not left its prison.

My dear Ursulines have prayed with me for yourself and your blessed family, and we are very grateful for your kind remembrance of us.

If you are well enough, write me a few lines. My paternal regard to the dear Josephine. Have you any news from William and Richard?

To all your dear Sisters I beg to be most respectfully and affectionately remembered.

You are every day with me before the Lord, and you know how much I love you, in the bowels of Jesus Christ.

Your brother and devoted servant,

✠ JOHN, BISHOP OF BOSTON.

MR. HARPER TO THE REV. MR. DUBOIS, AT MT. ST. MARY'S.

BALTIMORE, *Sept.* 30*th*, 1820.

MY DEAR SIR,—Our accounts respecting Mrs. Seton are of a nature to give us great alarm on her subject. We know and feel how severe a loss she would be to all with whom she is in any manner connected, among whom, none, perhaps, except her daughter, will feel it

[1] Original in English except first line.

more than we. It may be a consolation to be assured, on our part, that our feelings and views toward her daughter have undergone no change, except that the interest which we take in her is greatly strengthened since we have been more intimately acquainted with her. While we live she shall never want a protector and friend; and we shall be richly repaid for any thing that we can do for her, by the pleasure and benefit her society and example will confer on our children. Be so good, my dear sir, as to communicate this to her excellent mother, with the assurance of our most ardent wishes for her welfare and happiness.

With the greatest respect, I am, dear sir, your most obedient servant,

ROBT. G. HARPER.[1]

Elizabeth had been ailing since the month of September, 1820, and in November, her malady, an abscess on the lungs, increased violently. She had made a religious retreat in July, and was prepared patiently and Christianly to bear the sufferings that accompanied the passage from this life to that ETERNITY which for years had been her meditation and the object of her intense desires. She was constantly attended during the fatal illness by

[1] I have given this letter out of a spirit of gratitude to so benevolent and distinguished a gentleman, who received my aunt into his hospitable house as one of his own daughters after her mother's death. Mrs. Scott also offered her a home at the time, but Josephine (Catharine) preferred, agreeably to her dying parent's injunctions, the society and protection of a Catholic family.

Robert Goodloe Harper was born near Fredericksburg, Va., in 1765. He served under General Greene "during the latter part of the Southern Revolutionary campaign," studied law at Princeton, was elected to the "National House of Representatives" in 1794, and in 1815 was United States Senator from Maryland. Died—*Integer vitæ scelerisque purus*—Jan. 15th, 1825.

her only remaining daughter; but her sons she never saw in this world again. The Sisters of whom she was the venerated Mother assisted her with all the cares of charity and the most devoted affection, and the Rev. Superior of the Community was unremitting in the discharge of those sacred duties which ease and even sweeten to a Catholic soul the otherwise tremendous hour of death.

On the 2d of January, 1821, Elizabeth Seton received the sacrament of extreme unction, but before anointing her Mr. Dubois exhorted the circumstant religious in her name, as she was too enfeebled to speak herself, that ever they should preserve "the strictest union and charity among themselves" and "great fidelity to their rules." She then "raised her dying voice and said: 'Dear ones, pray for me when I am gone, for I shall want it. I thank God for having made me a child of His *church:* when you come to this hour *you will know* what it is to be a child of the church.' A good while after, she said: 'When I have done wrong, I sincerely repented of it.' She also before requested the Reverend Superior to ask pardon in her name for the bad example she might have given in some little indulgences her great weakness required during her sickness."[1]

She lingered two days more, and died in the peace of

[1] This account is taken from a paper, now lying before me, which was drawn up by one of the Sisters present at the last moments of her spiritual mother. It has been in Mr. Bruté's possession, but in a note on the margin he says, "I know not who sent it to me."

Him *whom no one can have for his Father that has not the Catholic Church for his mother.*[1]

Her spiritual Daughters, who hold her memory in perpetual benediction, and emulate the example she has left them, have caused to be inscribed in her chamber of death the following:—

Here, near this door, by this fire-place, on a poor, lowly couch, died our cherished and saintly Mother Seton, on the 4th of January, 1821. *She died in poverty, but rich in faith and good works. May we, her children, walk in her footsteps, and share one day in her happiness. Amen.*

They likewise have erected over her remains, in the wooded and moss-grown grave-yard of St. Joseph's, a Gothic tomb, which bears on a tablet set into the exterior wall these votive words:—

SACRED TO THE MEMORY

OF

E. A. SETON,

FOVNDRESS.

[1] *Habere jam non potest Deum patrem, qui Ecclesiam non habet matrem.*—D. Cypriani, De Unitate Ecclesiæ.

APPENDIX.

THE "MACEDONIAN" IS HOMEWARD BOUND.—WILLIAM RETURNS.

"Pass we the long, unvarying course, the track
Oft trod, that never leaves a trace behind;
Pass we the calm, the gale, the change, the tack,
And each well-known caprice of wave and wind;
Pass we the joys and sorrows sailors find,
Cooped in their winged, sea-girt citadel;
The foul, the fair, the contrary, the kind,
As breezes rise and fall and billows swell,
Till, on some jocund morn, lo, land—and ALL IS WELL."[1]

WILLIAM TO ELIZABETH.

"MACEDONIAN," OFF BOSTON LIGHT,
June 19th, 1821.

MY BELOVED MOTHER,—At last my fondest wishes appear on the point of being realized, and happiness, like a star from behind the clouds of a dark and stormy night, seems breaking on my view. But, alas, the horizon is not yet clear—and my poor, trembling star, how easily overclouded! You may imagine how anxiously I wait your first lines. The last I received from you was dated in May, 1820, one year and more back; and what great changes one year may produce, I fear to think on.

[1] Lines copied by Mr. Bruté for William, and illustrated by a very pretty pen-and-ink sketch.

Do write quick, and let me know how you are—let me know all. Kiss Kitty for me, and remember me to our friends at the Mountain. I shall keep my long stories until we meet: in fact, I feel too wild to say more.

Ever your

WILLIAM SETON.

He soon obtained permission to leave his ship and hasten down to Maryland, not having yet heard from any one a word of his mother's death; but at the village of Emmitsburg, on his way to the Sisterhood, he met Mr. Bruté, who handed him, with tears that told all, his unopened letter of the 19th. In this good priest he found the only one on earth who could console.

MR. BRUTE TO WILLIAM.

(*En tête* a pen-and-ink sketch: three graves, a cross emitting rays, around it the words, "*Yet a little while.*")

CHER WILLIAM,—I knew but yesterday, and from whom? Good Sister Rose. And at the very Sisterhood your happy last Sunday.[1] Judge the effect in my heart —and especially on that spot where I am so seldom that I might say better than two or three months that I spoke to her in that choir. I came away myself so happy. Opposite the lane I was ready to go a moment to the little wood, and talk of it with mother. Yet did not. Came home; would speak of it to you[2]—and then would not,—better not. At last, just now, reading for to-morrow

[1] Holy communion.

[2] He was staying at the college.

this pleasing Gospel she relished so much: "Yet a little while, and you shall see me,"[1]—I can not help, and your heart must receive kindly this one more,—may be now for long,—one last poor effusion of my contented one. Oh, do persevere. Your God and your eternity before all and above all. Your friend of the high seas.

Turn and keep it. S. BRUTE.

The following, which breathes all Mr. Bruté's most tender and elevated spirit, is what William was requested to keep. The first page is ornamented at top, bottom, at the sides, and between some of the lines, by appropriate pen-and-ink sketches.

William arrived
From the seas and shores so far,
William now comes
To Emmitsburg:
The Mountain,
The Valley,
Oh, the Valley.

The road that passes
Along the little wood,
The field, the fence,
The trees
That cover the graves—
Five graves—
But oh, the *one* grave!

One grave—
My mother—
Her William I—
Three years ago
I saw her last;
I see, I see her now!
My mother,
Do I not see you?

[1] John xvi.

Under these trees,
In that little inclosure:
My *mother;*
My sister Anna,
My little Rebecca,
Cecilia, Henrietta,
The good angels
All together there
Before I went away,
But now:
My dear mother.

No, my mother,
And all are in heaven.
I look above;
What a sight!
Shall I not go
And meet them
Faithfully,
Steadfastly,
Their good path
Of love
And service?

My God,
Now must I love Thee—
My heart has but Thee.
Friends too little when I
Have lost my mother:
But as if with her heart,
I love Thee my God,
Will serve Thee—I will.

Be good
Said my Anna, dying—
My Rebecca too:
But how does my mother
Repeat from her grave,
Ah, did repeat in her heart
For me, each of her last
Communions
To my Saviour:
Be my William good!

I the ten thousand miles from her,
I never more will see on earth!
How did her heart cry for me:
Be good.

I will, my God
I will join them all
In Heaven.

MR. BRUTE TO JOSEPHINE.[1]

MY DEAR JOSEPHINE,—The prayer I send is for you: "May the most just, the most high, and the most amiable will of God be in all things fulfilled, praised, and exalted above all, forever." It was one of her most familiar ones, and well-nigh the very last that she repeated while still in our midst.

The picture[2] for William, who can easily keep it as a mark in his prayer-book: Our Lord hanging on the cross; our good Mother at the foot; our common Father praying with such respect and resignation: his whole heart, ay, and ours too, expressed in his attitude,—the spirit of grace: his hope and ours. Pray for us.

S. BRUTE.

[1] Original in French.

[2] Pius VII., in exile, kneeling at prayer before a crucifix and a little image of our Lady of Sorrow that rests against it—a dove, the "Spirit that abideth forever" in the church, sends down upon the venerable pontiff the rays of grace to strengthen, console, enlighten. This, and the prayer printed on a slip of paper, used to be kept by Elizabeth in one of her books of devotion.

TO THE SAME, FROM MR. BRUTE.[1]

(A little sketch at top of five graves, last with a cross at the head. Above them, "Heaven, heaven! Yet still pray for us!")

Oh, these graves! Mother—such a mother! Such faith, such love, such spirit of true prayer, of true humility, of true self-denial in all, of true charity to all, truest charity! Such a mother! O Josephine, Emily![2] such Sisters. Annina, Rebecca—such sisters yonder. Mary at the Sacred Heart of Poitiers, and younger Elizabeth here. I love them still, in your own heart; but mark well, that our love of one another, all, all in this world, is all vanity, except it be for God, of God, in God!! You love yourselves, both so good—Emily and Josephine, just only to help one another the better to love and serve God, as you pass through this world. Pass, pass, pass, as little shadows,—so rapidly! for, pray, what will be twenty, forty years more to live *here below*, for those who hear, and delight to hear, that repeated cry of the altar: *Per omnia sæcula sæculorum?* Then so heartily say, *Amen!* What for two such resolute Christian souls as yours to say at Vespers (I recommend it always so much) the admirable Canticle of Mary? Eighteen ages in her immense glory! Oh, for that, then, for eternity! for God and our eternity. All in all!!!!

[1] Original in English. [2] Miss Harper.

[1]My dear Josephine,—I beg of you to accept this New Testament and the *Imitation*, as if coming from your good mother herself: you will thus be able to change, at times, from reading English to reading French. The beautiful heavens: they, in truth, are the whole object and the end of this life of a few days or a few years on earth! And, indeed, to live for heaven is, at the same time, to lead the happiest life upon earth. Is it not so, O mother? Answer from your *little wood.* Pray, now and then, for me.

S. Brute.

[2]*Sunday of the Holy Name of Jesus* (1821).

My Josephine,—Giving advice is such a poor thing for him who addresses a heart just bleeding from her living union to love, and wisdom, and experience itself, in their most sacred and persuasive forms. Still, to your faith is my right so high; to your kindness and good sense, my intention such a sufficient excuse; besides, I try to speak but from the grave, where all your treasure was laid. If I only repeat what yourself are the most sensible of, then it can not displease you; it can but strengthen and support the best intentions of your own (heart). Now, this my morning thought, very early at this table,—that after the first painful time of a parting, which is no real separation, or only exterior, and for so short a time, compared to the eternity coming on; after

[1] Original is in French.

[2] Original, as all the following, in English.

the indisposition which threatened, and, thanks to God, has not been so long and severe as it might have proved, you begin this week, to employ your time the most usefully that you will see good; let it be your consolation and offering to mother. After the long nursing and that sorrow which suspends all powers, occupation is a strange thing—without interest at first. Make it a pure offering of duty to mother, I said: "Oh, brighten up," she herself says. Only think that your good friends, and the young ones (particularly) will be but much pleased and edified at your courage. And suffer me to carry that same advice further on; I mean even when you find yourself amidst the attentions of any other friends, yield not entirely; seek to be resolutely employed and diligent, your many ways. Nothing looks so endearing and estimable; for, while friends think it their duty to be over-kind, and thus please themselves in goodness, they are, nevertheless, but the more sensible of the duty it leaves the other side, in a modest, laborious, and diligent soul. Do I say well? Do I say what said mother? I scarcely know,—so inexperienced at the things out of my wholly spiritual line, that all this may have but your smile and a merciful "My father says his best, but all of strange and odd turns enough." Well, well, I then put an end, my dear Josephine, and rely on your visitor, *within* your own heart, reviving continually, that best of inheritances so richly laid there by mother: pure, purest intentions in all; prudence, humility, self-denial, every best and truest suggestion of that solid piety and incomparable good sense of hers. She tried to leave all to her Josephine. God, our God! Pray for your poor friend,

S. Brute.

✠

ETERNITY.

One day more, my dear Josephine,—and so near that 4th. Can I pass the whole day without trying my poor little union to your sorrow? If a priest, and all for spirituals, is not this a most sacred care to be assumed among the heavenly ones, if God gave me grace for it? or if I knew better how to transmit, indeed, to your heart, the tender grace of that great Father of orphans, good Friend of sufferers, true Father, only Friend! Oh, my Josephine, though I write thus with tears, and not the first of the day—the first, happily, at the altar, and others since receiving back books so well used by mother; though I say, dear child, no heart but feels now your exceeding pain, yet God, your God, alone will remain within your own heart, the true Father and faithful Friend. This, our present world: so imperfect and unavailing its most precious things of sympathy and love. My own old mother, in France, whom, dear child, I will also see no more, no more than yours, who was also mine for kindness; my tender mother warned me thus; and to draw me nearer to God, always told me that He alone remains the unabated, faithful Friend. When all the hurry of life and business soon carries every one his usual ways—alas, may be often these days you see it—when it permits not, no, not the best of hearts and most willing to condole and comfort, to keep indeed much company, offer much real, soothing care to the wounded soul; God alone, our good God, my dear child, truly, God alone—at your prayer, your reading, or some musing with Him and thinking of mother; or, also, taking already, some little work in hand—keeps, within, His tender and faithful company with you,—speaks, within, of His divine rights and holy will, but with so much of love and grace for the poor child,—speaks, oh, surely, of your sacred trust to Him, above all,—of His providence to the least of His creatures, then how much more to His own divine image in ourselves; happy you to have honored it so well by the side of your sacred sufferer—so well in her and yourself. That side, my Josephine, let us turn wholly that side. Do, and settle gently, reasonably, what prudence and friends may show best; but feel the whole confidence and solace of it, to rest the side of God only. If you love Him and submit to Him, blessings will ever be abundantly fulfilled. Yes, if you *love* and submit—two words that will be continually coming to you from that holy grave, or rather, from beyond—love and embrace in all that most *high*, most *amiable* Will, as said your mother to the last; that Will so long, and to the last, her all. My dear child, if you do, morning and night, and often now, the day long, surely blessings will be abundantly fulfilled to you, even in that excess of the present grief. Will you, my good Josephine, kindly receive this poor, mortal father of the soul, as he comes round the bleeding heart? It is not, you see, assuming words he offers; how silent, rather, he would remain! He does but write over and over, or as from the heart of your own mother, repeat the only name which is all at once, duty, comfort, and hope: God, God, your good God, all in all! Father, Son, and Holy Ghost; holy, holy, holy saints and angels say, and mother: "Though we pray, we hope." Respectfully, my dear Josephine, S. BRUTE.

Take back, if you please, this picture sent to Bec; the sketch when but three—now five (graves)—and these two little books of *Kempis* and *Mme. de la Vallière.*

MR. BRUTE TO JOSEPHINE.

(Pen-and-ink sketch at top, of a grave and cross, under a spreading tree, and the date—*4th Jan'y,* 1821.)

MY DEAR JOSEPHINE,—Can I show, too often, my desires of your salvation? Ah, when now mother is silent, take, sometimes, your psalms, her psalms! in her Bible, and one verse or other. You will find her whole soul still warm to her God in yours. But what do I say! She (is) in the better place of love. I only mean to remind her Josephine what must have been the impressions, even while upon earth, and teach you humbly to seek for the same. I was just saying in my office, the 24th:—

"To thee, O Lord, I have lifted up my soul."

"In thee, O my God, I put my trust; let me not be ashamed. Neither let my enemies laugh at me: for none of them that wait on thee shall be confounded."

"Show, O Lord, thy ways to me, and teach me thy paths."

"Direct me in thy truth and teach me; for thou art my God, my Saviour, and on thee have I waited all the day long." . . . (How she did.)

"Remember, O Lord, thy bowels of compassion, and thy mercies that are from the beginning of the world."

"The sins of my youth and ignorances do not remember." (How humbly did she say.)

"According to thy mercy remember thou me, for thy goodness sake, O Lord."

"The Lord is sweet and righteous; therefore he will give a law to sinners in the way"—the way!!!

"He will guide the mild in judgment; he will teach the meek his ways." (Therefore be ever meek and humble.)

"All the ways of the Lord are mercy and truth, to them that seek after his covenant and his testimonies."

Let us, then, *seek*, dear child. Be happy; be good; be William and Richard good. Help them for it, by the most sweet and steady example. Pray for mother. Pray, also, for me, who will ever pray for you.

S. BRUTE.

Died on board the brig *Oswego*, June 26th, on her passage from Cape Mesurado to St. Jago, Richard B. Seton, Esq., of Baltimore, late United States Assistant Agent at Monrovia, aged 26 years.—*Boston Paper.*

MT. ST. MARY'S, *Sunday Evening,*
7th September, 1823.

MY DEAR WILLIAM,—Mr. Egan has informed us of the fatal news and the extreme affliction in which he left you and your good Kitty. Bear, I may almost say, with a few lines from your poor Bruté. Of consolation he will attempt no other but the continual motto of your dear mother: "He is all—all in all!" I was yesterday at her grave —wished you were. Saw the wildness of the three graves—of the five; then saw heaven—as we should so easily, in faith, and told them your heart of old and of now. I did, for you both, and me. I spoke to some of the Sisters. Mr. Hickey will have done so to all. I saw tears—he more. O *mother!* Friday I said here the mass of community for him, speaking a few words to the boys and to the young men. I noted what you told me of his kind remaining with that unfortunate colony.[1] I said my hope of his last fervent remembrances of our Lord, of his mother and holy sisters, Rebecca, Anna; and of his best moments for him, near them—and with yourself. Ah! I witness—O my God, my God! To-day I recommended him in town—mother ever so loved there. My William, bear with a devoted friend, and say, vouchsafe say, to your beloved and forever so dear, so truly respected sister, what you may for me. Be blessed both. "HE IS ALL! ALL IN ALL!" S. BRUTE.

TUESDAY OF PENTECOST.

MY DEAR JOSEPHINE,—Too kind and too great an invitation for that poor savage of the mountains. Yet it

[1] Jehudi Ashmun, who sailed for Africa in 1822, to take charge of a re-enforcement for the colony of Liberia, says of Richard Seton, in a letter to my aunt, of Dec. 28th, 1823, now lying on my desk:—

"To your dear brother I well may acknowledge my extensive obligations. He found me a solitary white man on this secluded coast; and from a spontaneous movement of generous feeling, offered to become my companion. He found me depressed with affliction, burdened with cares, and wasted to the weakness of childhood, by half a year's sickness. Too disinterested, alas! he offered to stay and supply more than sickness had deprived me of. . . . . . His open, undisguised character, the simplicity of his manners, and the native kindness of his heart, had won, perhaps, further on the affections of our black people than any other agent had ever done in so short a time. I have heard from them no other objection to Mr. Seton, but that he was *a white man;* the only fault which, with some of them, unfortunately, is held unpardonable."

requires a grateful acknowledgment, which I rather trust to one word of it that you will speak for me to Mrs. Caton, expressing my lively sense of respect better than I would succeed in any formal line. You can but know my heart for her and Mrs. Harper. But must I not, too, acknowledge your own kindness in calling for me yesterday? You *saw* our good president. Better, better still, if William had been here too; truly the two brothers. I the old brother of the high-seas—never to forget him or Josephine, never. What full conversation of *mother* had I yesterday, with Mgr. Flaget, with whom I crossed the seas my first time—just to be nearly at the very beginning of that valley, now of such an extensive blessing. O mother, mother, we said, could she ever have known what, in the secret of our dear Lord, was prepared to meet her simple offering of herself to His only glory and love, as He would Himself see best, only so purely, but the consequences so perfectly unforeseen to herself; nay, equally so to those who at first could have feared to suggest too much of sacrifice, if, as she used to tell me, any thing could be called sacrifice for God and for our eternity!—for God coming for us in Bethlehem, dying for us on the cross—for *eternity*, no less than Himself, enjoyed in *heaven*—face to face—with Mary and the saints, *forever*. All sacrifices were made with a heart that God Himself, whose grace accomplished them through it, did know, although to those who saw nearest that heart so duly felt. Your mother, Josephine, your dear mother, why do I try to speak of her to you? Excuse me almost; but dwell also a moment, as I was doing, with that good bishop, on the present consequences, far and wide; for from these parts could I not add that it prompted and encouraged his own wilds in Kentucky thus to bud and prosper. Monseigneur David[1] went; would have Sisters—had them—all also so beautifully blessed them. My dear Josephine, look from your vale to New York and every side; not the hundreds, but now far above the *thousand* of children blessed from heaven—I think so already, though we still pray, and must—by your mother. Now only my name of all respect and affection to you and William. Pray for me.

S. BRUTE.

Do excuse me; I dine at Dr. Chatard's, my old medical brother, and so offer only my best respects.

J. M. J.

MOUNT ST. MARY'S, *6th July*, 1831.

MY DEAR JOSEPHINE,—I feel most grateful, my good and respected child, for your kind letter of the 18th June, little deserving such attention and remembrance, except for my constant attachment to Josephine and William, which can cease but with life. My presence in Baltimore without seeing you, you notice in a friendly manner. I remained but two days, busy by the hour and moment, doubtful whether going so far,[2] I would find you—find you in the good family that I would have also to see, and just as exposed, by being too short at a visit, after years of absence, to give you pain. I did not go. But never mind; as the heart was once, to such an excellent daughter of such a mother, be sure it remains, and scarcely fears that you could doubt it, or be displeased from your own, at

[1] Titular of Mauricastro *in part.* and coadjutor of the Bishop of Bardstown.
[2] She was with her aunt, Mrs. Post, in New York.

my apparent want of proper *empressement*. I may say the same for William. I know not whether he received my first, directed to Washington, or a second, just before I received yours, which, on hearing *something* most interesting for him, I could not check my expressing the cordial share of his old Bruté in it, his *own way*. Confirm to both the warm wishes of their happiness I cease not to form, and many a time I offered to our Lord for them. What remembrance of that distant 1815 your letter brings to me, since you are with your respected aunt, so extremely kind then to me, who owed it to her love for him with whom I could rather feel proud and delighted.

Indeed, through the whole family it was the same most amiable reception, and even when returning alone, invitations were repeated in the most polite manner. I almost dare ask you, as you will see the moment, to renew the expressions of such respectful and grateful feelings as have ever since remained in my heart—in 1824, in 1815. Now, my good child and my William, your poor Bruté *the same to you* and all you love and mother loved—all. . . . . . I am glad you saw our good M. Bertrand. I have no letter since that fatal July.[1] He never wrote without the many lines about mother, Bec, and you. You are kind to notice the pain I have felt at the disasters of my country, and you heard, it seems, that I was so much affected by them. Yet, yet, I would be sorry that your old priest miss his proper settling with God. But yesterday, it was once more one of our most frequent meditations with the seminarians. The Will—only Will "all in all"—all in the general providence of the universe, heaven

[1] Alludes to the revolution that placed Louis Philippe on the throne of France.

and earth—all in our whole life, indeed, crowded with such mercies as to oblige us to boundless habitual confidence and resignation, and all, all *this* day, *this* hour, which can be the *last* . . . . . But I defer *preaching* you and William (until when you come), you preaching the better by all that I ever saw in Josephine since I knew her, and of which many an excellent line reminds me so well, in the good letter which I answer. Good-bye, excellent child, love still—and William, as much as he respects and loves you both,

S. Brute.

You know how pleased all have been here and at the valley, at your kind commissions. Perhaps M. Purcell[1] may see you or William in New York, for which he set out from here. How pleased with what you say of Emily![2] Could I ask to be remembered, respectfully?

Mr. Bruté was called, in 1834, to greater and more important duties, being appointed first bishop of Vincennes, with a diocese comprising the whole State of Indiana and the eastern half of Illinois. He received the Apostolic bulls in the month of May, while giving a retreat to the Sisters at St. Joseph's, and was consecrated by his old friend, Bishop Flaget, at St. Louis, on the 28th of October following. It was not given him to exercise the fullness of the priesthood long, but during the few years that he occupied his see, he was "as the rainbow giving light in the bright clouds, and as the flower of roses in

[1] The present Archbishop of Cincinnati.
[2] Mrs. (William) Seton, daughter of the late Nathaniel Prime, of New York.

the days of the spring, and as the lilies that are on the brink of the water, and as the sweet smelling frankincense in the time of summer."

This holy man, *whose steps were guided by the light of God*, was called to his eternal reward on the 26th of June, 1839.

"Blessed are they that saw thee, and were honored with thy friendship."—*Ecclesiasticus*, xlviii. 2.

MOUNT SAINT MARY'S COLLEGE, EMMITSBURG, MD.,
Feast of the Purification, 1868.

On Tuesday evening last, in the dim twilight, William Seton, son of Mrs. Seton, the sainted foundress of St. Joseph's of the Valley, was consigned to his final resting-place in the Mountain grave-yard.

The corpse came by rail from New York, his late residence, in charge of his son, William Seton, Esq. It was his earnest wish through life and in death, to have his remains laid to rest at Mt. St. Mary's, the home of his school-boy affections and shrine of his oft-repeated pilgrimages. Another son had the happiness of offering the requiem mass over his honored father's remains, at St. Francis Xavier's Church, Sixteenth Street, in the presence of the Most Reverend Archbishop McCloskey and a large assemblage of the clergy and laity of New York. The Right Rev. Dr. Roosevelt Bayley, bishop of Newark, and some of his clergy, were also present.

When the approach of the hearse from Frederick was signaled, towards the end of the five o'clock recreation, the slow tolling of the passing-bell gathered the boys to attend the *cortége* to the grave-yard.

Owing to the lateness of the hour, but few of the neighboring people, and only two of the Community from St. Joseph's, Sisters Martha and Bernardine, were present. These venerable ladies were among the first of Mother Seton's spiritual daughters. The sacred ministers and the seminarians, in surplice, met the corpse at the church door, and walked in procession to the grave. Not a gust of wind stirred the flicker of the candles, as the last prayers were said; a thin veil of snow covered the noble landscape, to the distant mountain-chain that bounds the horizon; and from the hill-side where we stood, could be faintly seen the outlines of the little Gothic chapel, in the convent grave-yard, beneath whose pavement Mother Seton reposes, still keeping silent watch over the living and the dead.

Letter in *Catholic Telegraph*, of Cincinnati.

FINIS.

Alice Murray.

A Tale. By Miss MARY J. HOFFMAN, authoress of "Agnes Hilton."

1 vol., large 12mo, beveled, cloth $2.00

"Alice Murray" has received from the entire Catholic Press very high praise. The following extract is from the "Baltimore Catholic Mirror":

"We would like to see such books as this brought out by our publishers. Since we must have works of fiction, we should endeavor to encourage a New School of light literature in complete opposition to the poisonous stuff with which booksellers' shelves are filled nowadays. To effect this, we must have pure-minded writers, and courageous publishers, who will not pander to the depraved tastes of the day, but look to the moral worth of a book, before they calculate whether it will sell. 'Alice Murray' combines all the conditions necessary to success in this New School of American literature. It is a picture of American life—natural, interesting, and well written. It breathes throughout a thorough Catholic spirit. In other words, it realizes the great desideratum for the family library."

The Mission Book of the Sacred Passion.

A Manual of Prayers, Practices, and Meditations for preserving the fruits of the Mission. Compiled from the most approved sources, with the approbation of the Most Rev. J. MCCLOSKEY, D. D., Archbishop of New York.

Neatly bound, in various styles of binding, from 75c. to $5.00 per copy.

A True Idea of Holy Communion.

By MGR. SEGUR. Approved and recommended by His Holiness Pope Pius IX.

Cheap edition for distribution:

Enameled paper cover $0.15
" " (per 100)..................10.00
Flexible cloth .... .25
Cloth extra .... .35

Extract from a recent letter of Rt. Rev. W. H. Elder to the publisher of Segur's "Holy Communion."

"I know hardly any book more suited for universal circulation by cheap price than this little book of Mgr. SEGUR's. What he recommends is the key to the reforming of weak Catholics, and the inflaming of piety throughout the country.

"Your faithful servant in Christ,

"WILLIAM HENRY ELDER,

"Bishop of Natchez."

Catholic Anecdotes, Parables, and Tales.

By PERE BONAVENTURE and others.

1 vol. 18mo, cloth.................................$1.00

No more instructive and edifying book than this could be placed in the hands of a young reader. Each parable or example interests the reader, and makes a deep impression upon the mind, not easily effaced or forgotten.

The Library of Good Example; for the Young.

Consists of the following twelve volumes at forty cents per volume; or done up in neat boxes at $4.80 per box:

The Indian's Cloak. The Poor Priest. The Battle of Lepanto. Sister Beatrice. The Keys of Poictiers. Guendaline. Young Communicants. Seraph of Assisium. The Traveler. Jovinian. The Dark Valley. The Way of Heaven.

Historical Sketch of the Order of St. Dominic.

By LACORDAIRE.

1 vol. 12mo, cloth, beveled.........................$1.00

This remarkably able and eloquent production is issued in beautiful style.

It is not merely a vindication of the Order of St. Dominic, but a grand exposition of the divine life of the church, and of her influence upon civilization and society. It is a book for the times.

IN PRESS.

The Flemings.

By MRS. ANNA H. DORSEY, authoress of "Conina," &c.

The Old Gray Rosary.

By MRS. ANNA H. DORSEY, authoress of "Conina," &c.

The Byrnes of Drumgoulagh.

By ALICE NEVILLE.

The Ferryman of the Tiber.

An Historical Tale.

Translated from the Italian of Madame A. K. DE LA GRANGE.

The Particular Examen.

For the use of the Brothers of the Christian Schools.

By the Very Honored Brother PHILIPPE, Superior-General.

This is a work of great excellence, and unsurpassed as a guide to the fulfillment of the duties of a religious life.

It is equally well adapted to people living in the world.

CPSIA information can be obtained
at www.ICGtesting.com
Printed in the USA
BVHW040731020221
599223BV00009B/411